AMARONE
della Valpolicella
DENOMINAZIONE DI ORIGINE CONTROLLATA
Classico
2000

Vitigni
Corvina Veronese 70%, Rondinella 25%, Molinara 5%.

Area of production
The grapes are produced in the vineyard of the Bertani Estate in Villa Novare, in the heart of Valpolicella classica. The soil is marl- calcareous, with the best expositions of all Valpolicella for the vineyard.

Vinification
A selection of the best, perfectly ripe and healthy bunches is then transported to the loft-extremely airy rooms situated in the wine cellar garret - and laid out on cane mats ("arelle") for the drying. After about 120 days withering, the grapes reach a sugar content of about 24/25°C. At half of January grapes are picked from the bunches and press. Then the grapes are vinified with an initial very slow fermentation, that follows to the period of maceration (about a total of 50 days) has given to the wine high level of noble alcohols and glycerine, very important elements for the elegance and softness of the taste.

Ageing
About 6 years in Slavonian oak casks (the capacity varies from 8 hl to 60 hl) and an aging period of at lowest 12 months in the bottle.

Organoleptic description
The wine is a deep, dark garnet red. The classical cherry flavours of Amarone are immediately perceptible to the nose, with the preponderant notes of Marasca and sour cherry. The wine presents a great variety of characters, from fresh fruit to jam, which offer a very harmonious lasting taste, alternating with spicy elements. The ample nose has a sweet impact and spreads in a continuous chain of sensations. The wine opens up in the mouth with all the red- berry fruits, besides vanilla in soft, heavy-duty cloth.

Analitycal data
Alcohol: 15,00%.

TWO HUNDRED AND NINETY-THREE
TRADITIONAL TYPES

ITALIAN
CHEESE

A guide to its discovery and appreciation

Slow Food Editore

Edited by
Roberto Rubino, Piero Sardo,
Angelo Surrusca

Collaborators
Enrico Azzolin, Francesca Baldereschi,
Andrea Barmaz, Hansi Baumgartner,
Andrea Bertucci, Gino Bortoletto,
Pier Bottà, Michele Bruno,
Guido Calvi, Dionisio Castello,
Valerio Chiarini, Angelo Concas,
Bepi Damiani, Cristiano De Riccardis,
Vittorio Ducoli, Luca Fabbri,
Carlo Fanti, Vincenzo Ferrara,
Giampaolo Gaiarin,
Armando Gambera,
Paola Gasparotto, Davide Ghirardi,
Marco Giraudo, Nadia Innocente,
Gino Larosa, Clara Laurita,
Giuseppe Licitra, Carmelo Maiorca,
Nicolò Migheli, Stefano Olla,
Nereo Pederzolli, Michele Pizzillo,
Raffaella Ponzio, Pippo Privitera,
Bepi Pucciarelli, Vito Puglia,
Carmine Ragusa, Marco Riva,
Cinzia Scaffidi, Massimo Scarlatti,
Altobella Sigilli, Lillino Silibello,
Anna Sulis, Enrico Surra

Editorial committee
Bianca Minerdo, Gigi Piumatti,
Giovanni Ruffa

Translation editor
Giles Watson

Translations
Helen Donald, Michael Farrell,
Giles Watson

Co-ordinating editor
Maria Vittoria Negro

Art director
Dante Albieri

Graphic design
Stefano Pallaro

Layout
Maurizio Burdese, Francesco Perona

Photographs
Giuseppe Cucco, Paola Di Fabio,
Tino Gerbaldo, Marcello Longo,
Marcello Marengo, Gianluigi Matta,
Maurizio Milanesio, Marco Regalati

Cover
Foto © Image Source/Corbis/
Grazia Neri

Offset litho
Imago, Marene (Cuneo)

Printed by
Rotolito Lombarda, Pioltello
(Milan)

Slow Food Editore srl
Via della Mendicità Istruita, 14-45
12042 Bra (Cuneo)
Tel. +39 0172 419611
Fax +39 0172 411218

For advertising enquiries contact
Slow Food Promozione srl
Ivan Piasentin, Enrico Bonura,
Carla Pattacini, Gabriele Cena
Tel. +39 0172 419611
Fax +39 0172 413640

Websites: www.slowfood.it,
www.slowfood.com

ISBN: 88-8499-090-4

We wish to thank the following companies and organisations for kindly supplying cheeses

Valle d'Aosta

Assessorato agricoltura e risorse naturali
  Direzione Assistenza Tecnica
  Quart (Aosta)
Il Capretto, Issogne (Aosta)
Institut Agricole Régional, Aosta
Les Ecureuils, Saint-Pierre (Aosta)
Walser Delicatesse, Issime (Aosta)

Piedmont

Agrinatura Occelli, Farigliano (Cuneo)
Arbiora, Cessole (Asti)
Casa del Formaggio, Saluzzo (Cuneo)
Cooperativa Agricola Mottarone,
  Armeno (Novara)
Il Cornale, Magliano Alfieri, (Cuneo)
Cedis, Bra (Cuneo)
Giolito, Bra (Cuneo)
Guffanti, Arona (Novara)
Stagionatura Valcasotto
  Pamparato (Cuneo)

Lombardy

Consorzio di Tutela Bitto
  e Valtellina Casera, Sondrio
Consorzio Tutela Provolone Valpadana,
  Cremona
Ganassa, Ballabio (Lecco)
Guffanti, Arona (Novara)
Ol Formager, Bergamo

Trentino-Alto Adige

Caseificio di Primiero, Mezzano (Trento)
Consorzio Trentingrana-Concast, Trento
De Gust, Varna (Bolzano)
Taberna Imperiale, Silvi Marina (Teramo)

Veneto

Caseificio Roncolato, Roncà (Verona)
La Casearia di Carpenedo
  Povegliano (Treviso)

Friuli-Venezia Giulia

Maria Carmen Spironelli
  Pontebba (Udine)

Latterie Friulane, Campoformido (Udine)
Tosoni, Spilimbergo (Pordenone)
Trattoria La stella
  Meduno (Pordenone)

Liguria

Autra, Savignone (Genoa)
Cooperativa Casearia Val di Vara,
  Varese Ligure (La Spezia)
La Bottega di Angela Maria,
  Molini di Triora (Imperia)
Pasquale Usai, Stella (Savona)

Emilia Romagna

Amerigo dal 1934, Savigno (Bologna)

Tuscany

Il Forteto,
  Vicchio di Mugello (Firenze)
San Polo, Pienza (Siena)
Vecchio Mulino,
  Castelnuovo Garfagnana (Lucca)
Zummo, Pistoia

Umbria

Il Bacco Felice, Foligno (Perugia)

Marche

La Ripa, Orciano di Pesaro (Pesaro)
Esperya, Loreto (Ancona)

Lazio

Cooperativa Agricola Stella,
  Amaseno (Frosinone)
Cooperativa Produttori Cisterna,
  Cisterna di Latina (Latina)
La Tradizione, Rome
Pane e Vino, Frosinone

Abruzzo and Molise

Aromatario, Castel del Monte (L'Aquila)
Esperya, Loreto (Ancona)
Pecorino Hat Atri di Lino Rocini,
  Atri (Teramo)
Taberna imperiale, Silvi Marina (Teramo)

Puglia
Tarantino, Gravina (Bari)
Taberna Imperiale, Silvi Marina (Teramo)

Campania
Antonello Di Masi, Albanella (Salerno)
La Baronia, Pontelatone (Caserta)
Madaio, Eboli (Salerno)

Basilicata
ANFOSC, Bella (Potenza)
Istituto Sperimentale per la Zootecnia,
    Bella (Potenza)

Calabria
Agenzia Regionale per lo Sviluppo
    e i Servizi in Agricoltura, Cosenza

Sicily
Antica Bottega, Bra (Cuneo)
Assessorato Regionale Agricoltura
    e Foreste Sezione Operativa no. 8
    Sant'Agata di Militello (Messina)

Assessorato Regionale Agricoltura
    e Foreste Sezione Operativa no. 29
    Palazzolo Acreide (Siracusa)
Assessorato Regionale Agricoltura
    e Foreste Sezione Operativa no. 59,
    Mezzojuso (Palermo)
Consorzio di Ricerca Filiera
    Lattiero-Casearia, Ragusa
Salvatore Passalacqua,
    Castronovo di Sicilia (Palermo)
Taberna Imperiale, Silvi Marina (Teramo)

Sardinia
Bonu, Cagliari
Cisalpino, Savigliano (Cuneo)
Ente regionale di sviluppo
    e Assistenza Tecnica in Agricoltura,
    Cagliari
I Sapori della Tradizione, Cagliari

Preface

Since the landmark first edition of this guide was published in 1999, many things have changed in the world of Italian cheese. From our point of view, the most significant change is that the use of raw milk in cheesemaking, which we believe to be crucial for excellence, has become widely accepted and applied. Today, labels proudly bear the words *a latte crudo*, and even in the remotest of areas people know that pasteurisation is synonymous with loss of character. This important cultural battle has been waged and won by Slow Food, in collaboration with allies like ONAF and Roberto Rubino and his team. It is a major step forward on the road to recovering cheese as a source of pleasure, as well as a food.

One other source of pride is that over the last few years, small-scale, marginal cheeses – the forgotten products – have not disappeared. In fact, many have found a new lease of life, attracting new interest on the part of consumers. There can be no doubt that the Presidia project, which holds forty-four cheeses and lays great emphasis on mountain dairy products, has helped to create a new awareness among consumers and public bodies. The vast number of cheese-related events, fairs and competitions that crowd the calendars of Italy's municipalities are object proof of this renewed interest. When the first edition of the *Cheese* food fair was held at Bra, and the first edition of this book was published, that interest was much less intense. It is no coincidence that we compared cheese as a cultural phenomenon to an underground karst river, waiting to emerge into the daylight. The *Cheese* fair enabled that river to burst back into full view. There were many, generous helpers on hand to encourage this phenomenon, but our most urgent warning at that first edition of *Cheese* was that the welcome new attention for cheese ran the risk of appearing too late, when the market was already compromised and monopolised by industrial products. Luckily, this is not the case. The two hundred and ninety-three cheeses in this guide, about a hundred more than were featured in the first edition, bear witness to the fact that cheesemaking is alive and well. Even small-scale products have achieved levels of output sufficient to justify inclusion here.

But the picture is not entirely a rosy one. Currently, the high-quality food and agriculture sector is going through a very difficult period. We allude in particular to the gap in prices that separates a few well-known producers from the rest. It is also a gap that regards visibility, financial gratification for the cheesemakers and organisation in general. Alongside the high prices commanded by bitto delle valli del Bitto – to give just one example – we have parmigiano reggiano prices that are below the survival threshold. In fact, the price of Italy's emblematic cheese has never been lower. Many historic cheeses, such as mozzarella di bufala campana, asiago, pecorino romano, pecorino sardo and others, are clearly in commercial difficulty.

In short, where there is a significant supply of the product, consumer response is unsatisfactory. We should be asking ourselves whether we have contributed to building up a virtuous market for niche products, while penalising those made on a large scale. Perhaps we have. It is clear that the new awareness of raw milk, to take one example, has led to lower levels of appreciation for cheeses made with pasteurised milk. Yet parmigiano reggiano is a superb raw milk cheese, made by hundreds of small-scale cheesemakers who comply with impeccably drafted regulations. What to do, then? What is the reason for this crisis? Are we simply talking about a change in taste? I do not believe so. For Italians, grana-type cheese is like mother. It is the first great love of our lives. The simple fact is that the aggressive promotion strategies adopted by large-scale distributors for this particular product have jeopardised its appeal, and led to its perception as a commodity product. Price is the crucial factor in purchase decisions. In times of crisis like the present, commodities feel the effects of promotional pressure more than other products. They also run the risk of attack by imitations or vaguely similar products from abroad. Parmigiano reggiano has been exposed to this slow, insidious aggression for years. Small-scale producers generally have fewer problems in gaining a fair market price, but they face other challenges. For one thing, they face difficulties in adhering to very strict, complicated DOP regulations. They struggle to make their facilities regulation-compliant, and to acquire the requisite health certificates that enable them to sell to retailers. Small cheesemakers find it tricky to gain a permanent place on the shelves of large-scale retail outlets, and inevitably come up against the bottlenecks in Italy's distribution system, one of the frailest and least developed in Europe. All in all, the market's health is far from florid, although it is in better condition than before. One reason for this – and one that impacts on all Italian cheeses – is that dieticians continue to discourage the consumption of cheese and butter. For the first time in years, we are witnessing a slow decline in consumption, in favour of fresh dairy products and milk derivatives.

In this worrying general picture, Slow Food cannot simply restrict itself to flaunting its Presidia as examples of virtuous promotion. We must ask ourselves questions, and start proposing a few answers. For example, we should be talking to public bodies and institutions about a full proposal for a specific small-scale cheesemaking mark, perhaps European, perhaps Italian, perhaps regional. We should be refocusing our education strategies, paying greater attention to marketing and communication-related issues. Perhaps we should also be considering specialised training for the makers of these typical products. But let's not get carried away with all this gloom and doom. We should not forget the good work that has already been done, and to which these pages bear witness. This guide is an extraordinarily useful tool for reviewing Italy's cheese heritage, and identifying new opportunities for pleasure. Ten years ago, all this would have been unthinkable. There is good reason to be optimistic.

Piero Sardo
Slow Food Foundation for Biodiversity

Slow Food Manifesto in defence of raw-milk cheese

Raw-milk cheese is more than a wonderful food, it is a deeply embedded expression of our finest traditions. It is both an art and a way of life. It is a culture, a heritage and a cherished landscape. **And it is under threat of extinction!** Under threat because the values it expresses are in opposition to the sanitation and homogenisation of mass produced foods.

We call on all food-loving citizens of the world to respond now to the defence of the unpasteurised cheese tradition. A defence of a food that has for hundreds of years inspired, given pleasure and provided sustenance but is now being insidiously undermined by the sterile hand of global hygiene controls.

We call for an end to all discriminatory regulations from EU, WTO, Food and Drug Administration and other government Institutions that needlessly restrict citizens' freedom of choice to purchase these foods, and threaten to destroy the livelihood of the artisanal craftsmen who produce them.

We deplore attempts by regulatory authorities to impose unattainable standards of production, in the name of protecting human health.

We believe that such impositions will have the adverse effect of that intended. The bacteriological health of our unpasteurised dairy products is destroyed by overzealous sterilization procedures. So will the health of human beings be destroyed through a diet of sterile food. Without any challenge, our immune system will fail and our medication become ineffective. Moreover the unique flavour and aroma of the cheese are conserved by non-pasteurisation.

We therefore call upon those who have it in their power to safeguard the diversity and complexity of our regional foods and the health and stability of our rural communities to act now and ensure a flexible, fair and appropriate regulatory framework; sensible controls and a positive disposition concerning the future.

Be aware - that once the knowledge, skills and commitment of this culture have been lost, they can never be regained.

Contents

The thirty-one DOP
(Protected Designation of Origin) zones

Asiago
Bitto
Bra
Caciocavallo Silano
Canestrato Pugliese
Casciotta d'Urbino
Castelmagno
Fiore Sardo
Fontina
Formai de Mut
Gorgonzola
Grana Padano
Montasio
Monte Veronese
Mozzarella di Bufala Campana
Murazzano
Parmigiano Reggiano
Pecorino Romano
Pecorino Sardo
Pecorino Siciliano
Pecorino Toscano
Provolone Valpadana
Quartirolo Lombardo
Ragusano
Raschera
Robiola di Roccaverano
Spressa delle Giudicarie
Taleggio
Toma Piemontese
Valle d'Aosta Fromadzo
Valtellina Casera

Families of Cheeses

Classification methods

Given the huge variety of products, it is not possible to identify a single general method of cheese classification. Generally, categories are defined on the basis of the characteristics of the cheese itself, or of the cheesemaking technology. As these parameters are not qualitatively comparable, each family may be combined others.

The most obvious criterion for differentiating cheeses is the origin of the **milk**. Five main families can be identified from the types of milk most commonly used around the world:

cow's milk, or *vaccino* in Italian;

ewe's milk, or *pecorino*;

goat's milk, or *caprino*;

buffalo's milk, or *bufalino*;

mixed milk, or *a latte misto*.

Cheeses can be classified on the basis of their **fat content**, or the percentage of fat measured as a proportion of dry matter. This gives the following categories:

fat, with fat in dry matter above 42% (whole milk);

semi-fat, with fat in dry matter ranging from 20-42% (part-skimmed milk);

low-fat, with fat in dry matter below 20%.

We can also identify the following cheese types on the basis of **water content:**

hard, with less than 40% water;

semi-hard, with 40-45% water;

soft, with 45-60% water;

On the basis of **cheesemaking technology**, cheeses can be classified as:

uncooked: the curd is cut, but not cooked;

semi-cooked: the curd is cut and then cooked at a temperature below 48°C.

cooked: the curd is cut and then cooked at a temperature of 48-56°C.

stretched curd: the curd ripens in warm acid whey for a few hours and is then stretched by hand;

pressed curd: pressure is exerted on the cheese for a varying length of time (usually 1-24 hours) to encourage expulsion of the whey before the outer rind forms;

blue or veined: the body presents diffuse blue and green veining caused by mould that has formed either naturally or after the deliberate perforation of the rounds;

bloomy rind: a layer of whitish microflora-induced mould forms on the surface of the rind. Characteristic of soft cheeses, especially those from France;

washed rind: the outer rind is washed periodically with brine or water and alcohol solutions. Characteristic of soft cheeses.

The final method of classification is by **maturing period**. The categories distinguished are:

fresh, to be consumed within a few days of production;

briefly matured, for up to one month;

medium matured, from one to six months;

slowly matured, for more than six months.

Cheese types

Dairy products

Dairy products are made by acid fermentation of milk, cream or whey, and may be subdivided into fermented milks and ricottas. The use of **fermented milk** among eastern peoples dates back long before the Christian era. Fermentation is a fairly slow natural process. Bacteria present in, or inoculated into, the milk transform lactose into lactic acid. The proteins gelatinise to form a semi-solid coagulate. If yeasts are present as well as bacteria, alcoholic fermentation will take place, as in kefir, the traditional dairy product of the Caucasus. Higher temperatures accelerate the fermentation process. Fermented milks include yoghurt, Sardinian gioddu and prescinseûa from Liguria.

Yoghurt is obtained from the combined action of two kinds of bacteria, *Streptococcus thermophilus* and *Lactobacillus bulgaricus*. It can be made with whole, skimmed, concentrated or powdered milk. Yoghurt is described as **set** when fermentation takes place directly in the jars, in which case it has a more compact structure. **Unset** yoghurt ferments in large containers and the product is packaged later. In this case, it has a runnier consistency and in some cases is liquid. Yoghurt must be consumed very fresh because it contains milk enzymes. Yoghurts may be low-fat, containing less than 1% fat, standard, with a fat content of about 1.1%, whole milk (3-3.5% fat), natural, natural sweetened, aromatised and sugared, or fruit.

Ricotta is obtained from whey, the liquid that separates from the curd during cheesemaking. Its name, from the Latin *recoctus* meaning "recooked", reveals the product's classical origins and explains how it is made. In addition to the unsalted version, there is also ricotta salata, which is dry-salted and matured for 15-30 days, and mature ricotta, which ages for several months. Ricotta is made over almost the whole of Italy, as well as in France, Greece, Spain and Portugal.

Fresh acid-set cheeses

The cheesemaking method is very straightforward. The cheese is obtained from an acid-set curd, generally precipitated by the combined action of souring and a small quantity of rennet. Milk and aromatic enzymes form, making the body soft and not very firm. Fresh cheeses are white and rindless. The body is smooth and the aromas faint. On the palate, they are clean-

tasting and pleasantly acidulous. Fresh cheeses are rich in proteins, contain a considerable amount of water, and have a high milk-to-cheese yield. The category includes cheeses like robiola and caprino (goat's milk cheese). These very soft, near liquid products are also known as **white cheeses** and are sold in jars or other sealed containers.

Soft cheeses

This large category includes two groups of soft, generally rennet-set cheeses. Soft cheeses have a high water content (45-55%) and mature for anything from a few days to six months. The first group includes crescenza, stracchino, casatella trevigiana, murazzano, toma di Langa cheeses, casu axedu, bonassai, raviggiolo and squaquarone. They have a soft white, or straw-white, body and are rindless, or present a very thin skin. These products mature for only a few days. Their aroma profile is straightforward, ranging from soured milk to vegetal notes of herbs and dried berries. The second group embraces short to medium mature cheeses that age for a few weeks or months, such as Lombardy's quartirolo, toma from Piedmont and the caciotta cheeses characteristic of central and southern Italy. The body is soft and elastic, often presenting eyes, and ranges in colour from ivory-white to straw-yellow depending on the length of the maturing period. The outer rind is thin, greyish and may present white or reddish moulds. It will be lightly furrowed if the cheese was wrapped in cloths during shaping.

Bloomy rind and washed-rind soft cheeses

In this category of cheese, the effects of maturing are evident above all on the outer surface. It is sometimes referred to as

"centripetal maturing" as it proceeds from the outer rind towards the centre of the cheese. A close look at a slice will reveal that under the rind, the body is runnier, the colour, fragrance and aroma are more intense and the taste is tangy. Nearer the centre of the cheese, the body is drier, firmer, lighter in colour and less pungent in flavour.

A **bloomy rind** is usually obtained by spraying the still-soft rind of the fresh cheese with spores of *Penicillium candidum*. The entire surface of the cheese is covered in a light but thick, dry down that is felt-like in texture and greyish-white in colour. The fuzzy bloom, which is redolent of moss, grassland, watermeadow and attractive vegetal notes, is perfectly edible. Italy's scimudin and many French cheeses, such as brie, camembert de Normadie, caprice de dieux, chabichou and crottin de Chavignol, all present a bloomy rind.

Washed-rind cheeses are obtained by sponging the outer surface with brine. The purpose of washing is to eliminate undesirable moulds and other impurities, and to encourage the growth of *Oospora crustacea*, a micro-organism that gives the rind a distinctive orangey yellow or reddish colour. These cheeses are smooth, moist and may present traces of the washing solution. The washed rinds, which are not always edible, have intense, piquant, feral aromas. Examples of washed-rind cheeses are taleggio, epoisses de Bourgogne and reblochon.

As maturing progresses, both bloomy rind and washed-rind cheeses produce ammonia. An aroma of ammonia, if limited to the rind, does not mean that the cheese is inedible. But if the body of the cheese smells of ammonia, it is no longer fit for consumption.

Blue or veined cheeses

Bleu is the French name for cheeses whose body is streaked with blue or grey-green veining. The cheese looks as if it has been sprinkled with parsley (*erborin* in the Milanese dialect), hence the Italian name for these cheeses, *formaggi erborinati*. It was in France that in the mid nineteenth century, Antoine Roussel perfected a technique for making blue cheeses from mouldy rye bread. The bluish colonies of mould on the bread developed the characteristic blue veining when they came into contact with the still-fresh cheese. At one time, this process was entirely natural, as is still the case with castelmagno. Today, however, the formation of mould is usually encouraged by inoculating *Penicillium* bacteria into the milk, and subsequently perforating the cheese to introduce air. This is the method used for gorgonzola, strachitund and other small-scale Alpine pasture products.

There is a wide range of French cow's milk blue cheeses, including bleu d'Auvergne, bleu des Causses, fourme d'Ambert and bresse bleu, which has a bloomy, down-covered rind. In Great Britain, there is the cow's milk stilton, and in Denmark, danablu. The most celebrated ewe's milk blue cheese is the French roquefort. Still in France, there are the well-known goat's milk persillés of Savoy. Almost all of these are compact, semi-hard cheeses with blue veining, caused by spontaneous microflora, which appears when maturing is well under way. Finally, there are mixed (cow's-goat's-ewe's) milk blue cheeses such as the Italian murianengo, Spain's cabrales and the Greek kopanisti. Blue cheeses tend to be tangy, and often very savoury, presenting strong aromas of mould and fat. The mould should be evenly distributed through the body. To achieve this, the perforations in the body

should be open for as long as possible, to encourage the circulation of air. If the body is pressed too hard, or there are too many holes, the *Penicillium* will only develop along the walls of the perforation.

Stretched curd cheeses

Stretched curd cheeses are typically Italian, and Italy is the largest producer. The group embraces provolone Valpadana as well as many other cheeses from central and southern Italy, and the islands. These products, very different in texture and in length of maturing, include burrata, burrino, caciocavallo, mozzarella, provola and scamorza cheeses, stracciata from Molise and vastedda del Belìce from Sicily. Their common feature is a cheesemaking technique that leaves the body particularly elastic. After ripening for a period of time, the curd is immersed in hot or boiling water and stretched with wooden sticks.

Pressed, hard and semi-hard cheeses

There are many cheeses of this type in Italy. They are made with rennet-set, very slightly soured raw or pasteurised milk. Since these cheeses are generally matured, special care is taken to ensure that all the whey is expelled. Crucial stages in cheesemaking are the meticulous cutting of the curd, which is performed twice in the case of some premium craft cheeses like castelmagno and bra d'alpeggio, the transfer of the curd into hoops and pressing. There are three sub-categories, **uncooked**, **semi-cooked** and **cooked**. The differences have already been discussed in the section on classification methods. There are not very many uncooked cheeses, and most of them are found in Piedmont (bra, castelmagno, raschera and others). The list of semi-cooked cheeses is a long one, but there are fewer types of cooked cheese.

Traditional cheesemaking

The photographs illustrate the procedures necessary to produce a **Raschera Quadrato di Alpeggio,** starting with the cutting of the soft curd. The preceding stages – the arrival of freshly drawn raw milk at the dairy, the inoculation of liquid calf's rennet, covering the container with a woollen cloth, and coagulation – are visually uninteresting. Let's take a look. First the mass of soft curd is agitated with a fork-like *spino*. Then the whey is removed and the curd is poured into a container lined with a hemp cloth. It is mixed vigorously by hand. Then it is knotted up in the cloth before undergoing a first manual pressing for about ten minutes on a wooden board with a draining channel. The bundle is then put into a square wooden mould and stones are placed on top to press the curd for five days. The last photograph

shows the pressed curd when it has just been removed from the mould. Obviously, the entire sequence of operations is done by hand. The cheesemaker's skill remains paramount. It should also be noted that cheesemaking is carried out in clean and tidy, if unsophisticated, surroundings in full compliance with public health regulations. In other words, traditional production is not incompatible with hygiene.

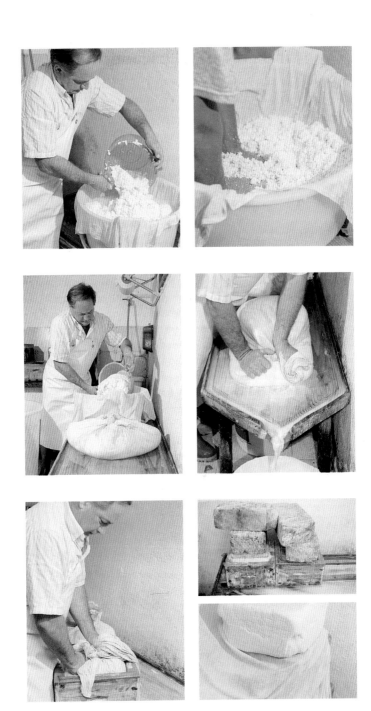

Industrial cheesemaking

Making **Parmigiano Reggiano** is not actually an industrial process. In fact, the reverse is true. Although this prestigious DOP consumes oceans of milk to produce millions of cheeses every year, production is split up among 600 or so *caselli* – small traditional dairies – that observe the same strict standards while still managing to present significant variations on the classic theme. The accompanying photographs illustrate how Parmigiano Reggiano is also a perfect example of standardised cheese production involving modern technology and a rigorous regime of hygiene controls. The differences with respect to craft-scale or *malga* (mountain dairy) cheesemaking are very obvious, even though the method does not jeopardise the product's traditional characteristics. We see the huge troughs where the cream is allowed to rise and the enormous conical vats

where the milk is coagulated and the curd is processed. Two separate cheeses are made from the soft curd in each vat, and we can follow their progress in the photographs until the outer rind is stamped with a unique mark, comprising the dairy number, the Consortium's symbol and the date of production. Salting is the final operation.

Maturing

Maturing begins when cold replaces warmth and damp takes over from dry in cheesemaking. Heat is the principal agent that curdles milk and separates curd from whey whereas lower temperatures and controlled humidity stimulate the micro-organisms and enzymes that modify the structure of the final product.

Maturing, also known as ageing or curing, alters the cheese's composition, promoting the fermentation of sugars, triggering proteolysis, the breakdown of proteins, and lipolysis, the breakdown of fats. The action of microbes and enzymes completely transforms a cheese's taste characteristics, altering its smell, taste, texture, digestibility and appearance, both inside and out. It is maturing that makes possible cheese's extraordinary variety. The photographs on these pages show a number of very different maturing environments.

Some are natural ambiences, where microbes and enzymes go to work spontaneously. Traditionally, cells and caves with temperature and humidity levels naturally suitable for ageing are the favoured locations. Over the years, these environments acquire a unique microflora that encourages the development of the chemical and physical properties of one specific cheese. But modern technology means it is also possible to recreate maturing rooms artificially. Environmental parameters can be monitored and the cheesemaker can intervene to modify the maturing process.

ITALIAN CHEESE

27

At the table

1. Buying cheese

Let's say you want to impress your guests at a dinner party with a tempting cheeseboard. How to go about it? The first thing is that the town where you live must have a good cheese retailer. It will by now be obvious that this is not something to take for granted. The specialised outlets that were once strongholds of quality and variety are going through a very difficult period. Under pressure from large-scale retail distributors, specialist cheese shops have had to fall in line with supermarkets, where pre-packaged industrial cheese holds sway and brand names dictate consumer choice. Few retailers search out new cheeses or have any desire to explain to customers that there are other options beyond their usual products. Few put quality above all else. In this market situation, it is almost impossible for knowledgeable consumers to put together an attractive, albeit perhaps limited, selection of cheeses. Should a restaurateur wish to offer a serious range of cheeses, he or she can turn to parallel sources of supply for there are still cheese wholesalers who are capable of putting together a good assortment. Otherwise, catering professionals in cheese-producing areas can build up the necessary contacts locally. Ordinary consumers cannot. Italy is a cheese-producing country of the first order but only an average consumer of cheeses. Italians eat about sixteen kilograms each of cheese every year in contrast to the twenty-four kilos consumed by the "world champions" – the Greeks – and the twenty-three kilos of the French. Above all, we Italians are a little bit chauvinistic. For the most part, we eat Italian cheeses, especially local ones. As a result, the range of available non-domestic cheeses, most of which are French, comes almost exclusively from industrial producers. What to do, then? Well, we have to be patient. We must study what guides there are, listen to experts and resign ourselves to the inevitability of having to make do with a limited range for our board. Very fresh cheeses should in any case be avoided. You will certainly not find them on the very best tables. However, if you can obtain morning-fresh supplies from a producer, you might want to include a special baked or flavoured ricotta made from buffalo's or ewe's milk. But it has to be out of the ordinary. Mozzarella is not a good choice for it releases moisture and is difficult to slice. If you want to present a particularly good mozzarella – and it must be buffalo's milk – then serve it with fresh tomato and make it the centrepiece of your table. Next, bear in mind that five is the perfect number, and should include ewe's or goat's milk cheeses, depending on the region. Any self-respecting cheeseboard should have at least one or two examples of pecorino (ewe's milk) and caprino (goat's milk) cheese. Avoid products flavoured with herbs, chilli pepper, walnuts, spices and so on. Great cheeses should be served on their own, or accompanied by bitter honey (mature cheeses), cognà (grape-must preserve, ideal for tangy cheeses) or perhaps by small chunks of pear. When arranging the cheeses on your board, start with the fresh-

The two knives illustrated are used to cut hard grana-type cheese. The toothed knife is for scoring the outer rind while the teardrop-shaped one is for cutting the cheese into portions.

est, provide each with its own knife, and let your guests help themselves. Always finish with a blue cheese (gorgonzola, roquefort or stilton). However, there is no set order for serving milder cheeses. Provided they are more or less equally ripe, you can present them as you prefer. If you do not know how long the cheeses were matured, taste them and start with the least tangy. Should you be able to get supplies from France – where there are forty-two DOP zones compared with Italy's thirty-one – remember that you will find the best quality where you see the words *fermier* (farm-produced) or *au lait cru* (made from unpasteurised milk) on the label. If you are offered cheese by the portion, investigate further. French *affineurs* (cheese maturers) are usually highly skilled. Bear in mind, too, that in Germany, Holland, Denmark, Belgium and Austria, ninety-nine cheeses out of a hundred are made industrially. However, the United Kingdom still has many good small-scale producers. If you go to Greece, you will find feta everywhere. There are twenty Greek DOP cheeses but they are hard to track down because production is limited and scattered across the country's thousands of islands. Spain has a good range of cheeses, especially ewe's milk varieties, and Portugal offers some pleasant surprises, but these products are rarely imported into Italy.

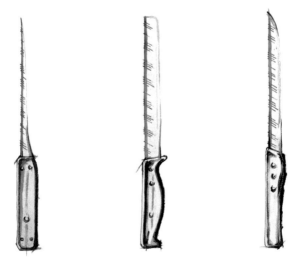

These three knives are used mainly for cutting fresh or soft cheese. The blade surface that comes into contact with the body is kept to a minimum.

2. Tasting cheese

How do you taste a cheese? Can you adopt the same tasting approach you would for a wine? Should tastings be blind, comparing similar products with assessments for appearance, nose and palate? In principle, yes, but there are some differences and difficulties.

First, it must be stressed that the term "tasting" should in theory only be applied to such operations as have a professional, or near-professional, purpose. Tasting means acquiring sufficient knowledge of a food product to be able to describe it with reasonable accuracy to another person. The more information we acquire, the more precisely will we be able to describe the product we are tasting. The question "What was that cheese like?" can be answered, "Nice", and that in itself is an assessment of quality. But our interlocutor will have gained no information, apart from a generic impression of approval. If you begin to describe the colour of the outer rind, the colour and consistency of the interior, the intensity and type of the primary and secondary aromas, the smoothness and appeal on the palate, the length of finish and so on, even without reference to the type of cheese or milk used, you will have supplied enough information for your interlocutor to recognise the cheese on tasting it, or at least to compare it with others. Obviously, it is unnecessary to go to the same lengths at home or in the restaurant. But it is also true that if you eat with the concentration you would dedicate to tasting, you will acquire more information – and greater pleasure – from your food. Above all, you will be reinforcing your defences against bad, adulterated or just plain boring food products.

Tasting categories

The theory and practice of cheese tasting are recent developments. They were first formulated in post-war France, and arrived in Italy in 1989, when ONAF, the Italian cheese tasters' organisation, was created. For many years, the DOP Consortia have been using tasting categories to assess their products' fitness for sale but the criteria adopted are relatively unsophisticated. Their purpose is to establish whether the cheese is free of obvious defects, and that the DOP standards are complied with. A tasting worthy of the name, however, will attempt to identify the specific taste characteristics of one particular sample at one particular moment in time.

Although most tasters are agreed on the primary categories – external appearance, sensations on nose and palate and typicality – of analysis, there is much debate over secondary ones – consistency, structure, eyes, oiliness of the body, overall harmony, aftertaste and so on – as well as vocabulary. Tasting cheese poses a genuine language problem because there simply aren't enough words available.

A working party co-ordinated by Marco Guarnaschelli Gotti met at the Occelli di Farigliano cheese dairy a few years ago to draw up a preliminary cheese-tasting dictionary. Contributions have also come from ONAF, with its tasting note profile, and from Slow Food's Taste Workshops. Thanks to this experience, we can now sketch out a first, provisional, dictionary of cheese tasting.

Visual examination

Leaving aside comments on the overall presentation, that is the shape, the side, top and bottom, which are of technical interest only, the outer rind is assessed for **appearance** (thin, thick, smooth, clean, orange-peel, crusty, rough, dry, moist, dappled, cracked or mouldy) and **colour** (white, chalk-white, milk-white, cream, ivory, straw-yellow, wax-yellow, golden, ochre, hazel, reddish, grey or black), the body for **colour** (milk-white, chalk-white, alabaster, cream, ivory, straw-white, wax-yellow, orange, hazel, ochre, veined, tending to green/grey/blue) and **consistency** or **texture** (smooth, buttery, chewy, chalky, chalky-crumbly, granular, rock-like, rock-like and flaky, spongy, dry, exuding droplets under the rind, with deep/small/large eyes).

Nose

The taster will assess the intensity and quality of the olfactory sensations, taking into account that not just the dominant primary aromas should be evaluated. After a few seconds, complementary aromatic notes emerge and these are crucial to the originality, or complexity, of some cheeses. At this point, the taster may proceed to a description of the aromas perceived, using wine vocabulary where possible, or appropriate terms identified specifically for cheese. One preliminary remark should be made. If the taster notes a dominant smell of ammonia, this means the cheese is overripe. Other critical indicators are rancid or acetone notes, but while these may be part of the tasting profile of some very ripe cheeses, ammonia is not.

Where possible, we have identified families of smells, listing them from the freshest to the most oppressive, which border on being defects.

The following smell families can be identified:

cream / buttermilk / acetone, butter / fat / rancid, white flowers / herbs / hay, honey / hazelnut / almond, vanilla / spices, bitterish / ginger / bitter, yeast / earthy, wool / barnyardy / billy goat, sourish / sour / sharp, vine leaf / woody / cheese cellar, cooked / smoky / burnt, noble rot / mushroom / white truffle, cabbage (vegetal) / onion / garlic.

Individual tasters may add to or modify the list depending on their olfactory thresholds and tasting skills.

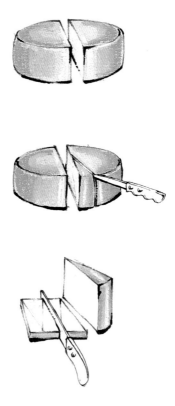

The above illustrations show how a round, high-sided, soft or semi-hard cheese should be sliced into portions.

How to cut a pyramidal cheese. This shape is characteristic of some French goat's milk cheeses.

Palate

Gustatory evaluation should begin with a description of general sensations (sweet/savoury/salty, fresh, sharp/burning, hard/round/fat) and the intensity and quality of the aromas (faint, intense, powerful, elegant, distinct, unusual, milky, bitter). It should then describe the gustatory and aromatic impressions perceived, identifying, for example, the following notes: buttery / developing lactic acid, sourish, buttermilk, sour or yoghurt, sweet or sweetish enzymes, bitterish/almondy, chestnut, hazelnut, honey, cooked, toasted, hay, garlic, onion, wool, vine leaf, dry, piquant or pungent, mould or mushroom, rancid.

It is then necessary to decide whether the impressions perceived are balanced and what overall sensation the cheese elicits. In other words, is the taster's perception thin, fondant or melt-in-the-mouth, silky, buttery, crystallised or lacking in structure? Finally, there are two other crucial characteristics to be considered in cheese tasting: length on the palate and suasiveness. Length (short, long or very long) is defined independently of saltiness or piquancy, which can be modified during cheesemaking and are not expressions of the cheese's complexity.

In contrast, suasiveness is very similar in some respects to palatability. Whereas palatability is a quantitative judgement, suasiveness is qualitative. Both, however, are assessed by verifying what proportion of the mouth and tongue's taste receptors the cheese stimulates. The opposite of suasiveness is pungency, which indicates a distinct, strong taste sensation limited to one group of receptors. Suasiveness refers to a wide, full richness of taste and aromas.

A dictionary of tasting

Aftertaste
The sum of the gustatory impressions perceptible in the mouth after swallowing the cheese. The aftertaste is assessed in terms of the quality and duration of perception (see **Length**).

Aroma
The sum of the odorous compounds and fragrances of a substance that are perceptible by the olfactory bulb. Odorous molecules are perceived by a retronasal – not direct nasal – route. Aromas may be animal, milk, vegetal and so on.

Balance
The balance of a cheese is the degree of congruence of the various sensations perceived during tasting. The more harmonious the relationship, the better the cheese is organoleptically balanced.

Colour
Referring to the body of a cheese and, if specified, of the outer rind. Colour depends on the milk used (neither goat's not buffalo's milk contains the yellow pigment, beta carotene) and maturing. The colour of the body may range from milk-white to brownish. The colour of the rind may be the result of treatment it has received.

Consistency
The sum of the sensations that emerge from chewing the cheese, and from its adherence to the taster's palate and tongue, to assess the structure of the cheese, hence the alternative term, "mouthfeel". A preliminary evaluation of protein breakdown should be made by moulding the cheese between thumb and fingers, if possible. Consistency is classified as crumbly, elastic, firm, fondant or "melt-in-the-mouth", dry, rubbery, flabby and so on.

Deformability
The tendency of the cheese, once in the mouth, to progressively lose its shape or yield before breaking up.

Elasticity
The tendency of a sample of cheese to recover its original shape after compression and deformation.

Flavour
The sensation perceived by the taste receptors, produced on introducing a food product into the mouth. Flavours may be sweet, bitter, salty, sour, attractive, unpleasant and so on.

Friability
The tendency of the cheese to crumble into small fragments.

Small, high-sided cheeses should be first sliced and then divided into servings by cutting the slices in half.

Granularity
The perception of small, granular particles during mastication of a piece of cheese.

Hardness
The cheese's resistance to slight pressure of the jaws.

Length
Indicates the duration of olfactory perception via the retronasal passage. In assessing length, perceptions of saltiness and piquancy should be ignored as these qualities may be modified during cheesemaking and are irrelevant to the intrinsic complexity of the cheese.

Liquescence
The sensation produced when a cheese sample melts rapidly in the mouth.

Olfactory complexity
Having ascertained the cheese's purity, or the absence of defects, on the nose, the taster identifies the main odorous components and their intensity. An overall assessment of the nose may be made to indicate the olfactory complexity of the cheese.

Organoleptic analysis
see **Sensory analysis**

Palatability
The sum of the tactile sensations perceived inside the mouth, indicating the number of sensory cells stimulated by the sample and the quality of those sensations. In general, palatability is determined quantitatively from the fat-derived sensations present but quality will also depend on the cheese's overall balance (see Balance).

Retronasal perception
The sum of the olfactory impressions perceptible in the mouth af-

ter swallowing the cheese.

Sapidity
The quality exhibited by an appetising, full-flavoured, mouth-filling cheese with good length on the palate.

Sensory analysis
The exploratory examination of a food product by means of the five senses or organs of the human body (sight, smell, taste, hearing and touch).

Shape
The external appearance of the cheese, expressed as a solid geometrical figure of small (in grams) or large (in kilograms) dimensions. Circular, square, conical, quadrilateral, tangerine-shaped, sausage-shaped, pear-shaped and so on.

Smell
A sensory quality perceived by sniffing. Smell indicates the sensations perceived by the olfactory epithelium when stimulated by odorous molecules entering the nasal passage directly.

Suasiveness
see **Palatability**

Two methods of dividing a round, low-sided, soft or semi-hard cheese into portions - the so-called "European cut" and the "North American cut".

 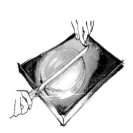

Above left is a professional wire cheese-cutter for soft cheeses. On the right, the same operation is being carried out with a knife held in both hands.

3. Principal defects

Fresh acid-set cheeses

Fresh acid-set cheeses may have two main defects. The flavour may be too acidic or the cheese may exude whey. Acidity is due to excessive fermentation of the milk and whey may present because of insufficient draining, a curd that is too finely cut, or excessive souring.

Soft cheeses

The outer rind may be wrinkled, and detach easily to show a layer of dripping, liquid body, a defect caused by a grey-white mould of *Geotricum candidum*. The micro-organism makes the rind fatty and waterproof, preventing normal draining. Low-acid cheeses that are insufficiently drained or stored in poorly-ventilated rooms may develop patches of a kind of cat's whisker-like *Mucor* bacterium that grows in the vicinity of *Penicillium candidum*. When the whiskers break, they leave undesirable grey patches. One of the most frequent defects of the body is chalkiness in the central part of the cheese. The body becomes dry and chalk-like in appearance. This may occur because of hurried draining stimulated by excessively high maturing temperatures, or the use of over-acidic milk. The contrasting defect is runniness, which can lead to the structural collapse of the cheese onto itself. Runniness is due to accelerated breakdown of the caseins caused by insufficient initial lactic fermentation. A bitter taste is a defect that can have several different causes, including psychrotrophic micro-organisms, too much salt or cheesemaking errors.

Stretched curd cheeses

Defects in fresh stretched curd cheeses include swelling, putrescence and the presence of whey, peeling, mould and excessive hardness or softness of the body. Swelling is due to the presence of coliform micro-organisms. Putrescence and whey are caused by contamination with spore-forming germs. Peeling derives from acid-saline imbalances in the cheese and the liquid in which it is kneaded. Mould comes from the storage and maturing environments and body defects are the consequence of poor cheesemaking.

Mature stretched curd cheeses are more likely to present delayed swelling, cracks in the surface, excessive flaking, a bitter flavour or undesirable colouring. Delayed swelling is caused by butyric clostridia that also encourage the widespread formation of large eyes. The excessive flaking, or detachment, of the body is due to excessive acidity during fermentation. Cracks on the surface are due to hurried drying. A bitter taste is the result of too much rennet or not enough attention to hygiene. Poor hygiene, in conjunction with microbial or chemical processes, may also cause undesirable colouring of the cheese.

Pressed curd cheese

Frequent defects in pressed curd cheeses are early or delayed swelling, flaking, surface mould, sandy body texture and bitter flavour. Early swelling can appear during pressing, when coliforms and yeasts are the cause. Delayed swelling due to butyric and propionic bacteria also causes large, undesirable eyes and, in the case of butyric bacteria, turns the cheese rancid. Flaking, the horizontal detachment of the body inside the cheese, may be caused by excessive acidity of the milk, excessive setting, salting or pressing, or by variations in temperature during maturing. Tufts of undesirable mould on the surface may be caused by excessive moisture in the body or by the external environment. Sandy texture may be caused by cooking the curd for too long, or by excessive salting. Finally, proteolytic micro-organisms like mesophilous Streptococcus bacteria are the reason for a bitter flavour.

4. Conserving cheese

How should you keep a cheese at home? Or rather, what do you have to do to make sure its taste characteristics do not deteriorate? First of all, it is necessary to distinguish between maturing (sometimes called curing, ageing or ripening) and conservation, which are two distinct processes, the latter being subsequent to the former. With the exception of fresh cheeses, maturing is an indispensable stage in cheesemaking. Conservation, however, is optional and generally has detrimental consequences for the product's taste profile. It is therefore advisable to conserve cheese for as brief a period as possible.

The fundamental parameters that govern maturing are ambient temperature and humidity - one only has to think of the cheese caves of Valsassina, the mountain huts of Castelmagno, the vast maturing sheds for Parmigiano Reggiano, or even the spotless warehouses used for semi-mature industrial cheeses. It goes without saying that the same temperature and humidity ought to – but obviously cannot – be maintained when storing cheese at home, where the difficulties of proper cheese conservation are compounded by other factors. Maturing involves the entire body of the cheese, whether it is large like some varieties of provolone or smaller, like caciocavallo cheeses. Conservation, in contrast, usually involves sliced or portioned cheeses, so other chemical processes come into play. For example, cheese oxidises fairly rapidly on the surface, which gives the body a brown colour. Processes such as proteolysis, and the intensification of the product's taste and smell, may reach dangerous levels, and UV rays in daylight may break down the cheese's fatty substances and vitamins. Cheese is a complex aggregate of organic substances that begin as milk and acquire different molecular structures and appearance, depending on the age of the individual type. The life cycle of cheese is fairly short and the time taken after initial shaping for the product to reach full maturity is brief. And that's it. When the product is overripe, the consumer is no longer a taster but a vaguely disconcerting devourer of smelly fermented milk.

Cellar and refrigerator
The problem of storing cheese at home can be at least partially solved by purchasing small portions from a reputable retailer for

consumption within a few days. Only those who live well away from the dry, polluted city atmosphere, and have cool cellars where food products can be stored in the cold and dark, should contemplate buying less frequently and in greater quantity. Such lucky cheese lovers might even want to revive the ritual of the gourmets who once used to buy whole immature cheeses directly from Alpine cheesemakers to age it in their own cellars. Each day, these connoisseurs would observe the progress of maturation and carefully clean the outer rind.

Sadly, old-fashioned larders no longer exist. The modern equivalent is the section of the refrigerator where the temperature is near – but never below – freezing. In it, we can store our slice of cheese, after first wrapping it in polythene, greaseproof paper or tin foil. Slices should be kept separate and wrapped individually. Otherwise, there is a risk of physical

Here is how to cut square or rectangular soft or semi-hard cheeses. The corners will have a greater amount of rind so cutting should ensure equal proportions of body and rind for all portions.

contact and the consequent transmission of aromas or mould. Some connoisseurs prefer to keep hard or mature cheeses separate from softer or younger products. For hard cheeses, experts recommend wrapping pieces of grana or pecorino, for example, in an odourless, freshly laundered hemp or cotton cloth, before placing them in a small, ventilated larder. If the body is reasonably dry, the cloth-wrapped cheese may also be put in a perforated polythene bag and then stored in a cool dark place. But check the cheese's state of conservation regularly as blue mould may appear on the surface. Remember, too, that keeping cheese at home is influenced by the time of year. In summer, temperature and humidity may reach critical levels so a refrigerator is an absolute must. Finally, the cheese should be taken out of the refrigerator, unwrapped and allowed to breathe for half an hour to an hour before it is consumed.

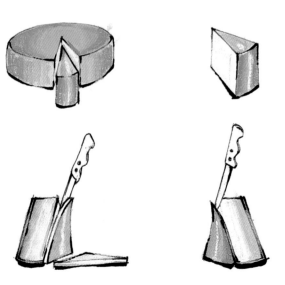

Another method of portioning a round, high-sided hard cheese. Note particularly the correct method of removing the rind from mature cheeses. Always begin from the centre, cutting towards the exterior.

A dictionary of cheese

Acidity
The chemical property of milk due to the presence of acids and acid groups. Acidity tends to rise naturally after fermentation, the formation of lactic acid from lactose, and lipolysis, or the liberation of fatty acids. It plays a fundamental role in the coagulation, or curdling, of milk.

Bloomy rind
A bloomy, or mouldy, rind is caused by surface microflora (Mucor and Penicillium) that generate a grey-white mould. Characteristic of soft-ripened cheeses such as Taleggio and Camembert.

Blue cheese
see **Veining**

Brine
see **Salting**

Butter
The term "butter" is legally defined in Italy as "the product obtained by the mechanical processing of cream taken from cow's milk, from cow's milk whey, or from a mixture of these products". The mechanical operation involved is churning. This entails the agitation of the cream to encourage the rupture of the external membrane of fat and separate the watery component (buttermilk). The removal of fatty elements in liquid form incorporates all the components of the cream and gives butter its special structure.

Buttermilk
see Butter

Casein
The most plentiful of the proteins in milk, accounting for about 80% of the total. It is made up of various fractions (alpha, beta and kappa) that coagulate to form curd when attacked by enzymes or acidity (see **Curd**).

Caves
Sheltered, stable, natural environments where some cheeses are matured, especially soft and blue cheeses. Known as grotte in Italian. Cool and damp, their temperature and humidity are regulated by cold, moist air entering through cracks in the rock. The caves of Valsassina, for Taleggio, and the so-called *fleurines* for maturing Roquefort, are two examples.

Cheese cellar
A suitable place for maturing cheeses, with optimal light, temperature and humidity conditions for promoting the physiological processes involved in ageing.

Cheese moulds
see Hoops

Coagulation
Coagulation, or curdling, is the fundamental transformation in cheesemaking. A number of factors, including acidity, temperature, mineral salts in the milk and inoculation with rennet, cause the precipitation of the casein to form the curd and separate it from the whey. When the precipitation of casein is caused by acidity, this is known as acid coagulation (for cheeses such as robiola di Roccaverano, quark, mascarpone and others). Rennet-based coagulation involves inoculation with rennet and is used for the majority of cheeses.

Colostrum
Milk secreted by the mammary gland in the first days after parturition. It has a different chemical composition from ordinary milk.

Cooked and semi-cooked cheese
A category of cheeses characterised by cooking of the just-cut curd

to promote separation from the whey, render the curd more elastic and encourage clotting. Cooking temperatures range from 44-45°C (semi-cooking, as for fontina, asiago, bitto and others) to 54-55°C (cooking, as for grana padano, parmigiano reggiano, emmental and so on).

Cream
An important milk product that rises to the top of standing milk, or is separated by skimming in a centrifuge. It is used mainly for making butter but has many other applications in the confectionery industry. Cream contains 25-40% fat but the proportions of its other constituents are almost identical to those of the original milk.

Curd
The clotted portion of coagulated milk, which has transformed from the colloidal solution of casein in sol phase into a gel after inoculation with rennet, or the curdling of the milk. Curd is essentially casein in gelatinous phase that has been separated from the whey. This separation is the first stage in cheesemaking.

Curing
The final stage in cheesemaking and the one that determines the final condition of the cheese (see Maturing). Curing is carried out in special cheese cellars or caves, or in temperature-controlled cells. It may last for only a few days, in the case of soft cheeses, or continue for several years for some hard cheeses. During this stage, the cheeses must be regularly turned over and cleaned.

Cutting the curd
The mechanical operation of breaking the curd in order to promote the separation and expulsion of the whey. The curd is cut with a special curd knife called a *spino* or *lira* in Italian. Initially, the soft curd is cut into large pieces. The operation is then repeated until the granules are of the dimensions required. The lumps for fresh, soft cheeses are walnut or hazelnut-sized, sweetcorn-sized for uncooked pressed cheeses and the size of a grain of rice for cooked hard cheeses.

Detachment of the body
A physical modification of the internal structure of the cheese, which tends to become detached from the rind lengthways,

forming irregularly shaped cavities. The defect is due to poor handling of the curd.

DO (Designation of Origin)
Recognition of a cheese in compliance with Italian law no. 125/1954, the second article of which states: "Designations regarding cheeses produced in geographically defined zones, in compliance with long-standing local customs, and whose product characteristics derive principally from the special conditions of their production environment, are recognised as Designations of Origin".

DOP (Protected Designation of Origin)
Recognition of a cheese or any other food product in compliance with EC Regulation 2081/1992, the second article of which states: "Designation of Origin means the name of a region, a specific place or, in exceptional cases, a country, used to describe an agricultural product or a foodstuff originating in that region, specific place or country, and the quality or characteristics of which are essentially or exclusively due to a particular geographical environment with its inherent human and natural factors, and the production, processing and preparation of which take place in the defined geographical area".

Draining
see **Synaeresis**

Enzyme
A complex organic substance that promotes certain chemical reactions. Milk contains about sixty different enzymes, some of which are extremely important for cheesemaking. The chymosin, pepsin and lipases contained in rennet (see Rennet) are also enzymes.

Eyes
The holes that form in the body of the cheese after acid fermentation, which produces gas, especially carbon dioxide. Eyes are usually small and uniform in size, although there are some exceptions, such as Emmental. In this case, the eyes are large and distributed extensively as a result of the action of propioni-bacteria, which transform lactic acid into propionic acid and carbon dioxide.

Fat

The principal component of milk, where it is found in the form of suspended globules enclosed in a phospholipid and vitamin-rich membrane. The proportion of fat in milk varies from one dairy species to another. It has significant nutritional value as a source of energy and vitamins. Fat is a fundamental component of cheese, contributing to its aroma and flavour. Cheeses are classified according to the fat content in the dry matter, expressed as a percentage – low-fat (less than 20%), semi-fat (20-42%) and fat (more than 42%).

Flaking

A defect, observed mainly in cooked hard cheeses and stretched curd cheeses, in which the body detaches in layers on the inside of the cheese. Flaking may be caused by hurried coagulation, the use of over-acidic milk, excessive salting or pressing, or by variations in temperature during maturing.

Fossa

A flask-shaped well, three metres deep, two metres across at the base and one metre across at the mouth, excavated out of the tufaceous rock at Sogliano al Rubicone (Forlì) and Talamello (Pesaro). To make formaggio di fossa, the cheeses are placed in the wells in mid August. The wells are then sealed air-tight, to be re-opened on 25 November, the feast of Saint Catherine, when the cheeses are taken out and put on sale.

Hard

Cheeses whose water content is less than 40%. Uncooked pressed cheeses and stretched curd cheeses, as well as cooked and semi-cooked cheeses, fall into this category.

Heat treatment

The application of heat to raw milk for at least fifteen seconds at a temperature of 57-68°C. After heat treatment, the milk should react positively to a phosphatase (enzyme) test. The aim of heat treatment is to reduce the native flora of the milk without altering excessively its cheesemaking properties.

Hoops

Special cheese moulds used to hold the curd after cooking. The curd may be left to drain (soft cheeses) or pressed (hard cheeses).

Hoops may be made of beechwood, metal or synthetic resin. The hoops give the side of the cheese its shape and can be used to print marks of origin.

IGP (Protected Geographical Indication)
Recognition of a cheese or any other foodstuff in compliance with EC Regulation 1081/1992. IGP status differs from DOP in that a specific quality, reputation or other characteristic attributable to the geographical area, and the production and/or processing and/or preparation of the product in the geographical area, are sufficient for its award.

Inner rind
The superficial layer of the body, just under the rind, with a more intense colour and more marked taste because it is most affected by the chemical process of oxidisation. In soft cheeses, proteolysis occurs on the inner rind because of the surface microflora.

Inoculation of starter culture
The addition to the milk to be transformed into cheese of selected starter cultures of specific bacteria to promote fermentation of lactose and other components. The main culture media used are milk and whey. Starter cultures are therefore milk or whey-inoculated (natural growth of bacteria), or milk or whey-fermented (selected bacterial growth).

Lactose
The sugar found in milk, in which it is the most easily assimilated source of energy. In chemical terms, lactose is the union of one molecule of glucose with one of galactose, and is not common in nature. The presence of lactose in some nerve tissues is important. Lactose has no significance quantitatively in cheesemaking as it remains in solution in the whey. Its fermentation into lactic acid through the action of lactic flora is important because this influences the taste profile of the cheese.

Lipolysis
The breakdown of fats promoted by the presence of specific enzymes (lipase). Lipolysis is significant in the maturing process of some cheeses characterised by strong hydrolysis, or breakdown by water, of the fat. In pecorino and provolone,

maturing is promoted by rennet paste-derived lipase, and in gorgonzola by lipase from mould.

Marbling
see **Veining**

Maturing
The overall result of various chemical and physical processes involving the curd. They determine the texture of the body, the external appearance of the cheese, and above all its final aroma and taste. The temperature and humidity of maturing rooms must be regulated with extreme precision.

Milk
By international convention, milk is defined as: "The whole product obtained from the complete, uninterrupted milking of a healthy, well-fed, rested, female dairy animal. The milk should be collected carefully and hygienically, and should not contain colostrum. The unqualified indication, 'milk', indicates cow's milk. Cleaning of material and utensils should carried out in such a way that the composition of the milk cannot be modified in any way". The average composition of cow's milk is as follows: water 87-88%, fat 3.4-4.4%, proteins 3-3.5%, lactose 4.7-5.2%, mineral salts 0.8-1%. The milk of other ruminants is also suitable for transformation into cheese. Ewe's milk, goat's milk, both highly prized, and buffalo's milk are common alternatives.

Milk enzymes
Important micro-organisms (bacteria) for cheesemaking because they promote acidity and the precipitation of milk protein into a solid curd. They are mainly responsible for the taste profile of the cheese as they act on lactose and other major components of milk during fermentation. Bacteria, including milk enzymes, are in part removed by cooking and most are eliminated during pasteurisation. It is necessary to inoculate pasteurised milk with a starter culture in order to turn it into cheese (see Inoculation of starter culture).

Milking
The operation of drawing milk from dairy animals. Milking may performed manually or mechanically, and should serve the follow-

ing aims: to produce clean milk, and to encourage the complete expulsion of the milk without damaging the udder. Milk is secreted by animals as a result of the complex hormonal mechanism that regulates the mammary gland.

Mineral salts
Milk contains a number of minerals that are important in nutritional terms. Although poor in iron, milk is rich in calcium and phosphorus, both of which are present in proportions that can readily be assimilated by the bones of the breast-feeding infant. Calcium and phosphorus also help to maintain the balance of caseins and are important factors in coagulation.

Moulds
Micro-organisms belonging to the Eumycota division of the Mycota kingdom, of the genera Aspergillus, Mucor, and Penicillium, which live as saprophytes on organic substances and form an efflorescence with their fruiting bodies. The sometimes powdery efflorescence may be white, grey, greenish or even black (see **Bloomy rind and Veining**).

Mountain pasture
A mountain region used in summer for pasturing dairy herds, where the fodder plants contain flavour-enhancing compounds that give the milk special characteristics. The Italian term *alpeggio* implies the presence of a milking dairy. But there are many other names for mountain pastures, which vary from region to region. Two of the more frequently encountered are *malga* and *alpe*.

Nail
A dark inner rind, blackish in colour. This defect occurs when the cheese contains a very high percentage of fat, and when it is stored in a poorly ventilated room or on old shelving.

Outer rind
A superficial layer that forms on the cheese after salting, ripening and maturing. In soft cheeses, the surface microflora makes a crucial contribution to the texture and taste profile of the final product. In other types, the outer rind has the main function of protecting the cheese and exchanging gas and water vapour with the surrounding environment. The rind may be washed, oiled or paraffin-waxed to

prevent the growth of mould and the red colouring due to the presence of oospores. In certain cases, such as pressed cheeses, the rind is removed and replaced with a protective wrapping of polyvinyl acetate. Rinds may be smooth, rough, rush mat-patterned, lustrous, thin, yellow, ivory, brownish, pock-marked, cracked and so on.

Oxidation
A chemical process that affects cheeses after prolonged exposure to air. Oxidation produces visible modification of the body colour as well as alterations of the cheese's nose and palate as fatty matter becomes rancid.

Pasteurisation
The application of heat to raw milk for at least 15 seconds at a temperature of at least 71.7°C. After pasteurisation, the milk should react negatively to the phosphatase (enzyme) test. The aim of pasteurisation is to destroy all pathogenic germs and ensure the healthfulness of the milk while enhancing its low-temperature storage potential.

Pasteurisation (UHT)
Heat treatment of raw milk for at least one second at a temperature of at least 135°C. After UHT pasteurisation, milk should present no spoilage when stored at 30°C for 15 days. Milk is ultrapasteurised to enhance its shelf life, and may be refrigerated or kept at room temperature.

Penicillium
A genus of fungi that grows inside or on the surface of cheeses. *Penicillium roqueforti* is the main agent responsible for internal veining in roquefort, gorgonzola and similar blue cheeses. *Penicillium camemberti* acts on bloomy rind cheeses, such as camembert or brie.

Stretched curd
A cheesemaking technique involving immersion of the curd in hot, acid whey for several hours to remove minerals from the body and render it elastic. The curd is then kneaded and stretched in warm water at 70-90°C until it acquires the desired shape. Cheeses of this type include mozzarella, provolone, caciocavallo, ragusano and others.

Pressing

A technique used mainly for uncooked hard cheeses. Pressure is applied for a period ranging from one to twenty-four hours to expel whey before a sturdy outer rind forms.

Processed cheeses

Products obtained by melting cheeses with the application of heat. Processed cheeses are pasteurised and may contain added milk, cream, water, and salts. The texture of processed cheeses is compact, homogeneous and extremely elastic.

Proteins

Proteins are the fundamental components of milk whose functional properties determine the basic cheesemaking technique. They are nitrogenous compounds and may be classified into two large groups, caseins and whey proteins. Caseins are found in suspension in milk in the form of micelles. They precipitate under the effect of rennet or acidity.

Proteolysis

A fundamental process in the maturing of cheeses, involving the breakdown of complex casein molecules into simpler nitrogenous compounds (amino acids). Proteolysis is encouraged by specific proteolytic enzymes.

Quark

A fresh cheese made industrially using pasteurised milk. It is acid-coagulated and inoculated with a small quantity of rennet and then cold-chain stored. Quark should be consumed within a week or two of production.

Raw milk

Milk that has not been heat-treated, used for cheesemaking. Raw milk still has the original microflora it acquired from its environment. The microflora contribute to the taste profile of the final cheese.

Rennet

An extract of animal origin containing proteolytic enzymes (chymosin and pepsin) that coagulate casein. Generally obtained from the abomasum, or fourth stomach, of unweaned ruminants (calves, kids or lambs). Some rennets also contain lipases, enzymes that can catalyse the hydrolysis of fats and contribute to the sensory profile of the cheese. Commercially, rennet is available in a number of forms, and may be used as a liquid or in powder, pellets or paste. Other coagulants may be of vegetable or fungal origin.

Ricotta

According to Italian law, ricotta is not a real cheese because it is not obtained from the coagulation of casein in milk. It comes instead from the coagulation at high temperature (80-90°C) of the proteins in whey, a by-product of the processing of cow's, ewe's or goat's milk. From a nutritional point of view, ricotta is low in fat and rich in complete proteins.

Ripening

The stage of cheesemaking that comprises storing the cheese in a warm (24-28°C), humid room for a few hours (up to twenty four) in order to complete the fermentation process and synaeresis (for gorgonzola and taleggio, etc.).

Rising of the cream

A physiological process that takes place in standing milk as the fatty emulsion rises to the surface because of its relative specific weight. This phenomenon is exploited in the preparation of partially skimmed milk to be used for semi-fat cheeses, such as grana padano and parmigiano reggiano, or "parmesan", cheese.

Salting

The final treatment applied to cheese before maturation. Salt is a preserving agent and an antiseptic that inhibits the growth of micro-organisms. It also has an osmotic effect as the cheese releases whey and absorbs salt. Salting may take the form of dry-salting, in which the salt is sprinkled onto, or rubbed into, the outer surface, immersion of the cheese in vats of brine for a period of time that varies depending on its weight, or by the addition of salt to the milk or curd.

Side

The upright, slightly convex or concave, lateral section of cylindrical cheeses. The shape of the side is determined by the hoops used. The sides of almost all hard cheeses bear the cheese's name and/or mark of origin.

Skimming

The process of removing part of the fat from the milk. Milk is skimmed naturally by the rising of the cream (see Rising of the cream). The process may be mechanised and accelerated with the aid of cream-separating centrifuges.

Smoking

The process of exposing a food product to the action of certain components in the smoke released by the combustion of various vegetable substances. Smoke is deposited on the food product through the absorption of steam, in which superficial and interstitial moisture acts as an absorption vehicle. Many cheeses are conserved using this technique.

Soft cheese

Cheeses whose water content is more than 40%. This category includes fresh cheeses for immediate consumption (mozzarella, robiola, quartirolo and so on) and medium mature cheeses (such as gorgonzola and taleggio).

Starter culture
see **Inoculation of starter culture**

Swelling

A frequent defect of cooked cheeses, caused by gas-producing micro-organisms. Swelling is "premature" when it is caused by the fermentation of lactose by non-milk bacteria (Coli etc.) and "delayed" when it presents towards the end of maturing as a result of butyric or propionic fermentation.

Synaeresis

The set of phenomena provoking the expulsion of whey from the curd. Synaeresis occurs more readily in rennet-based coagulation than in the acid-promoted process, since the curd is less contractile.

Top and bottom

The two plane surfaces on which cylindrical cheeses rest. The top and bottom surfaces of a cheese may be flat, as in grana and parmigiano, convex, such as asiago pressato, or concave, as in some *canestrato* (mat-drained) cheeses. The top or bottom sometimes carries the cheese's mark of origin.

Top of the milk
see **Cream**

Typical Designation
Recognition of a cheese in compliance with Italian law no. 125/1954, the second article of which states: "Typical Designations are those relating to cheeses produced on Italian territory observing genuine, long-standing customs, whose product characteristics derive from special methods in the reproduction technique". Unlike Designation of Origin, Typical Designation is not related to the influence of environmental factors in the zone of origin on the finished product.

Uncooked cheeses
A category of cheeses made without cooking the curd after it is cut. Fresh cheeses and soft cheeses are all uncooked. Some hard or semi-hard cheeses, such as bra, raschera and castelmagno from Italy, cheddar from the United Kingdom and edam from Holland, are pressed and uncooked.

Veining
The distinguishing feature of blue cheeses whose body is veined with blue or green mould. Also called "marbling", veining is characteristic of some of Europe's greatest cheeses, such as Italy's gorgonzola, stilton from the United Kingdom and roquefort and other blue cheeses from France. The Italian word *erborinatura* derives from the Lombard dialect word *erborin*, meaning "parsley", a reference to the colour and structure of the body of such cheeses. The term used in French is *persillé*.

Washed rind
see **Outer rind**

Whey drainage
see Synaeresis

Whey
The liquid by-product of cheesemaking which contains lactose, whey proteins and mineral salts. Whey accounts for about 90% of the original milk. It is partially recycled in the cheese factory for

the preparation of starter cultures (see Inoculation of starter culture) and ricotta (see Ricotta). Whey is also used in the confectionery industry as a powder or concentrate, and as an animal feed.

Whey proteins
Proteins that are not precipitated by rennet or acidity and that remain in the whey in solution. The major whey proteins are lactalbumins and lactoglobulins. These proteins may be recovered in the form of ricotta, or cottage cheese. Colostrum is also extremely rich in lactalbumins and lactoglobulins, the first antibodies to be acquired by newborns.

Yield
The proportion of milk transformed into cheese during cheesemaking. Yield is expressed as a percentage in kilograms of cheese obtained per 100 kilograms of milk used. A yield of 10% is reckoned to be average, but the figure may range from 15-20% for very fresh products, to 7-8% for hard cheeses.

Yoghurt
Milk fermented by cultures of *Lactobacillus bulgaricus* and *Streptococcus thermophilus*. Pasteurised or heat-treated whole, part-skimmed or skimmed milk is inoculated with a specific starter culture, cooled and stored at 4°C until it is consumed. Yoghurt is sold as a "live" or "living" product.

Light cheeses

Under Italian law, low-fat cheeses are defined as cheeses whose fat content in dry matter does not exceed 20%. This category includes the cheeses and other dairy products popularly known as "light". The prototypes of the category are quark and cottage cheese. Both are made with low-fat or part-skimmed milk, and have been available in the markets of the United States and northern Europe for several decades. More recently, light products have appeared in Italy, partly as a result of diet and health-driven fashions. These fiordilatte and bocconcini stretched curd products, crescenza, ricotta and cow's milk caprino-type cheeses are made by a multinational company and reflect none of Italy's traditional cheese types. What is lightened is the cheese's fat content, equivalent to 3.5% in whole milk and comprising mainly saturated fatty acids. Yet fat is not an inert component of cheese. It is part of the structure of the curd, and enhances the product's spreadability, softness and above all flavour. Removing part of the fat inevitably poses problems for the sensory characteristics of dairy products. Traditional technology has been industrially modified so that the end product's softness is maintained even though the fat content has been reduced. The intervention involves modifying the times and temperatures employed for processing the curd, washing and rinsing it (using colder water encourages humidity retention) and the subsequent homogenisation process, or milling of the curd. Another expedient, used for processed cheeses, consists in adding fractions of whey proteins, sometimes obtained by ultrafiltration, or other additives such as carrageenins, alginates or starch derivatives used, for example, in the industrial production of ice cream. Light cheeses have about half the content and one third fewer calories than standard equivalents. Light mozzarella contains about ten grams of fat per 100 grams total weight, compared with 20 grams for the traditional product. Light crescenza has about 11 grams of fat, compared with 22 for standard crescenza. The drawbacks of light products are that they have a neutral sensory profile and chalky texture, and the additives they contain have nothing to do with cheese. It would seem wiser to eat smaller quantities of traditional products, so as not to forgo taste and quality.

Valle d'Aosta

Brossa

Fontina DOP

Formaggio a Pasta Pressata

Formaggio di Capra
a Pasta Molle

Formaggio Misto

Reblec

Salignoùn

Séras

Toma di Gressoney

Valle d'Aosta
Fromadzo DOP

Brossa

The traditional product of a poor economy, Brossa was once made exclusively for domestic consumption. It is obtained from whey left over from making cheese with the milk from Valdostana cows, ewes or goats. This is mixed with liquid *bôné*, obtained by souring the whey itself and/or ricotta whey produced by spontaneous lactic fermentation. The mixture is heated to 83-84°C. The fat rises to the surface under the effect of heat and acidity – the Italian name for Brossa is *fiorito*, which means "risen to the surface" – together with a small quantity of casein and albumin. When the layer has thickened sufficiently, it is scooped up in a spoon-shaped *spanarola*. After it has cooled and been gently whipped, the Brossa is ready for the table. It should be eaten within two or three days of production on its own, as an accompaniment for polenta, or in a less traditional style mixed with sugar and cinnamon.

Body: fine, grainy, almost liquid, cream-white in colour
Territory of origin: the entire region

COW'S MILK

Fontina DOP

There are various explanations for this cheese's name. Some link it with the mountain pastures of Fontin, in the municipality of Quart, others to the place name, Fontinaz, and still others to the surname of a family of cheesemakers. Whatever the truth, this is Valle d'Aosta's cheese *par excellence*. Yet, despite its popularity, the mountain dairy version in particular is a difficult cheese to make successfully. Only fresh milk from Valdostana cows is used. It must be raw and come from a single milking. In fact, the cheese is made twice every day. The milk is heated to no more than 36°C and inoculated with natural or industrial rennet. Coagulation takes 40-50 minutes. The next stage is to stir the soft curd and break it up roughly for the first time. After being left to stand for a short while, the curd is cut again until rice-sized granules are obtained. The mass is then semi-cooked and left to settle on the bottom of the vat. Next, it wrapped up in a cloth and placed in the moulds that give the side of the cheese its characteristic concave profile. The cheeses are then pressed for about 12 hours and turned over frequently before being transferred to a cool (10°C) room at 90-95% humidity. Here, they are turned over daily, and salted and washed with brine-soaked brushes every other day. This operation is repeated until the outer rind acquires its characteristic brown colouring. After this, the cheeses are matured in a natural environment, including caves, grottoes, former army emplacements – the co-operative dairy even uses an old copper mine. Maturing lasts for at least 80 days.

Rennet: liquid, powder or very occasionally pellet, calf's
Outer rind: firm, thin, dark yellow or reddish-brown in colour
Body: soft, fondant, with relatively few bird's eye-sized holes, straw-white to deep yellow in colour
Top and bottom: flat, 30-45 cm in diameter
Height/weight: 7-10 cm / 8 -12 kg
Territory of origin: the entire region
DOP status awarded on 12 June 1996, regulation no. 1107

The mark of this celebrated mountain cheese features the outline of the Matterhorn. The illustration shows the scattered eyes that can be seen when the cheese is sliced.

Formaggio a Pasta Pressata

The milk is heated to a temperature of 36-37°C and coagulated with powdered or liquid rennet. In the past, calf's rennet in pellet form was used. After 30-45 minutes, the curd is cut with a *lira* curd knife into granules the size of a grain of rice. The whey is expelled in the cauldron by vigorously stirring the soft curd and heating it to no more than 40-42°C for 15-20 minutes. The curd is then transferred into hoops and pressed with a weight. It is turned over three or four times. The next stage is salting. Traditionally, this is carried out dry, but occasionally a brine bath is used. The cheese matures for at least 60 days in cool, damp cellars. During maturation, the cheeses are turned over every three or four days and the rind is cleaned periodically with a salt solution.

Rennet: powder or liquid, calf's or kid's
Outer rind: fairly substantial, straw-yellow in colour, acquiring other tinges from the maturing environment
Body: compact, with faint eyes, white in colour
Top and bottom: flat, 10-30 cm in diameter
Height/weight: 5-15 cm / 0.5-5 kg
Territory of origin: the entire region

Formaggio di Capra a Pasta Molle

This cheese is made all over the region in valley floor farms, *mayens* (mid mountain huts) and in mountain pastures. Once, it was made in summer, when the cows were taken to the high-altitude pastures and the goats, which stayed on the valley floor, grazed on the meadows that were not used for haymaking. The milk is heated to a temperature of 36-37°C and coagulated with powdered or liquid rennet. In the past, calf's or kid's rennet in pellet form was used. After 30-40 minutes, the curd is cut with a *lira* curd knife into granules the size of a grain of rice. The whey is drained off in 10-15 minutes with no further application of heat. The soft curd is then placed in hoops and pressed by hand. It is turned over three or four times. Salting is carried out dry, but occasionally a brine bath is used. The resulting cheese matures for at least 20-25 days in cool, damp cellars, where it is turned over every three or four days. The rind is washed with a salt solution when the cheese is turned.

Rennet: powder or liquid, calf's and/or kid's
Outer rind: thin, pale in colour acquiring other tinges from the maturing environment
Body: soft, firm, white in colour
Top and bottom: flat, 10-15 cm in diameter
Height/weight: 5 cm / 300 g
Territory of origin: the entire region

COW'S, EWE'S AND GOAT'S MILK

Formaggio Misto

Mixed herds have always enabled the mountain farmers of Valle d'Aosta to get the most out of their territory. The best pastures are kept for their cows, leaving the scrubby and least accessible areas for goats and sheep. A mixture of all three kinds of milk, in proportion that vary depending on the time of year, is coagulated in 40-60 minutes at a temperature of 36°C. The curd is cut with a *lira* curd knife into lumps the size of a grain of rice. The whey is expelled in the cauldron by vigorously stirring the soft curd and heating it to no more than 40-42°C for 15-20 minutes. The curd is then transferred into hoops and pressed by hand or with a weight. It is turned over three or four times. The cheese is then dry-salted and matured for at least 60-90 days in cool, damp cellars. During maturation, the cheeses are turned over every three or four days, and the rind is cleaned with a salt solution.

Rennet: powder or liquid, calf's or kid's
Outer rind: fairly substantial, straw-yellow in colour, acquiring other tinges from the maturing environment
Body: compact, with faint eyes, white in colour
Top and bottom: flat, 10-30 cm in diameter
Height/weight: 5-15 cm / 0.5-5 kg
Territory of origin: the entire region

COW'S MILK

Reblec

The dairy-produced version of this cheese, made with the surface portion of the curd, should not be confused with traditional Reblec, the cheesemaking process for which is relatively complex. The cream that has risen is skimmed off and heated to a temperature of 35-40°C. Next, sufficient rennet is added to coagulate the cream in one and a half hours. The soft curd is lifted out whole in a cloth and placed in a perforated container in a warm, humid room. Here, the excess whey drains off. The curd, however, remains fairly moist, ripening in the meantime. Reblec can be consumed as soon as the curd has formed but in any case should be eaten two or three days of production. It may be sprinkled with sugar or cinnamon. The former President of Italy, Luigi Einaudi, who often holidayed at By in Valpelline, used to love this cheese.

Rennet: liquid, calf's
Body: creamy, soft, still moist with whey
Height/weight: irregular
Territory of origin: all over Valle d'Aosta, almost exclusively in mountain dairies

Salignoùn

Technically, Salignoùn is not a cheese but a ricotta. It comes from the German dairy tradition, and in particular the Walser heritage. To make Salignoùn, fairly fatty, fresh ricotta, obtained by adding milk or cream to the whey, is used. It is kneaded with salt and powdered red chilli pepper, or paprika, which gives it its characteristic deep pink colour and markedly piquant flavour. Some cheesemakers also add wild herbs or dried flowers from the mountain pastures. The aromatised product is then shaped into balls, which are placed inside the hood of the hearth to dry and absorb a little smoke. There is also an unsmoked version, to which garlic is added during kneading. Salignoùn is generally made for consumption in the home and is rarely found on sale. It is an excellent cheese to serve with beer.

Body: crumbly, fatty, usually aromatised with herbs and spices
Weight: variable
Territory of origin: Lower Valle d'Aosta

Séras

Séras is a ricotta with an ancient tradition. Also known as *sérac* or *ceré*, it is made with the left-over whey from cheese-making with milk from Valdostana cows, sheep or goats. When made from ewe's or goat's whey, a maximum of 10% ewe's or goat's milk may be added to the mixture. The whey is heated to a temperature of 85-90°C and the curd that floats to the surface is skimmed off with a strainer called a *potse forete*. It is transferred to perforated rectangular moulds, where it drains for a few hours. Séras should be eaten fresh, but it may also be matured for a few months if smoked.

Body: soft, grainy
Top and bottom: flat, rectangular
Height/weight: 10-20 cm / 0.2-3 kg
Territory of origin: the entire region

Toma di Gressoney

Until the 1950s, Toma was made in three valleys in Valle d'Aosta, Gressoney, Champocher and Évançon. Today, only a few farmers continue to make this kind of cheese, as almost all the milk from the mountain pastures is used to make fontina (see entry). But around Gressoney-Saint Jean, there are still a number of small-scale, but very interesting, traditional products. On the summer pastures, some of which are 2,200 metres above sea level, cheesemakers still produce Toma di Gressoney, a classic uncooked Alpine toma made in slightly smaller, taller rounds than other similar products. The technique used is typical for a semi-fat cheese. Raw milk from the evening milking is left to stand for 24 hours and then skimmed by allowing the cream to rise to the top. The morning's milk, slightly skimmed after standing for 12 hours, is mixed with milk from the previous evening. The mixture is then heated to 35°C and coagulated with liquid calf's rennet. The curd is milled into very small granules that are removed from the whey and transferred to wooden hoops. The rounds are then salted, usually dry. Toma di Gressoney cheeses weigh three to five kilograms and are 5-12 centimetres high, with a diameter of 20-30 centimetres. The rind is smooth, slightly oily and shades from reddish to brown-grey in colour as maturing progresses. The body is straw-yellow in colour and has a few eyes. Toma di Gressoney is matured for at least three months, and has distinctive attractive aromas of moss and mushrooms. On the palate, pepper and vanilla notes lead into a finish reminiscent of beef broth. The cheese is capable of acquiring an even more exciting sensory profile if allowed to mature for a much longer time (up to one and a half years). Sadly, logistics and convenience mean that most Toma di Gressoney today is sold fresh. The Slow Food Presidium was set up to convince the producers to extend maturing and, where possible, restructure abandoned cellars.

Rennet: liquid, calf's
Outer rind: smooth, slightly oily, reddish to brown-grey depending on maturing
Body: with a few eyes, straw-yellow in colour
Top and bottom: flat, 20-30 cm in diameter
Height/weight: 5-12 cm / 3-5 kg
Territory of origin: the municipalities of Gressoney-Saint Jean and Gressoney-La Trinité in the province of Aosta

Toma di Gressoney matures for at least three months but is capable of acquiring an even more exciting sensory profile if allowed to age for a much longer time (up to one and a half years). The Slow Food Presidium was set up to convince producers to extend the maturing period.

Cow's, and goat's milk
Valle d'Aosta Fromadzo DOP

Valle d'Aosta Fromadzo DOP is made with cow's milk from two milkings that is left to stand and skimmed after the cream has risen to the top. It may contain up to 10% goat's milk. A medium-fat version is also made, for which the milk is left to stand for 12-24 hours, as well as a very low-fat type, in which case the milk stands for at least 36 hours. After skimming, the milk is heated to 34-36°C and inoculated with calf's rennet. When it has coagulated, the soft curd is cut into rice-sized granules and the temperature is raised to 42-45°C. At this point, the curd is placed in cheese hoops, called *feitchie* in the local dialect, where it is pressed and turned over three or four times a day. The rounds are then dry-salted, initially every other day, and then less and less frequently. After salting, the cheeses are matured in temperature-controlled rooms at 60% humidity, where they will remain for a period ranging from 60 days to about one year. Valle d'Aosta Fromadzo DOP, which can also be designated in French, has a straw-yellow outer rind that tends to shade into grey with the passage of time, also acquiring reddish tinges. The body is firm, with a few small or medium-sized eyes. The proportion of fat in dry matter is less than 20% in the low-fat version, and 20-35% for the medium-fat. DOP regulations permit aromatisation with the seeds or other parts of aromatic plants.

Rennet: liquid, calf's
Outer rind: fairly firm, straw-yellow tending to reddish-grey in colour as maturing progresses
Body: firm, elastic, with faint eyes, milk-white to deep yellow in colour
Top and bottom: flat, 15-30 cm in diameter
Height/weight: 5-20 cm / 1-7 kg
Territory of origin: the entire region
DOP status awarded on 1 July 1996, regulation no. 1263

Fortunately, production of this classic Alpine cheese is on the increase after a long period of near total absence from the market.

The producers

Amedeo Blanch
Località Ville Ozein, 29
Aymavilles (Aosta)
Tel. +39 0165 902286
Fontina Dop

Caseificio Artigiano Variney
Località Petit Quart
Gignod (Aosta)
Tel. +39 0165 256880
Brossa, Fontina Dop, Séras

**Consorzio Produttori
Fontina della Valle d'Aosta**
Corso Battaglione Aosta, 27
Aosta
Tel. +39 0165 44091
Fontina Dop

Cooperativa Produttori Latte e Fontina
Via Superstrada, 2
Pré-Saint-Didier (Aosta)
Tel. +39 0165 87850
Fontina Dop

Cooperativa Produttori Latte e Fontina
Regione Croix Noire, 10
Saint-Cristophe (Aosta)
Tel. +39 0165 35714
Fontina Dop

Cooperativa Produttori Latte e Fontina
Località Frissonia di Sopra
Valpelline (Aosta)
Tel. +39 0165 73280
Fontina Dop

Cooperativa Valle del Marmore
Località Evette, 26
Valtournenche (Aosta)
Tel. +39 0166 92132
Fontina Dop, Séras

Rina Ducret
Frazione Bettex, 11
Valsavarenche (Aosta)
Tel. +39 348 2942773
Fontina Dop

Evançon
Via Nazionale, 7
Località Glair
Arnad (Aosta)
Tel. +39 0125 968818
Fontina Dop, reblec, salignoùn, séras,
Valle d'Aosta fromadzo Dop

Secondo Ferrè
Località Champlong Martignon, 2
Villeneuve (Aosta)
Tel. +39 0165 95040
Fontina Dop

Giulio Girod
Frazione Colombit
Fontainemore (Aosta)
Tel. +39 347 5444280
Toma di Gressoney

Il Capretto
Frazione Pied de Ville
Issogne (Aosta)
Formaggio a Pasta Pressata, Formaggio
di Capra a Pasta Molle, Formaggio Misto

Bruno e Giuseppe Jeantet
Via Clementine, 17
Cogne (Aosta)
Tel. +39 0165 74469
Fontina Dop

Innocenzo Jeantet
Località Buthier, 1
Via Clementine, 10
Cogne (Aosta)
Tel. +39 0165 74773 - +39 0165 74397
Fontina Dop

La Famille
Frazione Les Iles, 151
Brissogne (Aosta)
Tel. +39 0165 762082
Fontina Dop

Alfredo Lateltin
Località Mettien
Gressoney-Saint Jean (Aosta)
Tel. +39 347 3086832
Toma di Gressoney

Lidia Laurent
Località Champsil
Gressoney-Saint Jean (Aosta)
Tel. +39 347 0052072
Toma di Gressoney

Les Ecureuils
Località Homené Dessus, 8
Saint-Pierre (Aosta)
Tel. +39 0165 903831
Formaggio a Pasta Pressata, Formaggio
di Capra a Pasta Molle, Formaggio Misto

Les Iles
Frazione Les Iles
Brissogne (Aosta)
Tel. +39 0165 762143
Fontina Dop, Ricotta, Salignoùn

Lo Dzerby
Località Ville, 21
Arnad (Aosta)
Tel. +39 0125 966067
Fontina Dop, Salignoùn

Carlo Squinobal
Località La Blatta
Gressoney-Saint Jean (Aosta)
Tel. +39 0125 355745
Toma di Gressoney

Elder Thedy
Località Gressmatten
Gressoney-Saint Jean (Aosta)
Tel. +39 349 6753609
Toma di Gressoney

Vallet di Pietro Severino
Località La Balma, 18
Donnas (Aosta)
Tel. +39 0125 807347
Fontina Dop

Piedmont

Bettelmatt

Bra d'Alpeggio DOP

Bra Tenero or
    Bra Duro DOP

Bruss or Bross

Cachat

Caprini Lattici

Caprino di Rimella

Caprino Ossolano

Caso or Toma di Elva

Castelmagno DOP

Cevrin di Coazze ●

Escarun

Formaggetta dell'Acquese

Formaggio a Crosta Rossa

Gorgonzola DOP

Macagn ●

Mezzapasta or Spress

Montébore ●

Mortaràt

Mottarone

Murazzano DOP

Murianengo or Moncenisio

Nostrale di Elva

Ormea

Ossolano d'Alpe

Paglierina

Raschera d'Alpeggio DOP

Raschera DOP

Robiola d'Alba

Robiola del Bec

Robiola di Ceva or Mondovì

Robiola di Cocconato

Robiola di Roccaverano
    Classica ●

Robiola di Roccaverano DOP

Saras del Fen ●

Seirass

Söra, Sola or Soela

Testun

Toma del Bot

Toma del Lait Brusch

Toma della Valsesia

Toma di Balme

Toma di Lanzo

Toma Piemontese DOP

Tomino di Talucco

Toumin dal Mel

Tuma di Pecora
    delle Langhe ●

Valcasotto

Bettelmatt

Bettelmatt is a particularly highly esteemed member of the toma family of cheeses from the high pastures of the Val d'Ossola. People say that the special flavour of the valley's tomas comes from a herb, known as *mottolina*, that grows only in Val d'Ossola. But it is the overall quality of the grazing that gives Bettelmatt its unique taste profile. Produced only in the summer months, Bettelmatt features a cheesemaking technique similar to that used for Gruyère. Whole raw milk is heated to 36-40°C in copper vats and coagulated in 25-30 minutes. The soft curd is then milled into pea-sized granules, left to stand for a short time, and cooked. The curd deposits on the bottom of the vat and is gathered up in a cloth and placed in hoops. After cooling, the curd is pressed mechanically for 12-24 hours. It then goes into brine for 10-15 days, or it may be dry-salted, after which it is left in a cool place to mature for a minimum of two months.

Rennet: liquid, calf's
Outer rind: rough, brownish tending to dark brown
Body: compact, softish, oily, with faint eyes, golden yellow or straw-yellow in colour
Top and bottom: flat, 30-40 cm in diameter
Height/weight: 10-15 cm / 5-7 kg
Territory of origin: Upper Val Formazza, in the municipality of Formazza, in the province of Novara, on the Bettelmatt Alp on the border with Switzerland, 2,100 metres above sea level

Bra d'Alpeggio DOP

The cheesemaking technique is substantially the same as that used for producing Bra in the lowlands. The main difference is that the tools used in the mountains are much less sophisticated and the procedure is almost entirely manual. The milk usually comes from Piemontese-breed cattle, kept in small or medium-sized byres and fed on local fodder. The DOP regulations also permit the addition of small quantities of ewe's or goat's milk. Milk from the evening milking, for example, is skimmed by allowing it to stand in tin-plated copper basins, which may be placed in running water. The following morning, the cream that has risen is removed with a spatula. Mountains dairies also employ a slightly higher coagulation temperature (32-35°C), heating the milk over by an open wood fire. A straw is inserted into the curd before it is cut to check that it has the desired consistency. When the straw stands up perfectly straight, the curd is ready for cutting. Before it is milled with a *spino* curd knife, the soft curd is cut into small cubes with a long, slender knife. It is then bundled up in a cloth and placed in a cheese mould, where it undergoes several pressing operations. These may be preceded by a rough division of the curd into sections to encourage draining of the whey. Mountain cheese presses comprise an inclined board of wood and a wooden lever, to which weights are applied. It should be remembered that Bra d'Alpeggio is only made during the summer months, from June to October, when the animals are grazed on mountain pastures.

Rennet: liquid, calf's
Outer rind: thin, elastic, straw-white for the Tenero (soft) version; hard, robust, brown or beige in colour for the Duro (hard) cheese
Body: ivory-white for Tenero, straw-yellow shading into ochre for Duro
Top and bottom: flat, 30-40 cm in diameter
Height/weight: 7-9 cm / 6-8 kg
Territory of origin: municipalities in the province of Cuneo classified as "mountain" in compliance with law 25 July 1952 no. 991
DOP status awarded on 1 July 1996, regulation no. 1263

Illustrated above are Bra cheeses matured for various lengths of time. Very mature Bra was once used for grating as a substitute for grana.

Bra Tenero or Bra Duro DOP

The product takes its name from the town of Bra, which was once the main centre for the maturing and sale of cheeses produced in the Cuneo Alps. Generic Bra cheese is made in the lowland dairies by coagulating usually pasteurised cow's milk from two milkings drawn on the same day, sometimes with the addition of small quantities of ewe's or goat's milk. Liquid calf's rennet is used, the milk being heated to a temperature of 27-32°C. The soft curd is cut into sweetcorn-sized granules with a circular movement using a Swiss-type *spino*, or curd knife. The curd may be cut a second time just before it is placed in moulds. The rounds are pressed, then salted – usually dry-salted – each day for six days. The Tenero, or soft, version may also be soaked in brine containing a 12% salt solution.

Rennet: liquid, calf's
Outer rind: thin, elastic, straw-white for the Tenero (soft) version, hard, robust, brown or beige in colour for the Duro (hard) type
Body: compact, elastic, with sparsely distributed eyes, dirty white to straw-white in colour for the Tenero cheese, firm, yellow-ochre in colour for the Duro version
Top and bottom: flat, 30-40 cm in diameter
Height/weight: 7-9 cm / 6 -8 kg
Territory of origin: the entire province of Cuneo and the municipality of Villafranca Piemonte in the province of Turin
DOP status awarded on 1 July 1996, regulation no. 1263

Bruss or Bross

Bruss, also known as *bross, brussu, bruz, bruzzu* or *buzzu*, is not a real cheese. It is a preparation that is normally made in the home to use up left-over pieces of cheese. The method of preparation varies with the cheeses used. Hard cheeses, for example, have to be grated or cut into small flakes. The cheese is then carefully kneaded and put into glass or earthenware dishes. A small amount of fresh milk is added to encourage refermentation. The dishes are then put in a cool place, where they will remain until fermentation is interrupted with a measure of alcohol or a distillate, such as grappa or cognac. In areas where robiola is produced, a fresh robiola cheese is cut into three pieces, which are then put into an earthenware jar with a measure of grappa or a glass of dry white wine. The jar is then left in a cool place for eight days before it is creamed by stirring the pieces twelve times. The operation is repeated on the fifteenth, twenty-eighth, thirty-fifth and forty-fifth days. The Bruss will be ready for the table when it has matured for seven weeks.

Body: creamy, easy-to-spread, ivory-white to straw-white in colour
Weight: variable
Territory of origin: various parts of the region, particularly in the province of Cuneo

Cachat

A preparation based on goat's milk and goat's milk cheese, Cachat is similar to bruss (see entry) but is more intensely aromatised, and has better balance on the palate. Pieces of left-over, but defect-free, goat's milk cheese are mixed with freshly milked goat's milk in special glass or earthenware jars. The mixture ferments rapidly, and is stirred several times a day. After the mixture has fermented for about three weeks, juniper distillate, or in some cases a leek-based infusion, is added. The jar is then sealed and stored in a cool place.

Body: soft, easy-to-spread, porcelain-white or milk-white in colour
Weight: variable
Territory of origin: Valle Stura in the province of Cuneo

Caprini Lattici

Caprino Lattico is a generic name for small (50-200 gram) cheeses made with whole goat's milk. The cheesemaking technique is based on rennet or lactic coagulation of the milk. Raw milk is left to sour indoors at a temperature of at least 20°C. The amount of rennet used is sufficient to ensure a starter effect for coagulation, and is lower than that used in rennet-only based souring. The milk is left to curdle for 18-24 hours at 18-20°C and then the curd is removed, taking care to break it as little as possible, and transferred to moulds. When the firm curd has reached the desired consistency, the moulds are turned over and left to drain for three to five hours. At the end of this process, aromatic herbs or spices may be added. The milk-white body has a fine, grainy texture and no eyes. There is no rind.

Rennet: liquid or paste, calf's or lamb's
Body: fine, grainy, with no eyes, milk-white in colour
Top and bottom: flat
Height/weight: 5-8 cm / 50-200 g
Territory of origin: the entire Piedmontese Alpine arc

Caprino di Rimella

Caprino di Rimella is a member of the extensive, albeit frag-
mentary, family of north Italian goat's milk cheeses, none
of which can be identified with any specific territory with the
exception of Roccaverano. These cheeses are normally made by
traditional, small-scale methods, mainly for local consumption.
That is also the case with this tomino-type product, set with
calf's rennet when it is to be eaten fresh, or lamb's rennet, to
bring out its piquancy, when it is intended for maturing. Raw
goat's milk is heated to about 18-20°C, after souring naturally.
A little rennet is then added and the milk is allowed to coagulate slowly. The resulting soft curd is transferred uncut to the
moulds, or else cut, shaped by hand, and left to drain on hemp
cloths. After three days, during which time it is dry-salted, the
cheese is ready for consumption.

Rennet: liquid or paste, kid's or lamb's
Outer rind: a barely formed skin, brownish white in colour when the cheese
is fresh, light brown when mature
Body: firm, soft, easy-to-spread when fresh, brownish white in colour
Top and bottom: flat, 8-9 cm in diameter
Height/weight: 2-3 cm / 200-300 g
Territory of origin: the entire Valsesia area, especially the municipality of
Rimella

Caprino Ossolano

Once upon a time, Val d'Ossola was a flourishing centre of goat's milk cheese production, but the tradition was gradually abandoned and is now almost extinct. Recently, goat's milk cheesemaking has been revived, thanks to the initiative of farmer-cheesemakers originally from Lombardy. The technique employed for Caprino Ossolano is substantially the same as for other mountain goat's milk cheeses. Produced from March to October, it is made by allowing raw goat's milk to sour and cool to 18°C. A little rennet is then added, and the milk is allowed to coagulate slowly. Next, the whole curd is put into moulds, where it is dry-salted and the whey is completely drained off. The cheese is ready for the table after it has ripened for three days.

Rennet: liquid or paste, kid's or lamb's
Outer rind: thin-skinned, cream-white or straw-yellow in colour depending on maturing
Body: soft, firm, cream-white in colour
Top and bottom: flat, 10-15 cm in diameter
Height/weight: 1-2 cm / 50-200g
Territory of origin: the municipalities of Domodossola, Varzo and Val Vigezzo

Cow's, ewe's and goat's milk
Caso or Toma di Elva

The name Caso in the Provençal language means "home-made". The soft curd is cut twice but is not cooked, unlike the procedure for making nostrale. Raw milk is heated to 30°C and liquid calf's rennet inoculated. It is left to coagulate for about one hour. The soft curd is then cut for the first time and allowed to set before it is cut up again, this time more finely into lumps about the size of a hazelnut. It is then left to ripen for three days before transfer into moulds to be pressed for two days. The rounds are removed and salted in a brine bath for at least 24 hours. Maturing in natural environments with abundant native flora may encourage the growth of blue-green mould, reminiscent of a Castelmagno cheese. When Caso is consumed fresh, after maturing for one or two months, the flavour is similar to bra or nostrale.

Rennet: liquid, calf's
Outer rind: rough, developing a brown colour with maturing
Body: porcelain-white, shading into brown, sometimes dappled with bluish mould
Top and bottom: flat, 20 cm in diameter
Height/weight: 15 cm / 2-6 kg
Territory of origin: the municipality of Elva

Castelmagno DOP

Thishis blue cheese takes its name from the municipality of Castelmagno, where it has been made since ancient times. There is a document dating from 1277 stipulating an annual rent for grazing lands to be paid in kind to the Marquis of Saluzzo in Castelmagno cheeses. The product is made from the cow's milk of two consecutive milkings, to which small amounts of sheep's or goat's milk may be added. The milk is poured into copper vats, heated slightly (35-38°C), and inoculated with liquid rennet. Coagulation takes 30-90 minutes, after which the soft curd is cut into walnut-sized lumps. The whey is removed as it rises. The curd is then left hanging for 15 minutes in a dry cloth knotted at the edges before it is cut into 5-8 cm cubes. It is then bundled up again in a cloth, where it will drain for one or two days. The bundles are subsequently packed into wooden tubs to stand for three or four days. At this point, the curd is milled very finely, kneaded again with coarse salt, placed in cheese hoops and pressed. After six days, the cheeses are taken out of the moulds and dry-salted for two days by rubbing, a process that may be repeated for 20-30 days. The cheeses are then left to mature in caves. Some makers perforate their cheeses to encourage the growth of mould, an operation reminiscent of the procedure for gorgonzola.

Rennet: liquid, calf's

Outer rind: smooth, straw-white when the cheese is young, rough, hard, brown veined with red in colour when the product is mature

Body: semi-hard, mould-ripened, pearl or ivory-white in colour marbled with blue-green veins from maturing

Top and bottom: flat, becoming rough with maturing, 15-25 cm in diameter

Height/weight: 15-20 cm / 2 -7 kg

Territory of origin: the municipalities of Monterosso Grana, Pradleves and Castelmagno in the province of Cuneo

DOP status awarded on 1 July 1996, regulation no. 1263

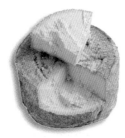 

Consumers today prefer white Castelmagno that has not yet developed the natural blue mould that is characteristic of the cheese when fully ripened.

GOAT'S AND COW'S MILK
Cevrin di Coazze

It is very easy to get to the mid-mountain slopes of the San-gone and Chisola valleys. Today, as in the past, the area is a popular holiday spot for Turin residents. It admirers have included intellectuals like Augusto Monti, Cesare Pavese, Leone Ginzburg, Giulio Einaudi and Luigi Pirandello. The area boasts a robiola-style local cheese, called Cevrin, or "goat's milk cheese" in the local dialect. In fact, pure goat's milk is almost never used to make it for varying proportions of cow's milk are added to the mixture. The milk comes from Camosciata delle Alpi goats. These agile, small to medium-sized animals have a reddish coat and magnificent back-curving horns, rather like those of the ibex, the wild cousin that shares its frugal lifestyle and ability to adapt to extreme conditions. The Camosciata delle Alpi is perfectly at home in high-altitude pastures, however poor. To make Cevrin, the milk is inoculated with liquid calf's rennet, subsequently undergoing a slow coagulation that is halfway between lactic and rennet-based curdling. The curd is milled and left to stand before being transferred to moulds that shape it into cheeses 20 centimetres across. Top and bottom are dry-salted, and then the cheese matures for at least three months in a mountain dairy or natural cellar. During maturing, Cevrin requires constant attention, for it has to be turned and cleaned daily. The round cheeses vary in weight from 0.8 to 1.5 kilograms. The side is ten centimetres high. Top and bottom have a diameter that ranges from 15 to 18 centimetres. The amber rind is moist and wrinkled. The slightly grainy body is yellowish on the outside, shading into white towards the centre. Mature Cevrin has a very intense, lingering nose, with aromatics that range from feral to dry wood and freshly scythed meadow. On the palate, hints of hazelnut and butter mingle with occasional tangy notes. The aim of the Slow Food Presidium is to promote the cheese by setting up a new distribution network that will encourage the recovery of goat breeding and boost production of goat's milk.

Rennet: liquid, calf's
Outer rind: wrinkled, moist, amber in colour
Body: slightly grainy, yellowish on the outside, white near the centre
Top and bottom: flat, 15-18 cm in diameter
Height/weight: 10 cm / 0.8-1.5 kg
Territory of origin: Val Sangone, in particular the municipalities of Coazze and Giaveno in the province of Turin

Cevrin di Coazze matures for at least three months in mountain dairies or natural cellars. Maturing is a labour-intensive process since each cheese has to be turned and cleaned daily.

Escarun

The name of this cheese comes from a word meaning "small flock" in the Provençal language that is still spoken in a few valley communities in the province of Cuneo. Until recently, the shepherds who spent the winter on the hills produced what was known as *formagg dl'escarun* (small flock cheese). In homage to this ancient tradition, one Farigliano-based dairy today makes Escarun using ewe's or goat's milk from spring grazings and the first high-altitude grazings of summer. The dairy uses the *a pasta rotta* (milled curd) technique, similar to the cheesemaking procedure for castelmagno (see entry). The curd is cut after souring and transferred to bundles to be squeezed and drained. The following day, it is milled again and the cloth used to wrap it is changed. Finally, it is placed in moulds, where it is pressed by hand. Ideally, Escarun should be matured for at least four months. Maturing takes place in cellars at Valcasotto. During the maturing period, the cheese may acquire a faint natural veining.

Rennet: liquid, calf's
Outer rind: thin, orange-peel texture, grey-white in colour tending to straw-yellow
Body: compact, delicate, slightly crumbly, white in colour
Top and bottom: flat, 17-18 cm in diameter
Height/weight: 13-15 cm / 3-3.5 kg
Territory of origin: the municipality of Farigliano in the province of Cuneo

Formaggetta dell'Acquese

Formaggetta dell'Acquese is made with goat's and cow's milk from one or more milkings drawn during the same day, and may contain a small proportion of ewe's milk. The milk is poured into small cylindrical containers, where it sours at room temperature in 8-24 hours after inoculation with a small quantity of liquid rennet, thanks in part to the action of milk enzymes. After coagulation, the contents of the cylinders are poured slowly into moulds. This is a very delicate operation as the curd should not break up. When the whey has been drained, one surface is salted by hand. A few hours later, the second surface is also salted. Formaggetta dell'Acquese is ready for the table in 8-12 hours, but can be matured for about one month.

Rennet: liquid, calf's
Outer rind: very thin skin, ivory-white tending to straw-yellow or brownish in colour with maturing
Body: fresh, soft, firm, white in colour
Top and bottom: flat, with faint edging, 10-14 cm in diameter
Height/weight: 4-5 cm / 400-600 g
Territory of origin: the Acqui Terme area, in the province of Alessandria

Formaggio a Crosta Rossa

This cheese is also known as Rebruchon, a name that clearly derives from the famous Savoy cheese reblochon, which in the local dialect means "second milking". This particularly fat-rich milk is ideal for making creamy cheeses. On the Italian side of the mountains, a similar cheese is made, although it obviously cannot use the DOP-protected reblochon name. The milk is filtered and heated to 35°C, then coagulated in about 30 minutes. The soft curd is then cut into walnut-sized lumps, first with a *spanarola* curd knife and then with a *lira*. After about ten minutes, the whey is drained off. The curd is then gathered up in a hemp cloth and placed in moulds, where it is lightly pressed. The rounds are removed from the moulds and placed in dry rooms, where they are dry-salted on top and bottom every other day. Brine salting is also employed. Finally, the cheeses are moved into increasingly cold rooms, where they will complete their maturation in about 20 days.

Rennet: liquid, calf's
Outer rind: thin, soft, oily, reddish yellow in colour
Body: soft, fatty, exuding droplets of whey, sometimes with faint eyes, ivory-white or straw-white in colour
Top and bottom: flat, 12 cm in diameter
Height/weight: 4-5 cm / 0.3-1 kg
Territory of origin: Val Susa, especially the area of Novalesa

Gorgonzola DOP

Gorgonzola is a blue cheese, called *erborinato* in Italian from the Lombard dialect word for the "parsley-green" colour of the mould. Cow's milk is pasteurised and heated to 30°C before inoculation with *Penicillium roqueforti* mould, milk enzymes and liquid calf's rennet. After 25-30 minutes, the soft curd is cut, first into 3-4 cm squares. These are allowed to stand in the whey for about ten minutes before they are cut more finely into walnut-sized lumps. After being bundled into thin knotted cloths, the lumps are drained for about half an hour. The firm curd is then transferred into perforated cylindrical moulds that are placed for about 24 hours on inclined boards, known as *spersori*, to encourage draining of the whey. Subsequently, the moulds are moved to the damp (96% humidity), warm (20-22°C) ripening rooms for four or five hours. They are then dry-salted. Today, high labour costs have induced some cheesemakers to use brine baths for salting instead. About one month later, the cheeses are perforated. This was once carried out with needles of seasoned wood but nowadays steel or copper needles are inserted into the top and bottom of the cheese, an operation that encourages an even distribution of mould. Gorgonzola *a fermentazione naturale* (naturally fermented), also known as *del nonno* (Granddad's) or *antico* (old-fashioned), is produced in very limited quantities. It has much more conspicuous marbling, a crumblier body, and a much tangier flavour than the standard version. The cheesemaking technique is similar, but some producers still leave the curd, which is precipitated in the evening, hanging from a stand overnight to drain and acquire the naturally occurring vein-producing mould present in the room. Another version, known as *a due paste* (two-curd), has today almost completely disappeared. It was made by leaving the curd from the evening milking overnight and pouring onto it the milk from the following morning's milking.

Rennet: liquid, calf's
Outer rind: rough, moist, tending to a reddish colour when mature
Body: raw, compact, white or straw-white in colour marbled with blue-green from mould (veining)
Top and bottom: flat, 25-30 cm in diameter
Height/weight: 16-20 cm / 6-13 kg
Territory of origin: the provinces of Novara, Vercelli and Cuneo, and the municipality of Casale Monferrato in Piedmont and the provinces of Bergamo, Brescia, Como, Cremona, Milan and Pavia in Lombardy
DOP status awarded on 12 June 1996, regulation no. 1107

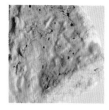

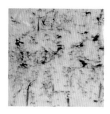

The photograph below highlights one of Gorgonzola's most popular features with today's consumers – its creaminess. The photographs on the left illustrate the difference in the body of a standard Gorgonzola and the two-curd type. The special version has more marked veining and is less moist.

Macagn

Macagn is a typical mountain cheese made from whole raw cow's milk. It takes its name from the Maccagno Alps, on the regional border with Valle d'Aosta at the mouth of Valle del Vogna. Today, the cheese is made in the mountains of the province of Biella and in Valsesia, especially in the Cervo, Sessera and Sesia valleys. Its main characteristic is that it is made at every milking, a method that probably evolved because of the need to take advantage of the milk's natural temperature. The cheeses weigh 1.7-2.3 kilograms, and have a diameter of 18-25 centimetres and a side 5-8 centimetres high. The rind is thin and smooth, and may present mould. The colour varies from straw-yellow to grey, tinged with yellow or orange. The body is compact, with a few scattered eyes. Straw-yellow in colour, it tends to gold as maturing progresses. Because it is made twice daily in summer, Macagn is particularly fragrant, the nose revealing notes of flowers and meadow grass. Generally a medium-mature cheese, Macagn is at its best after ageing for three to five months. If desired, it may be partnered with a wine that does not mask its delicate, lingering aroma. For fresh Macagn, a well-structured, non-aromatic white like Gavi, Erbaluce or Pinot Bianco is a good choice. A cheese matured for a few months will be more suited to a young Barbera, a Franciacorta red or an Oltrepò Pavese Pinot Nero. Macagn has all it takes to be a great cheese, starting with its superb raw material, whole mountain dairy milk. But further efforts are needed to raise the average level of quality and highlight the differences that derive from pastures or variations in cheesemaking methods while maintaining uniformity of production. The Slow Food Presidium was set up to achieve those ends. The Presidium brings together nine cheesemakers and is drafting production regulations to give this summer mountain dairy cheese a distinctive personality of its own.

Rennet: liquid, calf's
Outer rind: thin, smooth, varying from straw-yellow to grey in colour tinged with yellow or orange
Body: compact, elastic, with a few scattered eyes, straw-yellow in colour tending to gold with maturing
Top and bottom: flat
Height/weight: 5-8 cm / 1.7-2.3 kg
Territory of origin: the central and eastern parts of the Biella Pre-Alps and the mountains of Valsesia in the province of Vercelli

The main characteristic of Macagn is that it is made at every milking. This probably came about because of the need to take advantage of the milk's natural temperature.

Mezzapasta or Spress

This cheese is a ossolano or grasso d'Alpe (see entry) that has undergone prolonged maturing. The technique is distinct from that used for ossolano in that the milk is part-skimmed and the cheese is kept as dry as possible. After coagulation at a temperature of 30°C, the soft curd is cut and semi-cooked. When the curd has settled on the bottom of the cooking vessel, it is cut again. Next it is transferred into moulds, where it is vigorously pressed for several hours. The top of the round is then dry-salted, and the bottom is salted 24 hours later. After salting, the cheeses are placed in well-ventilated rooms at a constant temperature of 12-15°C. Maturing lasts for three-four months but may go on for as long as 12-14 months.

Rennet: liquid, calf's
Outer rind: smooth, medium thick, light or mid brown in colour depending on maturing
Body: elastic, firm, generally soft, with faint eyes, deep yellow in colour
Top and bottom: flat, 30-40 cm in diameter
Height/weight: 8-15 cm / 5-8 kg
Territory of origin: the upper part of the province of Novara, especially Val Formazza and Valle Antigorio

COW'S AND EWE'S MILK

Montébore

Montébore is named after a village in the Tortonese area of
Piedmont bordering to the south with Liguria and to the
east with Lombardy. The village is in Val Curone, between the
Grue and Borbera valleys. This formaggetta-style cow's and ewe's
milk cheese has a very long history. It is first mentioned in 1153,
but was probably invented before. In the late fifteenth century,
Montébore was the only cheese on the menu at the wedding ban-
quet of Isabella of Aragon and Gian Galeazzo Sforza. Production
continued without interruption almost until the present day and
in the mid twentieth century, 1,200 kilograms a year were still being produced. Then in 1982, the last cheesemaker decided it was
time to stop. It was thanks to the Slow Food Presidium that Montébore made a comeback in 1999. Two cheesemakers learned the
secrets of this ancient cheesemaking technique, following step by
step the instructions of Carolina Bracco, the last of the Montébore cheesemakers. The cheese is made with raw cow's (about
75%) and ewe's (usually 25%) milk. The curd is broken up with a
wooden curd knife and placed in moulds called *ferslin*, where it is
turned and salted. Three cheeses of decreasing diameter are removed from the moulds and allowed to stand for four or five
hours. They are then washed with warm, slightly salted water and
left to mature, one on top of the other, for a period ranging from
seven days to two months, in a curious wedding-cake shape that

was inspired by the village's ancient tower. The rind of Montébore is smooth and moist at first but with maturing becomes drier and wrinkled, varying in colour from white to straw-yellow. The smooth body may have a few eyes and is various shades of white in colour. Montébore can be consumed fresh, semi-mature (15 days) or as a grating cheese. If successfully matured, Montébore has a marked aroma of ewe's milk, even though the ewe's milk content is never more that 40%. There are faint feral and slightly spicy notes on the nose. On entry, the palate is milky and buttery, revealing a note of chestnuts with herbaceousness in the finish.

Rennet: liquid, calf's
Outer rind: smooth and moist when fresh, drier and wrinkled with maturing, white tending to straw-yellow in colour
Body: smooth, sometimes with a few eyes, varying shades of white in colour
Height/weight: 5-8 cm / 300-600 g
Territory of origin: the village of Montébore in the municipality of Dernice and neighbouring municipalities in the Curone and Borbera valleys in the province of Alessandria

Thanks to the Slow Food Presidium, Montébore made a comeback in 1999. Two producers began to make it again, following instructions supplied by the last surviving traditional Montébore cheesemaker.

Mortaràt

The name Mortaràt derives from the Italian for "mortar", in the culinary or perhaps the military sense, and was inspired by the highly distinctive sensory profile of this whole raw cow's milk cheese. According to local custom, Mortaràt matures for a brief period while covered or stuffed with aromatic spices. There are four traditional types. The oyster-shaped rind of Maccagnetta alle Erbe is covered in black pepper and mountain herbs. Its rind is soft and flavoursome, and should be eaten with the cheese. Maccagnetta alle Noci is stuffed with walnuts and then covered with maize flour. Both types weigh between 500 grams and one kilogram. There are cloves of garlic in the fresh body of Ciambella all'Aglio. The cheese, weighing two to four kilograms, matures under chopped garlic for one or two months and it, too, may be eaten with the rind. Mattonella al Rosmarino is similar in weight but rectangular in shape and matures under rosemary leaves. The scores on the rind are to help the cheese to dry and to enable the aromas of the herbs to penetrate into the body.

Height/weight: variable
Territory of origin: the province of Biella

Mottarone

Mottarone takes its name from Monte Mottarone (1,491 metres), known as the "mountain of the two lakes" because it lies between Lake Orta and Lake Maggiore. In the past, a number of dairy products were made in the area, but they were gradually abandoned as gorgonzola (see entry) became increasingly popular. In 1999, a small dairy began making the traditional *faterel* cheese again, modifying the ingredients (cow's milk only, instead of cow's and goat's milk) and renaming it Nostrano del Mottarone. The milk used comes from livestock farms at Armeno, Brovello, Gignese, Omegna and Sovazza on the slopes of the mountain. It is heated to 36-38°C and coagulated using natural calf's rennet. The curd is allowed to stand for about 40 minutes, and then it is cut and cooked at 42°C before being transferred to moulds and placed in a brine bath for 24 hours. Mottarone is ready to go on sale after 45 days but may also mature for more than two and a half months.

Rennet: powder or liquid, calf's
Outer rind: thin, uniform, ochre-yellow in colour tending to reddish
Body: soft, fondant, with evenly distributed, roundish or bird's eye-sized eyes, straw-yellow in colour
Top and bottom: flat, 18-22 cm in diameter
Height/weight: 4-5 cm / 4.5-6 kg
Territory of origin: the Monte Mottarone area in the provinces of Novara and Verbania

Murazzano DOP

The large family of Piedmontese robiolas has a number of illustrious members, such as Murazzano, traditionally obtained from Alta Langa ewe's milk, which was awarded DO status in 1982 and designated DOP in 1996. Today, it is increasingly difficult to find classic, pure ewe's milk Murazzano, not least because the DOP regulations permit the use of up to 40% cow's milk. Robiolas obtained from pure ewe's milk can bear the words *latte di pecora* (ewe's milk) on the label. The cheesemaking technique involves heating the milk to 37°C and inoculating it with liquid calf's rennet which has been diluted with water to help it disperse in the milk. Coagulation is takes 30 minutes. The soft curd is then roughly broken up into orange-sized lumps, which are left to stand for about ten minutes. The whey that drains off is removed. The curd is then broken again into hazelnut-sized lumps and removed from the whey. After standing for a short time, the firm curd is placed in hoops. Ten minutes later, it is turned upside down for the first time, and then turned again two hours later. One side is then dry-salted. Six or seven hours later, the cheese is turned over again and a second salting carried out. Next, the cheeses are placed in a lightly ventilated room on cotton cloths to absorb the whey that drains off. They ripen for seven to ten days, during which time they are turned over daily. At this stage, the

Murazzano is ready for the table but it may be left to mature for a further period of up to two months.

Rennet: liquid, calf's
Outer rind: thin skinned, milk-white or straw-white in colour
Body: soft, firm, sometimes with faint eyes, fine-grained and straw-white in colour
Top and bottom: flat, with a slight edging, 10-15 cm in diameter
Height/weight: 3-4 cm / 300-400 g
Territory of origin: 43 municipalities in the province of Cuneo
DOP status awarded on 12 June 1996, regulation no. 1107

Genuine Murazzano DOP should be wrapped in the classic triangular paper bearing the mark of the Consortium. The cheese may present faint eyes on being sliced.

Murianengo or Moncenisio

A cheese with a strong similarity to Gorgonzola, Murianengo has roots that may date back to more or less the same period as its more celebrated cousin. The earliest references to the cheese are from the eleventh century and the name derives from Val Moriana in Savoy. Some experts believe Murianengo and Moncenisio are two distinct types, but the cheesemaking procedure is almost identical. Milk, usually whole, is coagulated for 30-60 minutes. The soft curd is then cut, first into large lumps and then into hazelnut-sized pieces. It is then gathered up in a cloth and left to ferment for 24 hours in a wooden bucket. The old curd is then mixed with one half or one third of the new and the mixture is placed in moulds. It is lightly pressed, then dry-salted and the pressure is gradually increased. After 20 days, the rounds are transferred to the cellar, where they are perforated before standing for three months to allow the *Penicillium* mould to develop.

Rennet: liquid or paste, calf's
Outer rind: firm, rough, irregular, yellow shading into red in colour
Body: soft, buttery, firm, straw-white streaked with mould becoming dried and more heavily veined with maturing
Top and bottom: flat, 25-35 cm in diameter
Height/weight: 12-18 cm / 5 -12 kg
Territory of origin: the Moncenisio plateau, the southern slopes of Colle del Frejus and the Novalesa plateau

COW'S MILK

Nostrale di Elva

Nostrale is made at Elva, in Val Maira, along with the increasingly rare caso (see entry). Whole heat-treated or pasteurised milk is inoculated with enzymes and heated to a temperature of about 40°C. It is curdled with liquid calf's rennet in about 20 minutes. The curd is then broken up twice, first into large lumps, then into granules smaller than a hazelnut. It is heated to 42°C and stirred for ten minutes. The firm curd is transferred to moulds and turned for four or five hours. After 24 hours in a brine bath, the cheeses are set aside to dry. Nostrale di Elva normally matures for a minimum period of 30-40 days, but maturing may last for up to five or six months, or occasionally even longer.

Rennet: liquid, calf's
Outer rind: thick, white in colour tending to grey
Body: soft, with a few eyes, white tending to straw-yellow in colour
Top and bottom: flat, with faint edging, 25-40 cm in diameter
Height/weight: 6-10 cm / 3-7 kg
Territory of origin: the municipality of Elva in the province of Cuneo

Ormea

The cheesemaking process for Ormea is very similar to that used for Bra. Whole or part-skimmed raw milk is heated to 30°C and inoculated with liquid calf's rennet. It is then left to set. The soft curd is then cut in two stages. First, it is broken up by vigorous stirring, and then by pressing. It is next transferred to moulds, where it is subjected to gradually increasing pressure for four to six hours. When the hard-pressed curd is dry, it is dry-salted with coarse salt on the top and bottom alternately for a week. At this stage, the cheeses are moved to the maturing cellar. Fresh Ormea will stay there for one month but other types may remain for as long as eight months. Today, production of Ormea is in decline because cheesemakers prefer to make the better-known Raschera.

Rennet: liquid, calf's
Outer rind: thin, smooth, straw-white to beige or ochre in colour with maturing
Body: soft, firm ivory-white for the soft version, dry, golden yellow or ochre for the hard
Top and bottom: flat, 25-30 cm in diameter
Height/weight: 8-12 cm / 5-6 kg
Territory of origin: the municipalities of Ormea, Chiusa Pesio, Fontane, Frabosa Soprana, Garessio, Limone Piemonte and Pamparato in the southern part of the province of Cuneo

Ossolano d'Alpe

The version of this cheese made at a very special mountain pasture, the Bettelmatt (see entry) Alp, has achieved worldwide fame. However, other Ossolano d'Alpe mountain-dairy cheeses are equally interesting. Locally, this cheese type is also called Grasso d'Alpe. It is made only in summertime, using whole raw milk drawn from mountain grazing cows. The curd is milled into rice or sweetcorn-sized granules, and then cooked. When the curd has settled, it is removed in a cloth and placed in moulds. It is then pressed mechanically for 12-24 hours. After salting dry or in a brine bath, the cheese is matured in the cool natural environment of caves or cellars, a process that continues until the autumn. Ossolana d'Alpe cheeses are large, with a rough rind and a firm, soft, oily body that is golden or straw-yellow in colour.

Rennet: liquid, calf's
Outer rind: rough, brown tending to dark brown in colour
Body: firm, soft, oily, with faint eyes, golden or straw-yellow in colour
Top and bottom: flat, 30-40 cm in diameter
Height/weight: 6-8 cm / 5-7 kg
Territory of origin: the mountain pastures of Valdossola

Paglierina

In Piedmont, the name *paglierina* (or *paglietta*, or *d'la paja*, all meaning "straw cheese") indicates a vast range of usually fresh, flat cheeses, with or without a bloomy rind. In fact, it was the Quaglia dairy that first called one of its cheeses by this name about a century ago. Quaglia's cheese featured the distinctive marks on the surface that were once produced by the straw mats on which the product was placed to mature. The milk is coagulated at 38-40°C, and then the soft curd is cut into walnut-sized lumps with a curd knife. It is then placed in moulds to drain before ripening in a damp room at 25°C for about seven hours. After dry or brine salting, the cheeses mature in a cool, damp room until a white mould forms on the surface in 10-12 days. Maturing may be extended, in which case the cheese under the rind becomes creamier as a result of proteolysis.

Rennet: liquid, calf's
Outer rind: rough, elastic, with characteristic square or lined markings, sometimes with a bloom of white mould
Body: soft, firm, lustrous when fresh, firm, elastic, yellow in colour when mature
Top and bottom: flat, 10-15 cm in diameter
Height/weight: 32 cm / 300-500 g
Territory of origin: the provinces of Cuneo and Turin

Raschera d'Alpeggio DOP

Raschera may be called "d'Alpeggio" when it comes from locations more than 900 metres above sea level in the municipalities of Frabosa Soprana, Frabosa Sottana, Roburent, Roccaforte, Mondovì, Ormea, Garessio (only the Val Casotto area), Magliano Alpi (the area bordering on Ormea), Montaldo and Pamparato, all in the province of Cuneo. The cheesemaking technique is substantially that described for raschera DOP (see entry) but the mountain product offers aromas of Alpine herbs that further enhance the already outstanding taste profile of the variety. Production of the cheese, which is made in the summer months from June to the end of August, had been falling off in recent years as the Cuneo mountains became increasingly depopulated. It has now picked up again thanks to strong demand from wholesale markets and in particular from restaurants.

Rennet: liquid, calf's
Outer rind: thin, smooth, springy, reddish-grey sometimes tending to yellowish
Body: soft, elastic, with very few eyes, ivory-white in colour
Top and bottom: flat, 35-40 cm in diameter in the cylindrical version, the quadrilateral has sides 40 cm long
Height/weight: 7-12 cm / 5-8 kg
Territory of origin: areas more than 900 metres above sea level in a number of municipalities in the province of Cuneo
DOP status awarded on 1 July 1996, regulation no. 1263

Raschera DOP

Raschera is the traditional cheese of the valleys around Mondovì. Its name is echoed in many of the place names in the area, such as Lake Raschera, at the foot of Monte Mongioie, the Rascaira Alp and the name attributed to the area itself, Ruscaira. Raschera is made with cow's milk, although the DOP regulations permit the addition of ewe's or goat's milk. It must come from one or two milkings drawn on the same day. The milk should preferably be raw, and must come from Bruno-Alpina or Piemontese cows. Liquid rennet is added to coagulate the milk at a temperature of 27-30°C in a wooden container called a *gerla*. It is then covered with a woollen cloth for about one hour, until the curd forms. When the milk has coagulated, the soft curd is cut with a special tool known as a *sbattella*. The whey is then drained off with a hemp cloth and the firm curd, now called *prod*, is placed in moulds and pressed for about ten minutes. The *prod* is then cut again and pressed for a whole day. The cylindrical rounds are then dry-salted while the quadrilateral version is pressed again for five days with a wooden mould. Raschera is matured in cool, damp rooms on wooden shelves known as *selle* for at least 20 days. Some versions are however matured for as long as three months. The outer rind is grey-brown, and may acquire reddish marks while maturing. The body is ivory-white, springy and firm, with small, irregular eyes and a strong aroma of hay and buttermilk. With maturing, the nose tends to become slightly tangy and almondy.

Rennet: liquid, calf's
Outer rind: thin, smooth, springy, reddish-grey sometimes tending to yellowish
Body: soft, elastic, with very few eyes, ivory-white in colour
Top and bottom: flat, 35-40 cm in diameter in the cylindrical version, the quadrilateral has sides 40 cm long
Height/weight: 7-12 cm / 5 -8 kg
Territory of origin: the province of Cuneo
DOP status awarded on 1 July 1996, regulation no. 1263

Two square Raschera cheeses with the label indicating their origin. The green label attests a Raschera from a flatland dairy. Yellow is used for Raschera d'Alpeggio.

Robiola d'Alba

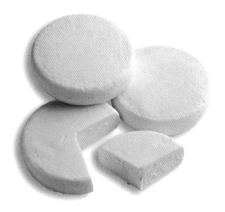

The name "Robiola" is believed to come from Robbio Lomellina, a municipality where this kind of cheese has been made since time immemorial, or perhaps from the Latin *ruber* (red), and its derivative *rubeola*, from the colour of the cheese's skin after maturing. In the province of Cuneo, the name *toma* is used for this cheese, although this is not strictly accurate because the term generally refers to large Alpine cheeses. Cheesemaking techniques, too, may vary considerably from area to area. Usually, cow's milk from a single milking is first coagulated at a temperature of 35-38°C. The soft curd is then broken up into hazelnut-sized lumps and transferred to moulds, where is stands for about eight hours at a temperature of 18-25°C. This is called "pre-maturing". The next stage is dry-salting before the cheese goes into a cool, damp room for up to eight days, in the case of the fresh version, or 40-50 days for the mature. Traditional Robiola d'Alba has a firm body that breaks cleanly when cut.

Rennet: liquid, calf's
Outer rind: white or faintly straw-coloured skin when fresh, grey-brown with reddish tones when mature
Body: buttery, soft, almost entirely free of eyes; cream in colour, shading into translucent straw-white with maturing
Top and bottom: flat, 10-20 cm in diameter
Height/weight: 2-4 cm / 200-400 g
Territory of origin: the whole of Valsesia, especially the province of Cuneo

Robiola del Bec

The name Robiola del Bec comes from the fact that this particular cheese is traditionally made only in the months of October and November, when the she-goats are on heat and are covered by the he-goat (*bec, buc* or *becco* in the Piedmontese dialect). The milk has a high fat content and the cheese obtained is very creamy. Milk from the evening milking is allowed to sour. The following morning's milk is added and the mixture is brought to 18°C. A little rennet is added and acid or lactic coagulation continues slowly for at least 24 hours. The soft curd is then carefully transferred to special moulds, where it remains for a day. For Robiola del Bec, the moulds are topped up as the cheese drains so that the side is higher than in other robiolas. Once the whey has drained off, white salt is added and the cheese is placed in a suitable room to ripen. The cheese is ready for the table after ripening for three days.

Rennet: liquid, occasionally paste, calf's
Outer rind: no skin when fresh, acquiring a rough, brown or straw-white rind that exudes droplets of whey with maturing
Body: firm, crumbly, soft, easy to spread, ivory or chalk-white in colour
Top and bottom: flat, 12-16 cm in diameter
Height/weight: 6-8 cm / 300-600 g
Territory of origin: the entire Robiola di Roccaverano production area and the Acqui area

Robiola di Ceva or Mondovì

R obiola di Ceva or Mondovì is one of the many varieties of robiola produced in the province of Cuneo. It is relatively little-known, partly because it is made on a very small scale. Nevertheless, it is a cheese that deserved to be more widely appreciated for its outstanding taste profile, thanks to the excellent quality Piemontese cow's milk that goes into it, and for the cheesemaking technique used, which is unlike that used for other toma or robiola cheeses. Coagulation takes place at a relatively low temperature (18-22°C) over a period of at least 24 hours. The soft curd is then gently broken up and transferred to the moulds. After draining for about two days, the cheese is dry-salted with white sea salt. Robiola di Ceva then completes its maturing period, which lasts an average of 20 days. At the end of this time, the rind will have a light bloom of white mould.

Rennet: liquid, calf's
Outer rind: soft, thin skin with a hint of bloom
Body: dry, supple, with no eyes, ivory-white tending to pale straw-yellow in colour with maturing
Top and bottom: flat, 15 cm in diameter
Height/weight: 2-3 cm / 200-350 g
Territory of origin: the entire Upper Val Tanaro

COW'S MILK

Robiola di Cocconato

This soft, white cheese has no rind and a mild, slightly acidulous flavour. It is firm on the outside and creamier inside. Whole raw cow's milk is heated at 38°C for half an hour and then inoculated with rennet. After about 30 minutes, the curd is cut into walnut-sized lumps with a *lira* (wire cheese knife). It is broken up again into lumps of the same size a quarter of an hour later. The curd is then removed and transferred to moulds. The cheeses are turned over and salted on both sides for 40 minutes and then left to stand for a couple of hours. After that, they ripen for a minimum of 24 hours, or up to five or six days.

Rennet: liquid, calf's
Body: soft, creamier near the centre, white in colour
Top and bottom: flat, 14 cm in diameter
Height/weight: 1-1.5 cm / 350-400 g
Territory of origin: the municipality of Cocconato in the province of Asti

GOAT'S MILK

Robiola di Roccaverano Classica

In all likelihood, few people know that the Robiola di Roccaverano produced on the rugged hills of the Langhe in the province of Asti is Italy's only historic goat's milk cheese, and the only one worthy of comparison with the celebrated chèvre cheeses of France. Formally at least, it is the only goat's milk cheese in Italy to have obtained DOP status. We say "formally", because the current production regulations allow Robiola di Roccaverano to be made using as much as 85% cow's milk, with only a minor proportion of ewe's or goat's milk. Happily, some long-standing goat farmers and cheesemakers have refused to accept this, and continue to make Robiola the way their forebears did 100-200 years ago. The Slow Food Presidium protects this group of small-scale craft producers and promotes Robiola di Roccaverano Classica produced exclusively with raw goat's milk. The traditional technique varies very little from one cheesemaker to the next, yet there are significant differences in the products themselves. The flowers, herbs and bacterial flora of pastures and farms are transferred to the cheese, making it possible to draw a "cru map" for Robiola, much as it is for wines. Unfortunately, the number of animals in local flocks has dropped dramatically over the years. The Roccaverano goat has largely been replaced by higher-yielding breeds. In 1990, there were only 200 goats left, but now the relaunch of Roccaverano Classico is driving major initiatives for the breed's protection. When eaten fresh, Robiola di Roccaverano offers an uncomplicated sensory profile. The nose has attractive notes of yoghurt, early-sprouting grass and hazelnuts, introducing a palate of astonishing appeal and flavour. When mature, the cheese has faint goaty nuances, and the nose foregrounds meadow and wild plant aromas. The palate is lifted by piquant and mossy notes, acquiring length and fullness in the finish. Roccaverano is also excellent when matured and conserved in oil. It is a perfect partner for a well-structured white wine.

Rennet: liquid, calf's
Outer rind: very thin skin, ivory-white tending to straw-yellow or brownish in colour with reddish streaks after maturing
Body: fresh, tender, firm, white
Top and bottom: flat, with faint edging, 10-14 cm in diameter
Height/weight: 4-5 cm / 400-600 g
Territory of origin: the municipalities of Bubbio, Cessole, Loazzolo, Mombaldone, Olmo Gentile, San Giorgio Scarampi, Roccaverano, Monastero Bormida, Serole and Vesime in the province of Asti, Cartosio, Castelletto d'Erro, Denice, Malvicino, Merana, Montechiaro d'Acqui, Pareto, Ponti, Ponzone and Spigno in the province of Alessandria

The flowers, herbs and bacterial flora of pastures and farms are echoed in the cheese, making it possible to draw a "cru map" for Robiola, much as it is for wines.

Robiola di Roccaverano DOP

R obiola di Roccaverano has a very ancient pedigree. It seems that the Celts who settled in Liguria made a very similar cheese. The name Robiola (*rubeola*) derives from the Latin *ruber* and refers to the reddish colour that the rind acquires with maturing. The cheese can be made with raw or pasteurised milk but in the latter case, milk enzymes as well as rennet are used to set the curd. Milk from two milkings on the same day is heated to 18°C and inoculated with liquid calf's rennet or, very occasionally but in accordance with ancient custom, with kid's rennet in paste. It is left to coagulate for 24 hours and then the unbroken curd is placed in plastic hoops for a further day. The product is then salted and left to ripen for three days in rooms with a controlled temperature of 15-20°C. The cheese will then be ready for the table, but it is often left to mature for a further 20 days, especially when it contains a high proportion of kid's milk. The current DOP regulations permit the use of up to 85% cow's milk, mixed with varying proportions of ewe's and goat's milk. However, cheesemakers are campaigning for a modification of the rules that would promote Robiola di Roccaverano made in the traditional manner, using no cow's milk. Robiola di Roccaverano is made in two Piedmontese provinces at Bubbio, Cessole, Loazzolo, Mombaldone, Monastero Bormida, Olmo Gentile, Roccaverano, San Giorgio Scarampi, Serole and Vesime in the province of Asti, and at Castelletto d'Erro, Denice, Malvicino, Merana, Montechiaro d'Acqui, Pareto, Ponti, Spigno and part of the municipality of Cartosio in the province of Alessandria.

Rennet: liquid, calf's
Outer rind: very thin skinned, ivory-white in colour, tending to straw-yellow or brownish with reddish streaks after maturing
Body: fresh, tender, firm, white
Top and bottom: flat, with faint edging, 10-14 cm in diameter
Height/weight: 4-5 cm / 400 g
Territory of origin: part of the provinces of Asti and Alessandria
DOP status awarded on 1 July 1996, regulation no. 1263

This is the only goat's milk cheese in Italy to enjoy DOP status, a tribute to the ancient origins of goat's milk cheesemaking in this part of Piedmont.

Saras del Fen

Saras or seirass (see entry) comes from the Latin *seracium*, related to *serum* meaning "whey". In the dialects of Piedmont and Valle d'Aosta, the word means "ricotta". The custom of wrapping the cheeses in hay arose from the need to transport ricotta from mountain pastures without damaging them or exposing them to attack by insects. This is the origin of the name Saras del Fen, or "hay saras". 11 producers are still active on the pastures more than 1,000 metres above sea level. Each has a personal cheesemaking technique, some adding milk, some pressing the cheese, some salting the ripening cheese, and others dry-salting. One producer on the Lausun Alp adds an infusion of herbs, spices and roots to the boiling whey. The common factor is that all use whey from just-made cheese. It is heated to 70°C and then brought almost to boiling point after the addition of milk or salts. The solids are then collected in a linen bag, which is tied, pressed and hung to drain. After 24-36 hours, the cheese is removed from the cloth, lightly salted and placed to dry for a couple of days on an inclined surface. It is then covered with hay and matured for no more than four months. Since it is a ricotta, Saras del Fen does not offer any great sensory complexity. Yet the addition of milk during cheesemaking, and the fescue grasses in the pastures, give it distinctive herbaceous and buttermilk notes that intensify with maturing, and may develop into pleasing notes of mould and damp cellar.

The palate is rich and appealing, with good persistence. It may present a creamy texture and a piquant note in the finish with ageing. The aim of the Slow Food Presidium is to protect Saras del Fen and to promote the food and agriculture of Val Pellice, a heritage that has come down to us over centuries of history. Crucial to this effort is the work of restaurateur Walter Eynard, whose celebrated Flipot restaurant has had this very special ricotta on the menu for more than 20 years, both as part of the cheese board and as an ingredient in a number of dishes.

Body: delicate, lumpy when fresh, compact, translucent, brownish-white or straw-yellow in colour when mature
Height/weight: variable / 2-5 kg
Territory of origin: the Mountain Communities of Val Pellice, Chisone and Germanasca, and Pinerolese Pedemontano, more than 1,000 metres above sea level, in the province of Turin

Eleven producers are still working on mountain pastures more than 1,000 metres above sea level. Each has a personal cheese-making technique.

Seirass

This most classic of Piedmontese ricottas is mainly available in winter. Low in fat and delicate in character, it has a distinctive aroma of fresh milk and a mild flavour. Its signature conic or truncated cone shape comes from the custom of making and distributing the cheese in small cloths. Whey left over from the production of toma cheeses is mixed with a small proportion of whole raw milk (about 10%) at a temperature of 40-50°C. The mixture is brought to the boil (90-100°C) and then stirred vigorously as it cools to obtain a compact mass that is easily removed. The Seirass is collected in cloths and hung to drain for 12 hours at a temperature of 20-25°C. It should be eaten fresh, within four or five days of production.

Body: delicate, soft, lumpy, snow-white or whitish in colour
Top and bottom: smooth
Height/weight: 8-15 cm / 0.5-1 kg
Territory of origin: the entire region

Söra, Sola or Soela

Söra is a typical mountain cheese, which is especially good in summer. Its origins are lost in the mists of time but it is mentioned by the historian, Tullio Pagliana, in a study of the lives of shepherds in the Upper Val Tanaro. The name derives from the dialect term that indicates the sole of a shoe because of the cheese's characteristic flat, square shape. The cheese itself is made with raw milk heated to 30-36°C and coagulated with liquid rennet. After the soft curd has been broken up, it is wrapped in a cloth to drain the whey. When dry, it is kneaded and then placed in moulds before being pressed. The subsequent stages involve dry-salting and then maturing, which takes place in fairly dry cellars at a temperature of 10°C.

Rennet: liquid, calf's
Outer rind: vestigial, thickening with maturing, straw-yellow in colour shading into brown
Body: soft, lustrous, firm, with faint eyes, cream tending to ivory or yellow in colour when mature
Top and bottom: flat, 15-25 cm in diameter
Height/weight: 3-4 cm / 2-4 kg
Territory of origin: mountain pastures at the head of the Tanaro river valley in the municipality of Ormea, in Valcasotto and in the valleys around Mondovì

Testun

The technique for making this classic mountain toma cheese is very similar to that used for bra. It differs in that only ewe's milk is used, or ewe's milk mixed with small quantities of cow's milk. Testun, which in the Piedmontese dialect means a "big, hard head", had almost completely disappeared from the market. Now, its extraordinary taste profile has earned it a reprieve. The milk is coagulated at 37°C and the soft curd is cut into hazelnut-sized pieces. It is then left to stand in whey for about an hour, after which it is wrapped up, kneaded and placed in moulds, where it is pressed. After pressing, the rounds are dry-salted on top and bottom alternately with sea salt. They are then placed in cellars or caves to mature for a period of ranging from two to twelve months or even longer. Once, very mature Testun was also used for grating.

Rennet: liquid, calf's
Outer rind: thin, often scored by the rush mats used for maturing, yellow-brown in colour
Body: firm, brownish-white or straw-white in colour, extended maturing may result in traces of marbling
Top and bottom: flat, sometimes with slight roughness, 30-36 cm in diameter
Height/weight: 8-10 cm / 4-8 kg
Territory of origin: the area of the province of Cuneo bounded by the river Tanaro and the torrential river Vermenagna, exclusively in mountain dairies

Toma del Bot

Toma cheeses are made from ewe's milk in Valle Stura under the name of Toma Valle Stura, or from cow's milk, in which case they are sold as Toma del Bot. Whole raw milk is heated to 37°C, and then coagulated with liquid calf's rennet for two hours. The soft curd is then broken up with a tool called a *bourcet* and allowed to settle on the bottom of the vat. Afterwards, a perforated cloth called a *reirola* is used to remove and press it before it is kneaded and shaped. The pressed curd is left so that the remaining whey can drain off, and then top and bottom are dry-salted for at least 24 hours. Toma del Bot is then cellared to mature for three months, during which time the cheeses are regularly turned over and, if necessary, moistened with brine.

Rennet: liquid, calf's
Outer rind: thick, rough, straw-yellow to brown in colour, depending on maturing
Body: soft, firm, straw-white or golden yellow in colour
Top and bottom: flat, 10-15 cm in diameter
Height/weight: 5 cm / 3-10 kg
Territory of origin: Upper Valle Stura in the province of Cuneo

COW'S MILK

Toma del Lait Brusch

Also called *toma brusca* (sour toma) or *toma 'd la cajà* (curd toma), Toma del Lait Brusch (sour milk toma) was traditionally made in mountain pastures. Milk from the evening milking is left to cool naturally for about 12 hours. When it has soured, and with the rising cream skimmed off, it is mixed with milk from the morning milking. The mixture is heated to 38-40°C and coagulates in about one hour after inoculation with powdered rennet. The curd is milled into lumps the size of a grain of rice, then wrapped in a cloth and drained for a quarter of an hour by pressing the curd by hand. Salt is added and the soft curd is kneaded and placed in moulds. The cheese is subjected to heavy pressure in the moulds for 24 hours, and is turned over two or three times during this period. The cheeses are then dry-salted and mature on wooden boards for two to five months.

Rennet: powder, calf's
Outer rind: firm, rough, hard, irregular, reddish-yellow in colour
Body: hard, crumbly, heavily veined after maturing
Top and bottom: flat, 25-35 cm in diameter
Height/weight: 12-18 cm / 5-12 kg
Territory of origin: the Susa, Sangone and Lanzo valleys in the province of Turin

Toma della Valsesia

Whole raw cow's milk is inoculated with liquid rennet. After about one hour, the curd is milled into lumps the size of a grain of rice and heated to 45-47°C. The curd is allowed to stand for five minutes and is then extracted. It is transferred to moulds, where it is pressed by hand. It stays in the moulds for 24 hours, during which time it is turned twice. The cheeses are removed from the moulds and allowed to stand for about one week on wooden boards. Salting may be dry, 12 hours each for top and bottom. Alternatively, the cheese may be salted in a brine bath for 24 hours, followed by drying for a further 24 hours, during which the cheese is turned. Toma della Valsesia then matures for a period two weeks to two months.

Rennet: liquid, calf's
Outer rind: thin, yellowish in colour
Body: tiny eyes, white or yellowish in colour
Top and bottom: flat, 20 cm in diameter
Height/weight: 8-10 cm / 2 kg
Territory of origin: all the municipalities in Valsesia in the province of Vercelli

Toma di Balme

Toma di Balme is made with the classic mountain cheese-making technique. If whole milk from a single milking is used, the cheese is not semi-cooked. The milk is heated to 37°C, inoculated with liquid calf's rennet and allowed to coagulate. The soft curd is then cut with a curd knife known locally as a *bourceret* into lumps the size of walnuts. It is allowed to settle and then removed using a perforated cloth called a *reirola*. Once drained, the curd is hand-kneaded and moulded roughly into shape. It is then placed on a special shelf called an *iloira*, where it remains for 24 hours until the whey has completely drained. Next, the tops and bottoms of the rounds are dry-salted for a further 24 hours. In the past, some cheesemakers also sprinkled pepper on their products. At this point, the cheeses are placed in a damp room, where they mature for an average of one month.

Rennet: liquid, calf's
Outer rind: smooth, thin, straw or golden yellow when fresh, thick, rough, dark brown in colour when mature
Body: firm, elastic, liberally scattered with eyes, deep yellow in colour
Top and bottom: flat, 20-40 cm in diameter
Height/weight: 8-15 cm / 3-11 kg
Territory of origin: some mountain dairies in the municipality of Balme (Cumba and Pian Gioé Giasset)

COW'S MILK

Toma di Lanzo

Toma di Lanzo is one of the territory-specific products that have never been included in the extensive family of the Toma Piemontese DOP. Its main distinguishing characteristics are its less regular shape and the pastures where the milk for the summer version comes from. After heating to 37°C, the milk is inoculated with liquid rennet and left to coagulate. The time required depends on the milk's fat content and the rennet used. Next, the soft curd is cut roughly and left to drain before a second cutting is performed to produce sweetcorn-sized granules. It is left to settle for five minutes and then transferred to cheese hoops, where it is pressed for two days. Dry-salting, which takes a week, is the next stage. Many cheesemakers still add salt to the curd when it is removed from the vat. The rounds are then placed in natural caves, where they ripen for one month and mature for at least three months. During this time, the cheese are turned over every day.

Rennet: liquid, calf's
Outer rind: smooth, medium-hard, brown or dark brown in colour
Body: firm, fairly hard during maturing, brownish-white or straw-white in colour
Top and bottom: flat, 30-35 cm in diameter
Height/weight: 10 cm / 4-8 kg
Territory of origin: Valle di Lanzo, particularly Val Grande and Valle di Ala

Toma Piemontese DOP

There is still debate about the origin of the word *toma*, which is widely used in Piedmont, Valle d'Aosta, France, Savoy, the Pyrenees and even Sicily. One possible explanation is that it refers to the precipitation of casein during coagulation and derives from the dialect word for "fall", *tomé*. In the great family of toma cheeses, Toma Piemontese is one of the most significant in terms of quantity, and the only one so far to enjoy DOP status. Milk from two consecutive milkings (or one only, if whole milk is used) is left to stand for up to 12 hours, if a whole milk product is desired, or for 24 hours for the semi-fat cheese made from milk skimmed after the cream has been allowed to rise. The milk is then put in a cheese vat, stirred gently and heated to 32-35°C before inoculation with calf's rennet. Forty minutes later, the curd is broken, and may also be reheated in a sort of semi-cooking process, until rice-sized granules settle on the bottom of the vat. The firm curd is then removed and placed in hoops where it is pressed, turned over and dry-salted with coarse salt on top and bottom for up to 15 days. Otherwise, the rounds may be salted in a brine bath for a period of 24-48 hours. The cheeses are then matured, usually in natural environments but sometimes in special rooms, where they are regularly turned over and brushed or washed with brine from time to time. Maturing lasts for at least 60 days for cheeses weighing over six kilograms and 15 days for lighter cheeses. Toma Piemontese DOP is produced nearly everywhere in Piedmont, especially in the hinterland of the provinces of Novara, Vercelli, Biella, Turin and Cuneo, in the municipalities of Acqui Terme, Terzo, Bistagno, Ponti and Denice in the province of Alessandria, and in the municipalities of Monastero Bormida, Roccaverano, Mombaldone, Olmo Gentile and Serole in the province of Asti.

Rennet: liquid or paste, calf's
Outer rind: smooth, elastic, straw-white to reddish brown in colour
Body: firm, springy, sometimes with faint eyes
Top and bottom: flat, 15-35 cm in diameter
Height/weight: 5-12 cm / 2-8 kg
Territory of origin: the provinces of Novara, Vercelli, Biella, Turin and Cuneo, as well as some municipalities in the provinces of Alessandria and Asti
DOP status awarded on 1 July 1996, regulation no. 1263

Toma Piemontese DOP – the label can be seen in the illustration – includes an astonishing range of Piedmont mountain toma-type cheeses of differing shapes, weights and maturing periods.

Tomino di Talucco

The traditional technique used to make this cheese begins with the heating of pure goat's milk to a temperature of about 85°C. When the milk has cooled to 38°C, it is inoculated with liquid calf's rennet and left to coagulate for 40 minutes. Next, the soft curd is carefully cut into largish lumps and then poured into moulds. A day later, top and bottom are dry-salted, although some cheesemakers salt the milk itself. The next day, Tomino di Talucco is ready for to be consumed fresh, but the local cheese-making tradition includes maturing. Once they have acquired a firm texture, the cheeses are placed in earthenware *ule*, or jars and sprinkled with black pepper or garden thyme and wild thyme.

Rennet: liquid, calf's
Outer rind: no rind when fresh, thin, hard, reddish yellow when mature
Body: fine-grained, soft, moist, chalk-white tending to brownish white with maturing
Top and bottom: flat, 5 cm in diameter
Height/weight: 32 cm / 50-500 g
Territory of origin: the villages of Grandubbione and Talucco in Val Chisone

Toumin dal Mel

Toumin was first made in the mid-nineteenth century on the slopes of Valle Varaita, later taking its name from the municipality of Melle, or Mel, where it was sold. The cheese is made by adding a little rennet to whole, freshly drawn milk and leaving the curd to stand at room temperature for a fairly long time that varies depending on the individual cheesemaker's style. Subsequently, the curd is cut into large lumps and then transferred into the traditional moulds with a skimming spoon. The moulds are turned over several times, salted on top and bottom, and placed in a cool, damp room to mature. Toumin dal Mel releases fresh, tangy aromas of buttermilk and yoghurt, with nuances of fresh hay that shade into mossy notes with maturing. On the palate, it is mild, full-flavoured and faintly sourish. In its territory of origin, Toumin dal Mel is used as a filling for the traditional Valle Varaita *ravioles*. With maturing, the nose tends to become slightly tangy and almondy.

Rennet: liquid, calf's
Outer rind: milky white skin when fresh, becoming porcelain-white with maturing
Body: fatty, raw, soft, with no eyes, milk-white in colour
Top and bottom: flat, 10-12 cm in diameter
Height/weight: 1-2 cm / 150-200 g
Territory of origin: the municipalities of Melle, Frassino and Valmala in Valle Varaita

Tuma di Pecora delle Langhe

Once, the farms in the Langhe hills would always keep a small flock of sheep. Ewe's milk, sometimes mixed with goat's milk, was used to make the typical local cheese, which was arranged in rush baskets for sale at the markets in Murazzano, Bossolasco, Alba, Dogliani and Ceva. Commonly known as Robiola or Tuma, the cheese acquired DOP status with the name of Murazzano (see entry) but the production regulations allow the use of up to 40% raw or even pasteurised cow's milk. The aim of the Slow Food Presidium is to recover the traditional cheese, obtained exclusively from raw Langhe ewe's milk mixed with a maximum of 5% goat's milk. The Presidium opted for a different name, Tuma di Pecora delle Langhe, to distinguish the traditional product. Langhe sheep used to be widely farmed and in 1950, there were over 45,000 animals in the area. Today, their numbers have fallen dramatically. Only 2,500 are left on about 60 farms in Piedmont and Liguria. The Langhe sheep is hornless and has a characteristic convex profile, white coat and long, nimble legs. Its milk is heated to about 37°C and coagulated with liquid calf's milk to make Tuma. The curd is milled and placed in moulds. Each cheese is turned over several times and salted. At this point, the cheeses are moved to a slightly better-ventilated room, where they are turned over daily. After 10-15 days, the cheeses are ready for the table, but will acquire greater complexity of flavour and aroma if matured for at least one month. The finished product is cylindrical and ranges in weight from 200 to 300 grams. It is rindless and the straw-white body is soft, sometimes presenting a few eyes. Traditionally, Tuma may also be conserved in glass, and is then called *tume 'n burnia* (toma in a jar) in the local dialect. The cheese can be conserved in its jar through the winter. Cheeses matured for at least a month can be grated or broken up and put in an earthenware jar, to which a little grappa is added, to make bruss (see entry). The perfect accompaniment for Tuma di Pecora delle Langhe, whether fresh or mature, is Dolcetto d'Alba or Dolcetto di Dogliani.

Rennet: liquid, calf's
Body: soft, sometimes with a few eyes, white or straw-yellow in colour
Top and bottom: flat, 12-15 cm in diameter
Height/weight: 2-4 cm / 200-300 g
Territory of origin: 50 municipalities in Upper Langhe in the province of Cuneo

The aim of the Slow Food Presidium is to recover the traditional version of this cheese, obtained with raw Langhe ewe's milk mixed with a very small proportion of goat's milk.

Valcasotto

This outstanding mountain dairy cheese, now almost impossible to find, is made with whole raw cow's milk to which small quantities of ewe's milk, or very occasionally goat's milk, have been added. The milk is heated to 38°C and inoculated with liquid calf's rennet. After it has coagulated fairly slowly, the curd is cut into walnut-sized lumps and then removed. It is ripened in a warm, damp room at a temperature of 26°C for a few hours. The firm curd is then placed in moulds, where the remaining whey is drained off. The next stages are salting in brine and maturing for 10-20 days at a temperature of about 5°C. Extended maturing produces a creamy body and a thicker rind that dramatically alter the cheese's taste profile.

Rennet: liquid, calf's
Outer rind: vestigial when fresh, rough, brown, streaked with reddish mould when very mature
Body: soft, ivory-white or straw-white in colour
Top and bottom: flat, 15-25 cm in diameter
Height/weight: 2-4 cm / 0.3-1 kg
Territory of origin: Upper Valle Tanaro, in mountain dairies on the border of Piedmont and Liguria

The producers

Carlo Abrile
Regione Ovrano
Roccaverano (Asti)
Tel. +39 0144 950687
Robiola di Roccaverano Dop

Alcide Accusani
Località Montecastello, 6
Spigno Monferrato (Alessandria)
Tel. +39 0144 91370
Robiola di Roccaverano Dop

Cesare Accusani
Regione Vaccamorta, 4
Montechiaro d'Acqui (Alessandria)
Tel. +39 0144 92077
Robiola di Roccaverano Classica

Claudio Adami
Via Viora, 19
Paroldo (Cuneo)
Tel. +39 0174 789074
Murazzano Dop, Tuma di Pecora delle
Langhe

Marco Aglì
Via Boschetti, 4
Bobbio Pellice (Turin)
Tel. +39 0121 957803
Saras del Fen

Chiaffredo Agù
Via Roma, 1
Garzigliana (Turin)
Tel. +39 0121 541584
Toma Piemontese Dop

Albrum di Gianni Matli
Via Provinciale, 45
Premia (Verbania)
Tel. +39 0324 602929
Ossolano d'Alpe

Arbiora
Via Consortile, 18
Bubbio (Asti)
Tel. +39 0144 852010
Robiola di Roccaverano Classica

Marco Arneodo
Via Vittorio Veneto, 1
Frazione Chiotti
Castelmagno (Cuneo)
Tel. +39 0171 986234
Castelmagno Dop

Silvia Barolin
Via dei Martiri, 59
Villar Pellice (Turin)
Tel. +39 0121 930015
Saras del Fen

Bassi
Via Sempione, 10
Marano Ticino (Novara)
Tel. +39 0321 97147
Gorgonzola Dop

Franco Bernardini
Frazione Viceno, 25
Crodo (Verbania)
Tel. +39 0324 61520
Bettelmatt

Giuliano Blengio
Regione Santa Libera, 46
Monastero Bormida (Asti)
Tel. +39 0144 88305
Robiola di Roccaverano Dop

Domenica Boaglio
Roure (Turin)
Tel. +39 368 3415553
Toma Piemontese Dop

Ermes Bonetta
Via Scuola, 17
Borgosesia (Vercelli)
Tel. +39 0163 25336
Macagn

Fratelli Bozio
Via Varei, 3
Sostegno (Biella)
Tel. +39 015 762900
Gorgonzola Dop,
Toma Piemontese Dop

Carla Bozzo
Frazione Baragiotta, 1
Pratosesia (Novara)
Tel. +39 0163 850495
Macagn

Laura Bruno
Via Belvedere, 20
Giaveno (Turin)
Tel. +39 011 9377159
Cevrin di Coazze

Buttiero e Dotta
Cascina Bula
Frazione San Gerolamo, 23
Roccaverano (Asti)
Tel. +39 0144 93183
Bruss, Robiola di Roccaverano Classica

Ca' Rumè
Frazione Mellea, 49
Murazzano (Cuneo)
Tel. +39 0173 797174
Murazzano Dop

Luciana Camera
Borgata Sprella, 58
Feisoglio (Cuneo)
Tel. +39 0173 831234
Murazzano Dop

Cascina Albertana
Regione Castignolio, 1
Netro (Biella)
Tel. +39 015 65330
Caprini

Cascina Amelia Ivaldi
Località Valle Caliogna, 51
Cavatore (Alessandria)
Tel. +39 0144 322457
Caprini

Cascina Rosa
Strada Pero, 2 a
Cantalupa (Turin)
Tel. +39 0121 352013
Tomino di Talucco

Caseificio Cooperativo Elvese
Borgata Serre
Elva (Cuneo)
Nostrale di Elva, Toma di Elva

Bruno Catalin
Via Beisilia, 11
Bobbio Pellice (Turin)
Tel. +39 0121 957735
Saras del Fen

Natalino Catalin
Borgata Teynaud, 23
Villar Pellice (Turin)
Tel. +39 0121 930245
Saras del Fen

Ivano Challier
Via Parco Orsiera, 2
Frazione Balboutet
Usseaux (Turin)
Tel. +39 0121 884234
Toma Piemontese Dop

Cooperativa Agricola Mottarone
Piazza della Vittoria, 9
Armeno (Novara)
Tel. +39 0322 900887
Mottarone

**Consorzio Tutela Formaggi
a Dop Raschera**
Via Mondovì Piazza, 1 d
Vicoforte (Cuneo)
Tel. +39 0174 563307
Raschera Dop

Consorzio Vittorino Vezzani
Via Richardette, 63
Sauze d'Oulx (Turin)
Tel. +39 0122 858060
Murianengo, Toma Piemontese Dop

Cooperativa Vallenostra
Località Valle, 1
Mongiardino Ligure (Alessandria)
Tel. +39 0143 94131
Montébore

Gian Mario Costa
Frazione Camasco
Varallo Sesia (Vercelli)
Tel. +39 0163 53578
Macagn

Cottino
Frazione Montà di Rodi
Località Cremoletti Inferiore
Viù (Turin)
Tel. +39 0123 697603
Toma Piemontese Dop

Maria Gabriella Cruciani
Piazza Cavour, 14
Cocconato (Asti)
Tel. +39 0141 907016 - +39 0141 907426
Robiola di Cocconato

Bartolomeo Decostanzi
Via Provinciale, 3
Melle (Cuneo)
Tel. +39 0175 978001
Toumin dal Mel

Armando Deini
Via Crino
Baceno (Verbania)
Tel. +39 333 3424910
Caprino Ossolano

Marina Della Piazza
Via Quarata, 16
Frazione Cosasca
Trontano (Verbania)
Tel. +39 0324 45617
Ossolano d'Alpe

Nicolino Demichelis
Via Campasso, 21
Cirié (Turin)
Tel. +39 011 9203313
Toma Piemontese Dop

**Dove Osano le Aquile
di Giacomo Isoardi**
Via Matteotti, 4
Castelmagno (Cuneo)
Tel. +39 0171 986160
Castelmagno Dop

Franco Durand Canton
Borgata Genteugna, 1
Bobbio Pellice (Turin)
Tel. +39 0121 957836
Saras del Fen

Letizia Filosi
Località Bugliaga
Trasquera (Verbania)
Tel. +39 338 3882461
Caprino Ossolano

Formazza agricola
Frazione Valdo, 36
Formazza (Verbania)
Tel. +39 0324 63169
Bettelmatt

Lidia Fresco
Frazione Pettani
Callabiana (Biella)
Tel. +39 333 2662877
Macagn

Bartolomeo Gallo Balma
Strada del Masero, 7
Castellamonte (Turin)
Tel. +39 0124 517309
Toma Piemontese Dop

Livio Garbaccio
Località Pianai
Civiasco (Vercelli)
Tel. +39 347 4564589
Macagn

Edis Garbella Tavernin
Frazione Capomosso
Mosso (Biella)
Tel. +39 333 7385729
Macagn

Garda
Via Vittorio Emanuele, 48
Albiano (Turin)
Tel. +39 0125 59666
Reblec, Toma Piemontese Dop

Franca Ghione
Cascina Bricco
Roccaverano (Asti)
Tel. +39 0144 93041
Robiola di Roccaverano Dop

Ernesto Giacomone
Frazione Roccapietra
Varallo (Vercelli)
Tel. +39 0163 52217
Caprini

Pier Flavio Giacomone
Frazione Rolando, 8
Mosso (Biella)
Tel. +39 015 741161
Macagn

Giovanni Giordano
Località Abate
Bossolasco (Cuneo)
Tel. +39 0173 793251
Murazzano Dop

Luciano Giovale
Via Cardinal Maurizio, 44
Giaveno (Turin)
Tel. +39 011 9377548
Toma del Lait Brusch

Fratelli Giraudo
Via Ariosto, 16
Acqui Terme (Alessandria)
Tel. +39 0144 324314
Formaggetta del Monferrato, Seirass

Sabina Gonnet
Borgata Costa, 1
Bobbio Pellice (Turin)
Tel. +39 0121 957928
Saras del Fen

Italo Gonnet Salomone
Via Podio, 6
Bobbio Pellice (Turin)
Tel. +39 0121 957838
Saras del Fen

Il Casolare
Via Umberto I, 2
Piasco (Cuneo)
Tel. +39 0175 797984
Toma Piemontese Dop

Imalpi
Regione San Marco, 2
Demonte (Cuneo)
Tel. +39 0171 955594
Cachat, Caprini

La Cascina dei Prapien
Regione Prapiano
Mosso (Biella)
Tel. +39 015 757162
Caprini, Toma Piemontese Dop

La Colma
Località Ortaiolo
Civiasco (Vercelli)
Tel. +39 0163 55635
Caprini

Laura Lacopo
Borgo Goria Superiore, 2
Elva (Cuneo)
Tel. +39 0171 997979
Nostrale di Elva, Toma di Elva

Francesco Lauria
Regione Caldasio, 119
Ponzone (Alessandria)
Tel. +39 0144 378868
Robiola di Roccaverano Classica

Erminio Lussiana
Borgata Ciausi, 17
Giaveno (Turin)
Tel. +39 011 9364006
Cevrin di Coazze

Fratelli Lussiana
Borgata Fornello, 38
Giaveno (Turin)
Tel. +39 011 9363903
Cevrin di Coazze, Toma del Lait Brusch

Marina Lussiana
Via Benna, 12
Coazze (Turin)
Tel. +39 011 9349351
Cevrin di Coazze, Toma del Lait Brusch

Ugo Lussiana
Via C.L.N., 41
Giaveno (Turin)
Tel. +39 011 9376982
Cevrin di Coazze

Aldo Macario e Maddalena Giorgis
Regione Cavanero, 1
Tetto Barlet
Chiusa di Pesio (Cuneo)
Tel. +39 0171 735288
Caprini, Sola

Franco e Antonio Mantello
Via Guglielmo Marconi, 27
Rassa (Vercelli)
Tel. +39 0163 737533
Macagn

Mario Martini
Via Colle del Mulo, 3
Castelmagno (Cuneo)
Tel. +39 337 233077
Castelmagno Dop

Silvano Matli
Via Provinciale, 63
Premia (Verbania)
Tel. +39 0324 602902
Bettelmatt

Lorena Michelis
Via Sotto la Rocca, 8
Prunetto (Cuneo)
Tel. +39 0174 99008
Tuma di Pecora delle Langhe

Pier Claudio Michelin Salomon
Borgata Alloeri, 6
Bobbio Pellice (Turin)
Tel. +39 0121 957795
Saras del Fen

Roberto Negrini
Via Marconi, 12
Domodossola (Verbania)
Tel. +39 0324 242201
Ossolano d'Alpe

Gianfranco Nervi
Cascina Caramello, 14
Roccaverano (Asti)
Tel. +39 0144 93155
Robiola di Roccaverano Dop

Gualtiero Oberto
Borgo Montone, 2
Ceresole Reale (Turin)
Tel. +39 0124 953179
Toma Piemontese Dop

Occelli Agrinatura
Regione Scarrone, 2
Farigliano (Cuneo)
Tel. +39 0173 746411
Escarun, Ormea, Robiola di Ceva,
Testun, Valcasotto

Adolfo Olzeri
Via La Torre, 27
Baceno (Verbania)
Tel. +39 0324 62140
Ossolano d'Alpe

Renato Paltrinieri
Corso XXIII Marzo, 209
Novara
Tel. +39 0321 402042
Gorgonzola Dop

Sergio Pautasso
Borgata Prato Bottrile, 15
Condove (Turin)
Tel. +39 011 9633866
Toma del Lait Brusch

Franco Perotti
Via Tegas, 9
Buriasco (Turin)
Tel. +39 0121 56401 - +39 339 6738604
Toma Piemontese Dop

Piccola Società Cooperativa La Masca
Regione Cova, 12
Roccaverano (Asti)
Tel. +39 0144 93313
Robiola di Roccaverano Classica

Silvio Pistone
Via Alba, 14
Borgomale (Cuneo)
Tel. +39 0173 529285
Toma Piemontese Dop

Oscar Plavan
Borgata Savoia, 7
San Germano Chisone (Turin)
Tel. +39 0121 58593
Saras del Fen

Produttori Toma di Lanzo
Comunità Montana Valli di Lanzo
Frazione Fè, 2
Ceres (Turin)
Tel. +39 0123 53339 - +39 0123 53491
Toma di Lanzo

Piero Rege
Borgata Coccorda, 4
Giaveno (Turin)
Tel. +39 011 9375920
Toma Piemontese Dop

Arturo Rizzolio
Regione Sessania, 1
Monastero Bormida (Asti)
Tel. +39 0144 88293
Robiola di Roccaverano Classica

Roggero
Via Provinciale, 36 a
Melle (Cuneo)
Tel. +39 0175 978197
Toumin dal Mel

Enrico Rossello
Cascina Sorito
Località Ceretta Cà Torba, 30
Roccaverano (Asti)
Tel. +39 0144 80217
Robiola di Roccaverano Classica

Danilo Rostagnol
Via Giordanotti, 15/2
Torre Pellice (Turin)
Tel. +39 0121 932996
Saras del Fen

San Martino
Corso Piemonte, 129
Saluzzo (Cuneo)
Tel. +39 0175 41912
Bra Dop, Paglierina, Raschera Dop,
Toma Piemontese Dop

Renzo Sandretto
Borgata Pratidonio, 31
Pont Canavese (Turin)
Tel. +39 0124 85101
Bruss, Toma Piemontese Dop

Santi
Corso Sempione, 49-55
Cameri (Novara)
Tel. +39 0321 472867
Gorgonzola Dop

SI di Santi e Invernizzi
Via Romentino, 100
Trecate (Novara)
Tel. +39 0321 783090
Gorgonzola Dop

**Società Cooperativa Agricola
Mombarone**
Via Circonvallazione, 33
Frazione Torre Daniele
Settimo Vittone (Turin)
Tel. +39 0125 757471
Salignoùn

Daniele Taddei
Frazione Uresso
Baceno (Verbania)
Tel. +39 0324 62127
Ossolano d'Alpe

Mariolina Taschetti
Regione Gorretta
Cessole (Asti)
Tel. +39 0144 80217
Robiola di Roccaverano Dop

Elsa Tourn
Via Maestra, 11
Rorà (Turin)
Tel. +39 0121 902341
Saras del Fen

Ugo Venara
Via Borgosesia, 10
Serravalle Sesia (Vercelli)
Tel. +39 0163 450313
Macagn

Don Roberto Verri
Regione Rocchino, 30
Serole (Asti)
Tel. +39 0144 94129
Robiola di Roccaverano Classica

Lombardy

Agrì di Valtorta

Bagòss di Bagolino ●

Bernardo

Bitto DOP

Bitto Valli del Bitto ●

Branzi

Caprino Stagionato

Crescenza

Fontal

Formaggella di Monte

Formai de Mut dell'Alta
    Val Brembana DOP

Grana padano DOP

Magnocca or Maioc
    or Maiocca

Magro di Piatta

Mascarpone

Pannerone di Lodi ●

Provolone Valpadana DOP

Quartirolo Lombardo DOP

Salva

Scimudin

Semigrasso d'Alpe or Livigno

Silter

Stracchino Tipico

Strachitund

Taleggio DOP

Tipico Lodigiano

Tombea ●

Valtellina Casera DOP

Zincarlin or Cingherlino

Agrì di Valtorta

This is a local cheese made in Valtorta, a small valley way off the beaten track. Whole, fresh-drawn milk is heated to 32-35°C and inoculated with rennet and a little soured whey, hence the name Agrì (*agro* means "sour" in Italian). Coagulation takes place in two to three hours and the curd is left to drain for two days on clean cloths. The firm curd is then put in ricotta moulds and left to stand for a day. It is salted by hand and almost always eaten straight away. It has a milky aroma and a slightly sour taste.

Rennet: liquid, calf's
Body: dry, soft, white shading into yellowish in colour after maturing for a week or two
Top and bottom: flat
Height/weight: 6-7 cm / 70-80 g
Territory of origin: Valtorta in Upper Val Brembana in the province of Bergamo

Bagòss di Bagolino

Bagòss di Bagolino is an uncooked cheese obtained from part-skimmed milk. It takes its name from the local nickname for the residents of Bagolino, a small municipality in Val di Caffaro, in the northern part of the province of Brescia. The cheeses are larger than average for mountain toma-type products, and usually weigh 16-18 kilograms, although some are as heavy as 20-22 kilograms. Bagòss di Bagolino is made with raw milk from Bruno Alpina cows. Following an ancient tradition, many producers add a spoonful of sugar when they are breaking up the curd. The production regulations demand at least 12 months' maturing, but the average is substantially longer (24 or 36 months). During maturing, the rind is brushed with raw linseed oil, which gives the cheese its characteristic ochre-brown colour. Known affectionately to locals as "poor man's grana", Bagòss di Bagolino is ideal for grating when mature. Nonetheless, it is mainly consumed as an outstanding cheese for the table. After the first 10-12 months' maturing, when the body starts to turn rock-hard and flaky, the cheese begins to reveal an astonishing breadth of sensory perceptions. The nose has strong notes of saffron spice that meld into green pasture and hay aromas. On the palate, the green notes are joined by a faint almondy sensation and a slightly tangy finish that tends to become more marked as maturing progresses. A fine partner for powerful, seriously structured red wines, like Sfurzat della Valtellina or Amarone, Bagòss di Bagolino is equally delicious with a glass of good Spumante Metodo Classico. The 55 producers in the Slow Food Presidium, members of the Cooperativa Valle di Bagolino, make their cheese by traditional craft methods. All use wood fires and large copper vats. In summer, they make cheese in the mountain pastures and in winter comply with strict production regulations that impose local hay as the only fodder. The Presidium promotes this great cheese and protects it from the many imitations circulating in the market. The original may be recognised by the distinctive mark that is applied to the side of the cheese.

Rennet: powder, calf's
Outer rind: smooth, slightly hard, oiled during maturing with raw linseed oil, orange-yellow in colour
Body: grainy in texture, with few eyes, straw-yellow in colour
Top and bottom: flat, 35-40 cm in diameter
Height/weight: 12-14 cm / 16-22 kg
Territory of origin: the municipality of Bagolino in the province of Brescia

During maturing, the rind is brushed with raw linseed oil, which gives the cheese its characteristic ochre-brown colour.

Bernardo

A classic summer cheese made in Alpine pastures, Bernardo is generally eaten fresh. Raw milk is coagulated at 35°C, then the curd is cut up coarsely and cooked at about 40°C. The curd is lifted out of the whey and a little saffron powder added. It is then wrapped in cloths and placed in moulds. The rounds are dry-salted while standing on wooden boards. After ripening for about 15 days, they are ready for the table. The fresh version has almost no rind, a reddish-yellow body and a delicate flavour. The less commonly found mature variety has a brownish-yellow rind, fairly evenly distributed, medium-sized eyes and a more intense aromatic flavour.

Rennet: liquid, calf's
Outer rind: almost entirely absent
Body: soft, mild-flavoured, reddish-yellow in colour
Top and bottom: flat
Height/weight: 3 cm / 1 kg
Territory of origin: the area around Clusone in the province of Bergamo

Bitto DOP

This cheese takes its name from the torrential river Bitto, a place name which may come from a Celtic root meaning "perennial", or a Germanic word for "bed". The Bitto flows through the valley of the same name, joining the Adda at Morbegno, where the famous Bitto fair is held. Bitto cheese is made only during the summer months, generally using traditional techniques, in mountain dairies or *calecc*, unroofed stone refuges that are covered with canvas when used. Fresh-drawn cow's milk, with a maximum of 10% goat's milk added, is slightly heated to a temperature varying from 39 to 49°C. It is then left to curdle for 20 to 40 minutes. The curd is milled into rice-sized pieces and cooked at 45-53°C for 20-60 minutes. The firm curd is then removed from the heat for a quarter of an hour and stirred continuously before being put in the moulds. The rounds are dry-salted with coarse kitchen salt every two or three days for three to four weeks. The outer rind of Bitto is thin and straw-yellow, going brown over time. The body is firm with sparse, bird's eye-sized eyes and a mild, fragrant flavour when the cheese is fresh. With maturing, which may go on for up to ten years, the body becomes firmer and harder, turning golden yellow. It also acquires a stronger, more aromatic, flavour, sometimes with a tangy edge. Maturing, which continues for at least 70 days, is always begun in the mountain dairies and completed in the cheese stores on the valley floor.

Rennet: liquid, calf's
Outer rind: thin, straw-yellow becoming brown in colour over time
Body: compact, with sparse, bird's eye-sized eyes
Top and bottom: flat, 30-50 cm in diameter
Height/weight: 8-10 cm / 8-25 kg
Territory of origin: the entire province of Sondrio, in particular Valtellina, and the municipalities of Averara, Carona, Cusio, Foppolo, Mezzoldo, Piazzatore, Santa Brigida and Valleve in the province of Bergamo
DOP status awarded on 1 July 1996, regulation no. 1263

Bitto can be aged for an extraordinary length of time. Some cheeses are matured for as long as ten years.

COW'S AND GOAT'S MILK

Bitto Valli del Bitto

The historic home of Bitto production is the Gerola and Albaredo valleys formed by the torrential river from which the cheese takes its name, in the province of Sondrio. Bitto is made in the mountain pastures of these valleys, at 1,400 to 2,000 metres above sea level. The cheese has some very distinctive characteristics. A series of traditional techniques bring out the quality of the product, as well as playing a crucial role in the conservation of the environment and Alpine biodiversity. The most important of these techniques is rotation grazing. Over the three summer months, the herd is led from pasture to pasture in stages that take it from lower-altitude grazing to the highest pastures. Along the way, traditional *calècc* (a contraction of *casa* and *letto*, meaning "house" and "bed") bothies act as temporary dairies so that the milk only has to travel a few metres, and can be processed before it loses its natural warmth. Another local practice is to take Orobica goats to the summer pastures with the herds of cattle. Goat's milk accounts for 10-20% of the content of Bitto, giving it a particular aromatic quality and persistence of flavour. Milking in the high pastures is done exclusively by hand, to ensure the health of the herd. The cheese is generally dry-salted so that as delicate a rind as possible forms, to guarantee more satisfactory maturing. All fodder supplements, additives, preservatives and selected enzymes are prohibited during the production process. The Slow Food Presidium was set up to promote mountain dairy production in the traditional cheesemaking area. Only the cheeses that are adjudged to be of outstanding quality and suited to special maturing – they can conserve superbly fragrant sensory perceptions even after maturing for a decade – are branded with the mark of the Valli del Bitto Producers' Association. The working practices adhered to by the association's members have a positive impact on both the quality of the cheese and the environment. It is crucial that this situation should be acknowledged by the market, and that the producers should receive fair remuneration for their fundamental role in conserving the environment. Once the mountain pastures have been abandoned, degradation quickly sets in and is almost impossible to reverse.

Rennet: liquid, calf's
Outer rind: thin, straw-yellow becoming brown in colour over time
Body: compact, with sparse, bird's eye-sized eyes
Top and bottom: flat, 30-50 cm in diameter
Height/weight: 8-10 cm / 8-25 kg
Territory of origin: the valleys of Albaredo and Gerola, and the neighbouring mountain pastures in the province of Sondrio

Over the three summer months, the herd is led from pasture to pasture in stages that take it from lower-altitude grazing to the highest pastures. Along the route, the traditional calècc *bothies serve as provisional dairies.*

Branzi

This variant of formai de mut takes its name from the village of Branzi. Raw milk is coagulated at 34-36°C for about half an hour. The soft curd is then milled into small pieces and cooked at 43-46°C for 30 minutes. Next, it is put into moulds, covered with cloths called *patte*, and pressed for about an hour. The rounds are dry-salted in the mountain dairies, or soaked in brine during the winter, when Branzi is made in the village's co-operative dairy. The cheese has a mild, delicate flavour that becomes fairly strong, or even tangy, with ageing. Despite the shared cheesemaking technique, Branzi may have a slightly different flavour and aroma depending on where it was made, particularly if in the case of the mountain dairy version. This versatile cheese has many uses in the kitchen and is an ideal accompaniment for polenta.

Rennet: liquid, calf's
Outer rind: smooth, thin, elastic, yellowish in colour
Body: soft, with faint eyes, straw-yellow in colour
Top and bottom: flat, 40-45 cm in diameter
Height/weight: 8-9 cm / 12-15 kg
Territory of origin: the municipality of Branzi and the neighbouring areas in Val Brembana in the province of Bergamo

GOAT'S AND EWE'S MILK

Caprino Stagionato

A whey-based starter culture is inoculated into lightly salted whole or part-skimmed raw milk, which is then heated to the minimum temperature necessary to provoke lactic, or acid, coagulation, which takes about 24 hours. Once the curd has reached a firm enough consistency, it is transferred to perforated moulds without milling. The moulds are left to stand for about 24 hours so that the whey can drain off completely. The small rounds are turned over several times and dry-salted. Caprino may be sold fresh, after ripening for three or four days, but in Valsassina it is traditional to leave the cheese to mature for at least 30 days. There are versions flavoured with parsley, garlic, chives and ground pepper. This is the mature version of Caprino, called *furmagin pasà*, or "over-ripe cheese", in the local dialect.

Outer rind: the skin tends to acquire a thin mould that turns reddish with age
Body: compact, smooth, moist, ivory-white in colour
Top and bottom: flat, about 3 cm in diameter
Height/weight: 10 cm / 300-500 g
Territory of origin: Valsassina and the municipalities of Intelvi and Montevecchia in the province of Como

Crescenza

Today, Crescenza is almost exclusively an industrial product. It apparently takes its name from the Latin word *carsenza*, meaning "flat bread", because if kept in a warm place, the cheese ferments, swells up and bursts open just like rising bread. Crescenza belongs to the family of stracchino cheeses. It is made from pasteurised milk which is curdled at 37°C for half an hour. The soft curd is broken up in two stages with a 30-minute break between milling operations. It is then stirred and transferred into special perforated moulds before ripening in a warm, damp environment at 22-24°C for five hours. Brine baths are used for salting. The cheese takes five or six days to mature and should be eaten immediately. It has a mild, delicate flavour and a milky smell. Because Crescenza poses conservation problems, two types are produced. The winter version has a softer, creamier body whereas Crescenza made in summer has a firmer body.

Rennet: liquid, calf's
Body: uniform, compact, buttery, with a melt-in-the-mouth texture, white in colour
Top and bottom: flat and variable
Height/weight: 4-5 cm / 1.8-2 kg
Territory of origin: the entire Po Valley

Fontal

Fontal is produced, most of it industrially, in much of northern Italy all year round. The name, which has been used since 1955, is a conflation of fontina (see entry) and emmental. Pasteurised cow's milk is inoculated with selected mesophilous Lactococcus starter cultures. Coagulation with liquid or powdered calf's rennet takes 25-35 minutes at 30-35°C. The curd is milled into medium-sized or small lumps and heated to 38-40°C. It is then removed and pressed with pneumatic presses to extract the whey. Salting, which may begin with the addition of salt while the curd is still in the vat, is completed by immersing the moulds in a brine bath. Fontal matures for 40-60 days at 8-10°C, and is then ready for the table. A semi-hard cheese, it has a mild flavour and a subtle aroma.

Rennet: liquid or powder, calf's
Outer rind: thin, smooth, compact, with reddish brown wax or plastic covering
Body: elastic, compact, uniform, semi-hard, with few sparsely distributed eyes, white or cream in colour
Top and bottom: flat, 30-40 cm in diameter
Height/weight: 8-10 cm / 8-12 kg
Territory of origin: the flatlands of Lombardy

COW'S MILK

Formaggella di Monte

Made from whole or slightly skimmed cow's milk, Formaggella di Monte is a semi-cooked cheese from the Brescian Alps. It is generally made in the summer months with a technique similar to that used for scimudin (see entry) in Valtellina. Cylindrical in form, the cheese has a diameter of 20-25 centimetres and a slightly convex side six to ten centimetres high. It varies in weight from 1.2-2 kilograms. The cheeses are dry-salted and then mature for an average of 20-30 days, although in some cases maturing may continue for several months. The rind is greyish and wrinkly. The body is white and compact but soft, and has small eyes. Formaggella di Monte's delicate flavour can be enjoyed when the cheese is fresh after only 15 days' maturing, or one month in the case of the traditional mountain dairy version.

Rennet: liquid, calf's
Outer rind: greyish, wrinkly
Body: white, compact, soft, with small eyes
Top and bottom: flat, 20-25 cm in diameter
Height/weight: 6-10 cm / 1.2-2 kg
Territory of origin: the Adamello Regional Park in the province of Brescia

Formai de Mut
dell'Alta Val Brembana DOP

Formai de Mut could be translated as "mountain cheese", but it has to be remembered that *mut* in the local dialect indicates the Alpine pastures, not the mountain itself. The herds are in fact fed exclusively on grass, either fresh or in the form of hay, from meadows lying 1,200-2,500 metres above sea level. Only during the winter months do the DOP regulations permit the diet be supplemented with mixtures of cereals, or maize or grass-based silage. Most Formai de Mut is, however, made during the summer. The milk is put into large, 300-400 litre vats (it takes ten litres of milk to make one kilogram of cheese) and curdled at 35-37°C in 30 minutes. After the soft curd has been milled into rice-sized pieces, it is semi-cooked at 45-47°C, taken off the heat and stirred. The firm curd is lifted out using special filtering cloths called *patte*. After being left to stand and drain, it is transferred to moulds, where it is turned over and pressed. Salt is added first to the curd, then the rounds are either dry-salted or immersed in brine baths on alternate days for one or two weeks. The rind is thin, compact and smooth with a straw-yellow colour that shades into grey with maturing. The body is a straw-white to ivory colour. It is firm, elastic and presents a scattering of eyes ranging from very small to bird's eye-sized. The flavour is delicate, fragrant and not particularly salty or tangy. After maturing for at least 40-45 days, Formai de Mut may be used in the preparation of a wide range of dishes. The mature version, which may be well over six months old, is an excellent table cheese.

Rennet: liquid, or rarely paste, calf's
Outer rind: thin, firm, smooth, straw-yellow tending to grey in colour when mature
Body: firm, elastic, with scattered eyes ranging from very small to bird's eye-sized, straw-white to ivory in colour
Top and bottom: flat or semi-flat, 30-40 cm in diameter
Height/weight: 8-10 cm / 8-12 kg
Territory of origin: Upper Val Brembana in the province of Bergamo
DOP status awarded on 12 June 1996, regulation no. 1107

Nowadays, Formai de Mut is produced all year round but the best cheese is still made in Alpine pastures during the summer months.

Grana Padano DOP

The origin of Grana Padano is disputed as both Lodi and Codogno claim to be its home. Today, it is made throughout almost the whole of the Po Valley, as far as Trento. Grana Padano is made all year round from the milk of cows fed on green and dried fodder, or silage. When silage is used, in wintertime, the cheese is also known as Vernengo. The raw milk from two milkings drawn on the same day is part-skimmed by allowing the cream to rise, and then transferred to ten-hectolitre copper vats that hold enough milk for two whole cheeses. Coagulation takes ten minutes at 31-33°C and then the soft curd is broken up into millet-sized pieces. It is then cooked, first at 43-44°C for a few minutes, and then at 54-56°C. When the curd is sufficiently acid and elastic, it is taken out using cloths and split into two blocks, which are put into separate moulds. The rounds are turned over several times and then salted in a brine bath for about 28 days. After this, they are ripened and aged in temperature and humidity-controlled rooms at 18-20°C and 85% humidity for 12-36 months. During this time, the rounds are constantly checked, turned over and cleaned. The rind is hard, smooth, thick and dark yellow or golden brown in colour. It must bear the mark of the Grana Padano Consortium. Only Grana Padano made in the province of Trento can be identified by its place of origin, with the

Trentingrana mark. The body is straw-yellow, finely granular and breaks away in flakes. There are no eyes. The palate is fragrant, with a strong yet delicate and never tangy flavour. Grana Padano can be used either as a table cheese or for grating.

Rennet: liquid, calf's
Outer rind: hard, smooth, thick, dark yellow or gold in colour
Body: fine-grained, tending to break away in flakes, straw-yellow in colour
Top and bottom: flat, 35-45 cm in diameter
Height/weight: 18-25 cm / 24-40 kg
Territory of origin: the provinces of Alessandria, Asti, Cuneo, Novara, Turin, Vercelli, Bergamo, Brescia, Como, Cremona, Mantua, Milan, Pavia, Sondrio, Varese, Trento, Padua, Rovigo, Treviso, Venice, Verona, Vicenza, Bologna, Ferrara, Forlì, Piacenza and Ravenna
DOP status awarded on 12 June 1996, regulation no. 1107

The Consortium mark, the number of the dairy and the date of production must be clearly visible on the rind of Grana Padano.

Cow's milk

Magnocca or Maioc or Maiocca

This cheese is made in Valchiavenna and the neighbouring valleys, and is in fact related to several Alpine tomas made in various other places. The production technique is similar to that used for casolet (see entry). Whole or slightly skimmed milk is heated and inoculated with liquid calf's rennet. After about 30 minutes, the soft curd is cut up fairly coarsely but not cooked, as it is for casolet. The curd is lifted out with cloths, left to drain and then put into moulds. Once the whey has drained out completely, it is either dry-salted or immersed in brine. Magnocca is placed in fairly damp cellars to ripen and is ready 16-30 days later, after which it can be left to mature for months, or even a year. The same cheese is made using the same cheese-making technique in Valtellina, where it is called *scimuda*.

Rennet: liquid, calf's
Outer rind: hard, compact, straw-white to grey in colour
Body: compact, tending to become crumbly with age, straw-yellow in colour
Top and bottom: flat, 25-30 cm in diameter
Height/weight: 8-10 cm / 10 kg
Territory of origin: Valchiavenna and Valle San Giacomo in the province of Sondrio

Magro di Piatta

This is one of Italy's lowest fat cheeses. In the Alpine pastures, freshly drawn milk is put into metal basins placed in running water. The milk is left in the basins for about 16 hours, after which the cream that has risen to the surface spontaneously is skimmed off. The milk is then heated to 35°C, inoculated with rennet and left to curdle. After an hour and a half, the temperature is increased and the milk is semi-cooked at 42°C for about 30 minutes, while being stirred continuously. The curd is then removed and placed in wooden moulds, where it is left for two days. Salting is carried out by taking the rounds out of the moulds and immersing them in salted whey. The rounds are then placed in fairly damp cellars to mature. After 60 days, Magro di Piatta is ready for the table, but ageing normally continues for a year or more.

Rennet: liquid or paste, calf's
Outer rind: compact, hard when mature, brownish-yellow tending to grey in colour
Body: fairly hard, crumbly, with small eyes, straw-yellow in colour, acquiring greenish tints with age
Top and bottom: flat, 25-30 cm in diameter
Height/weight: 9-12 cm / 6-7 kg
Territory of origin: Valdisotto and the Bormio area in general

Mascarpone

The name of this cheese apparently derives from *mascarpa*, a by-product extracted from the whey left over from making stracchino. The word may, however, simply be a synonym for ricotta. According to a more colourful version, its origin is the Spanish expression *más que bueno* (more than good) and it dates back to the days of Spanish occupation. Mascarpone, or Mascherpone, is made from cream obtained by centrifuging, or allowed to rise spontaneously. The fat content is variable, ranging from 25 to 40%. The cream is coagulated with organic acids by heating it in a double boiler for about ten minutes at 85-90°C and stirring continuously. The curd is left to stand in the whey for 8-15 hours at a low temperature and then removed with cloths. After standing again for a short while, the remaining whey is removed and the Mascarpone is ready for the able. Excellent sprinkled with sugar and cocoa, Mascarpone is also used in the preparation of custards and desserts. It is thought to have come originally from the areas around Lodi and Abbiategrasso.

Rennet: tartaric, citric or acetic acid
Body: creamy, soft, with a mild, creamy flavour that sours slightly after a few days, white in colour
Height/weight: variable
Territory of origin: the entire region

COW'S MILK
Pannerone di Lodi

Once misleadingly known as "white gorgonzola", even
though it is completely unrelated to Italy's best-known
blue cheese, Pannerone di Lodi owes its name to the local
word *panéra*, which means cream. The cheese itself is made exclusively with whole milk. Its distinguishing characteristic is
the total absence of salting in any form. Raw cow's milk is coagulated in 30 minutes at 28-32°C. The curd is then milled
into sweetcorn-sized lumps. Some of the whey is removed using basins known as *ramin* and then the curd is constantly
stirred as it is removed in cloths called *patte*. The curd is then
divided manually into moulds, where it stays for four to five
days at a temperature of 28-32°C as the rest of the whey drains
off. When they are removed from the moulds, the cheeses are
wrapped in special paper, bound in wooden hoops and ripened
for 24 hours. Maturing continues while the cheeses are kept at
room temperature for two or three days, before going into cold
storage at 4-6°C. The maturing process lasts for about ten days
in total. Pannerone cheeses, which are about 20 centimetres
high, are cylindrical in shape, weigh 12-13 kilograms and have
a diameter of 25-30 centimetres. The rind is thin, smooth and
straw-yellow in colour. The cream-white body is soft and fragrant, with a liberal scattering of eyes. The flavour, which derives from the action of bacterial flora in the absence of salt, is

complex and distinctive. A mild, appealing front palate introduces a distinctly almondy finish with a bitterish twist. It is this challenging flavour that has led to the cheese's near extinction. Before the First World War, Pannerone was widely produced all over the Lombard flatlands, the main centres of production being in the municipalities of the Lodi area. Today, there is only one producer left. The Slow Food Presidium, starting from this craft cheesemaker, has drafted production regulations and involved other small local businesses to ensure that this fine example of the cheesemaker's art will have a future.

Rennet: liquid, calf's
Outer rind: moist, thin, reddish-yellow in colour
Body: crumbly, not compact, with small, unevenly distributed cracks, ivory-white in colour
Top and bottom: flat, 25-30 cm in diameter
Height/weight: 20 cm / 12-13 kg
Territory of origin: Lodi and neighbouring municipalities

The distinguishing feature of Pannerone di Lodi is that it is made without any kind of salting.

Provolone Valpadana DOP

Provolone originally comes from the south of Italy, where it is a traditional cheese. Production had already spread to the Po Valley, and the area between Brescia and Cremona in particular, by the end of the nineteenth century. The name derives from the Neapolitan word *prova* or *provola*, used to indicate fresh samples of dairy products for tasting. Whole, raw milk, which may be heat-treated for the tangy version or pasteurised for the mild variety, is coagulated at 37-39°C. The curd is then milled into sweetcorn-sized lumps and cooked at 50-52°C. When the curd has acquired the desired consistency, it is kneaded and stretched in hot water at 70°C. It is then shaped and cooled. Provolone Valpadana DOP is sold in various formats, including salami-shaped, melon-shaped, tangerine-shaped, truncated cone, pear-shaped and flask-shaped (like a pear with a ball on top). Weight and size vary for each shape. The cheeses are then salted in a brine bath for a period that varies depending on their weight. The cheeses are tied with cords and suspended from special supports to mature. The rind is smooth, thin, shiny and golden in colour. The body is firm, and may present faint, sparse eyes. Slight flaking is acceptable in the tangy version. Straw-yellow in colour, Provolone Valpadana DOP has a delicate flavour if matured for less than three months. This is the mild version, made using calf's rennet. The flavour tends to become tangy with ageing, or if the milk is curdled with kid's or lamb's rennet, or both. An excellent table cheese, Provolone Valpadana DOP is also made in a smoked version. It is versatile in the kitchen, thanks to its stretchy texture and ability to melt and mingle with other ingredients. It is produced in four regions of northern Italy. In Lombardy, it is found throughout the provinces of Cremona and Brescia, and in some parts of the provinces of Bergamo, Mantua and Lodi. In the Veneto, it is made in the provinces of Verona, Vicenza, Rovigo and Padua. In Emilia Romagna, it is found all over the province of Piacenza and in Trentino, Provolone Valpadana DOP is made in many municipalities in the province of Trento.

Rennet: paste, kid's or lamb's for the tangy version, liquid, calf's for the mild cheese
Outer rind: smooth, thin, lustrous, golden
Body: firm, may have faint, sparsely distributed eyes
Top and bottom: variable, depending on the shape
Weight: variable, depending on the shape, from a few hundred grams to more than 100 kg
Territory of origin: the provinces of Cremona, Brescia, Verona, Vicenza, Rovigo, Padua and Piacenza, and some parts of the provinces of Bergamo, Mantua, Lodi and Trento
DOP status awarded on 12 June 1996, regulation no. 1107

Provolone Valpadana is the cheese with the widest range of shapes and sizes, which is indicative of how old the type is. Each cheese must bear the distinctive DOP mark.

Quartirolo Lombardo DOP

The name Quartirolo derives from the feed given to the cattle during the cheesemaking period and refers to fresh fodder from the fourth cut, the *quartirolo*, which is richer in fragrance and flavour. Quartirolo used to be called Stracchino Quartirolo della Val Taleggio, or Quartirolo di Monte. Today, it can be produced all year round, but the best Quartirolo is still made in the autumn, from early September to the end of October, with whole or part-skimmed cow's milk from two or more milkings. Coagulation takes place at a temperature of around 35-40°C in 25 minutes. The curd is milled into hazel-nut-sized lumps in two stages that depend on the changing level of acidity in the whey. The curd and whey are then put into moulds and ripened at 26-28°C for 4-24 hours. Salting can be dry or by soaking in brine. Soft Quartirolo matures in 5-30 days. After 30 days' ageing, it can be sold as Maturo (mature). Quartirolo di Monte is the version made in mountain dairies using milk freshly drawn from the cow, with no added enzymes. It is ripened in a naturally warm, damp environment and dry-salted. The rind is thin and pinkish white in the case of fresh cheeses, and a reddish grey-green in the case of more mature cheeses. The body is compact, with small lumps. It is normal for small pieces to break away. Crumbly and soft, the cheese acquires a melt-in-the-mouth texture as it ages. The colour darkens from white to straw-yellow with maturing. On the palate, it is slightly sour when young, becoming more aromatic and faintly bitterish with ageing.

Rennet: liquid, calf's
Outer rind: thin, pinkish white when young, shading into reddish grey-green as maturing progresses.
Body: firm, slightly lumpy, crumbly, soft, acquiring a melt-in-the-mouth texture with ageing.
Top and bottom: flat, rectangular 18-22 cm
Height/weight: 4-8 cm / 1.5-3.5 kg
Territory of origin: throughout the provinces of Brescia, Bergamo, Como, Cremona, Milan, Pavia and Varese
DOP status awarded on 12 June 1996, regulation no. 1107

Quartirolo may be eaten very fresh, when it is almost completely rindless.

When mature, Quartirolo resembles taleggio.

Salva

This cheese used to be made in May with the excess milk produced at that time of year. Salva (literally, "it saves" in Italian) was an appropriate name for a cheese that represented an economic lifeline for many dairies. The cheesemaking technique is the same as for quartirolo but the milk is processed at a higher level of acidity and the curd is milled into very small pieces. Pasteurised part-skimmed milk is curdled at 36°C for about 30 minutes. The curd is milled in two stages with an interval of 10-15 minutes. After being left to stand for a short while, it is taken out and placed in moulds. The rounds are then ripened at 25-30°C for 18-24 hours. Next, they are left to mature in cool rooms for a month. At this point, the cheeses are ready for eating or further maturing. Salva has a mild flavour when young, acquiring aromatic, forest-floor notes as it matures.

Rennet: liquid, calf's
Outer rind: fairly thick, hazel shading into dark brown in colour with age
Body: tiny, almost imperceptible eyes, may present slight flaking, straw-white in colour
Top and bottom: flat, rectangular 20-23 cm
Height/weight: 10-18 cm / 3-4 kg
Territory of origin: the Franciacorta district in the province of Brescia and a few municipalities around Bergamo and Cremona

Scimudin

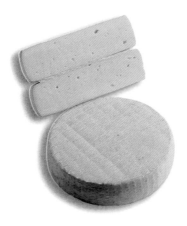

Scimudin is a smaller, and usually creamier, version of scimuda. Pasteurised cow's milk is inoculated with a milk-based starter culture and heated to induce coagulation. The curd is cut up coarsely and poured into moulds, where it is left until the whey has drained off completely. Once dry, the firm curd is removed from the hoops, dry-salted and immersed in brine. It is then transferred to maturing rooms, where it is left at a temperature of 3-6°C in 85-90% humidity for a minimum of three or four weeks.

Rennet: liquid, calf's
Outer rind: thin, with a thin layer of greyish-white mould
Body: firm, soft, with very small eyes, straw-white in colour
Top and bottom: flat or convex, 18-22 cm in diameter
Height/weight: 4-5 cm / 1.3-1.7 kg
Territory of origin: Upper Valtellina

Semigrasso d'Alpe or Livigno

In some mountain diaries, cheesemakers mix cow's milk with goat's milk, which gives the cheese a special, tangy flavour, but in most cases, only cow's milk is used. The milk is heated to 37°C and inoculated with calf's or lamb's rennet. After co-agulation, the mixture is left to stand so that the curd (or *scimuda*) separates from the whey. The curd is then cut using either a coarse or a fine *lira*, a wire cheese knife, according to the eye size required, and semi-cooked at 47°C, stirring continuously. This is the most critical stage of cheesemaking since the curd must be cooked slowly and carefully on a low heat for two hours or more. It is then taken out, placed in moulds and dry-salted or soaked in brine. Ripening may continue for as long as 60 days, while maturing can last for a year or more. Semigrasso d'Alpe may be eaten fresh, after three months' maturing, semi-mature after six months, when it is at its best, according to the experts, or in the hard version after 18 months' maturing.

Rennet: liquid calf's or lamb's
Outer rind: hard, compact, variable in colour, depending on the maturing period
Body: straw-yellow, medium-hard, with characteristically close-packed, evenly distributed, bird's eye-sized eyes
Top and bottom: flat, 30-40 cm in diameter
Height/weight: 8-12 cm / 8-14 kg
Territory of origin: Bormio, Livigno and throughout the Upper Valtellina area

Silter

In Val Camonica, *silter* is the name for the storeroom where cheeses are kept and matured. During the summer season, Silter is made in mountain dairies using traditional techniques. In winter, it is produced in the small dairies on the valley floor. The milk from the morning and evening milkings, or from several milkings, is curdled raw at around 30-32°C in 40 minutes. The curd is milled and cooked at about 46°C for half an hour. After being left to stand for a short while, the soft curd is transferred to hoops, where it ripens for a few hours. The cheese is then salted, either dry or in a brine bath. Silter matures for at least 100 days. If it is matured for more than 200 days, it can be sold as Silter Stagionato. When it has matured for a year, Silter can be used as a grating cheese.

Rennet: liquid, calf's
Outer rind: thin, straw-yellow tending to brownish in colour
Body: compact, with a few small and medium-sized eyes, straw-yellow in colour
Top and bottom: flat, 32-36 cm in diameter
Height/weight: 10-15 cm / 6-14 kg
Territory of origin: Val Camonica and the Pre-Alpine municipalities of the Sebino (Lake Iseo) area of the province of Brescia, from Pisogne to Sultano

Stracchino Tipico

O nce, Stracchino used to be made in the autumn from the milk of cows that were exhausted (*stracca* means "tired" in the local dialect) after walking for many hours from their summer pastures to the flatlands. According to another version, it was not the animals that were weary, but the milk they gave on the water-meadows of the Lombardy plains. Raw milk is coagulated at 30°C for about half an hour and the curd cut into slices of varying thicknesses. It is lifted out with cloths, drained and put into moulds, where it stays for a few days. The rounds are ripened on rush matting and are dry-salted. After a few days, the cheese is ready to be eaten. The fresh, creamy Straness version is eaten as soon as it is made while Stracchino dei Campelli is eaten after 15 to 20 days' ageing to bring out its special aroma, enhanced by the rhododendron flowers among which it matures. It has a melt-in-the-mouth texture and a sweet flavour with aromatic notes.

Rennet: liquid, calf's
Outer rind: barely discernible skin
Body: uniform, buttery, with no eyes, white or pale yellow in colour
Top and bottom: flat, circular or rectangular 20-25 cm
Height/weight: 5 cm / variable
Territory of origin: originally throughout the region but the production area is now much more limited. Stracchino di Nesso from the province of Como and Stracchino della Valle dei Campelli from the province of Bergamo are particularly well-known

Cow's milk

Strachitund

Strachitund – the name means "round stracchino" – has been made in Valbrembana since the latter half of the nineteenth century, but had practically disappeared by the 1970s. The tradition only survived thanks to the efforts of Guglielmo Locatelli from Reggetto di Vedeseta, supported by cheese maturer Giulio Signorelli. A few years ago, a small consortium was set up. The new group follows production regulations for this blue cheese and has boosted output from the previous 100 cheeses a year to today's 50 a week. Milk from Bruno Alpina cows is coagulated using liquid calf's rennet. The curd is milled into hazelnut-sized lumps, removed with a cloth and transferred to hoops in layers with 25-30% of the previous evening's cold curd. Strachitund matures for two months after dry-salting. During maturation, the cheese is turned over periodically. After about 40 days, the cheeses are perforated on the top, bottom and side to encourage the uniform growth of mould.

Rennet: liquid, calf's
Outer rind: wrinkled, thin, light brown in colour
Body: aromatic, full-flavoured, occasionally mould-ripened, pale to deep straw-yellow in colour
Top and bottom: flat, 25 cm in diameter
Height/weight: 15-18 cm / 4-5 kg
Territory of origin: Upper Val Taleggio

Taleggio DOP

This cheese originally seems to have been made in Val Taleggio, in the Upper Bergamo area, during the tenth and eleventh centuries. However, the name Taleggio has only been used since the early twentieth century. Taleggio cheeses matured in the caves of Valsassina, in the province of Como, are particularly prized. Thanks to deep fractures in the rocks, these caves have a unique mesoclimate that favours maturation and the growth of moulds on the rind. It is estimated that about a third of all Taleggio is matured in the mountains. Raw or pasteurised milk is coagulated at 30-36°C for 20-25 minutes. The curd is milled into hazelnut-sized lumps in two stages with a five or ten minute interval. It is then poured into moulds and ripened at 22-25°C. The squares are either dry-salted or soaked in brine. Maturation lasts for 25 to 40 days at a controlled temperature of 3-8°C and humidity of 85-90%. During this period, the cheeses are sponged down with brine to prevent undesirable moulds from appearing and to give the rind its classic pink colour. The rind itself is thin, yellowish or pink in colour, and covered in bloom from the special moulds that grow during ageing. The body is soft, with only a few eyes. Its straw-white colour is deeper under the rind because of the breakdown of proteins that takes place in the mature cheese. Mild and buttery on the palate, Taleggio develops a fuller, tangier flavour with prolonged maturing.

Rennet: liquid, calf's
Outer rind: thin, covered in bloom from mould during ageing, yellow or pinkish in colour
Body: soft, with only a few eyes, straw-white in colour, deeper under the rind because of the breakdown of proteins that takes place in the mature cheese
Top and bottom: flat, rectangular 18-25 cm
Height/weight: 5-7 cm / 1.7-2.2 kg
Territory of origin: the provinces of Bergamo, Brescia, Como, Cremona, Milan and Pavia in Lombardy, Treviso in the Veneto, and Novara in Piedmont
DOP status awarded on 12 June 1996, regulation no. 1107

Taleggio is one of the very few washed-rind Italian cheeses. To mature properly, it must be conserved in cool, damp caves.

Tipico Lodigiano

G ranone Lodigiano was first made in the twelfth century. Cistercian monks standardised the production technique, but the cheese gradually disappeared after the Second World War as smaller dairies closed, unable to compete with industrial production. For several years, four of the traditional local producers have been collaborating in a consortium to make a modern version of Granone. Thus was born Tipico Lodigiano. The cheese is made from October to May, when the cows are fed almost entirely on hay containing Ladino clover, which has also been selected as the logo with which the side is branded. Raw milk from two milkings, part-skimmed by being allowed to settle and then removing the cream that rises to the top, is coagulated with calf's rennet. The curd is milled into lumps the size of a grain of rice. After cooking, the curd is removed and transferred to hoops, where it is turned over several times. Salting is carried out in brine baths. Tipico Lodigiano matures for 20 months.

Rennet: liquid, calf's
Outer rind: thick, brownish yellow tending to pale brown in colour
Body: grainy, straw-yellow in colour
Top and bottom: flat, 40 cm in diameter
Height/weight: 22 cm / 35 kg
Territory of origin: the province of Lodi

Tombea

This cheese takes its name from Monte Tombea (1,950 metres), the mountain overlooking Valvestino, the small valley between Lake Idro and Lake Garda that marks the regional border with Trentino. Tombea is made in mountain dairies in the municipality of Magas, at the Cima Rest and Tombea pastures. Similar to bagòss (see entry), made in the nearby Val di Caffaro, Tombea also features the addition of saffron to the body and the cheeses are oiled to conserve them. It is produced from May to September, using raw milk from Bruno Alpina cows. The cylindrical cheeses are very large and weigh 7-14 kilograms. The rind is straw-yellow, tending to dark brown. The body is compact, does not flake and presents abundant, irregular eyes. Tombea has a spicy fragrance. With maturing, the nose acquires the meat stock notes characteristic of very mature, grainy cheeses. Full-flavoured and outstandingly appealing on the palate, it reveals a tangy note in the finish. Tombea is a fine partner for Spumante Metodo Classico, Valtellina Superiore or Oltrepò Pavese Pinot Nero. Most of the producers, who make a total of about 2,000 cheeses annually, are advanced in years. The cheese is hard to find and little known outside the region. There is a serious risk that the ancient art of making this cheese will be lost with the last surviving cheesemakers. If the high-altitude pastures are not made regulation-compliant, a superb quality raw material will also be lost. The Slow Food Presidium brings together the seven leading producers and is part of an overall project to protect the unspoiled natural environment in the Alto Garda Bresciano Regional Park, promoted by the local Valvestino Forestry Consortium and the Alto Garda Bresciano Mountain Community. The aims of the Presidium are to construct a cheese-maturing facility and restore the traditional pitched-roof thatched barns – some dating from seventeenth century – that were once the homes of the local farmers.

Rennet: powder, calf's
Outer rind: straw-yellow tending to dark brown in colour
Body: compact, with abundant, irregular eyes
Top and bottom: flat
Height/weight: 7-14 kg
Territory of origin: Upper Valvestino and the municipality of Magasa in the province of Brescia

Tombea has a spicy aroma that acquires notes of meat consommé with ageing. Its savoury flavour reveals a slightly tangy hint in the finish. Good wines to serve with Tombea are Spumante, Valtellina Superiore or Oltrepò Pavese Pinot Nero.

Valtellina Casera DOP

Valtellina has a wealth of unique local products that have survived to the present day thanks to the valley's isolated position. Valtellina cheeses reflect the special nature of cattle-farming in the area, which has a macroclimate that is unlike any other anywhere else in the Alps. At the end of the eighteenth century, a version of Bitto, the large-format cheese that keeps well and has better flavour and more character than many others, became the standard product on the valley floor. It was this cheese that today is known as Valtellina Casera. The product is made using Bruna Alpina cow's milk from two milkings, although it may come from more than two milkings if the milk is refrigerated. The milk is left to stand for 12 hours, to permit the spontaneous growth of microflora, and then part-skimmed by allowing the cream to rise. It is heated to 37°C and inoculated with calf's rennet. The curd is milled into sweetcorn-sized lumps and then semi-cooked at a temperature of 44°C for about 30 minutes. Next, the firm curd is left to stand in the whey for a while before being taken out and put into moulds. Traditionally, moulds were made of wood but in modern dairies this has been replaced with food-safe plastic. The rounds are then slowly pressed for 8-12 hours before being taken out and either dry-salted or soaked in brine. At this point, Valtellina

Casera is ready for maturing, which takes place in rooms with a minimum of 80% humidity, at a temperature of 6-16°C. Maturing takes a minimum of 60 days.

Rennet: liquid, calf's
Outer rind: firm, straw-yellow shading into grey-brown in colour
Body: firm, elastic, with sparsely distributed eyes, straw-white in colour
Top and bottom: flat, 30-45 cm in diameter
Height/weight: 8-10 cm / 7-12 kg
Territory of origin: the entire province of Sondrio
DOP status awarded on 1 July 1996, regulation no. 1263

Casera is Valtellina's valley-bottom cheese. Its an excellent table cheese and may be eaten either fresh or medium-mature.

Zincarlin or Cingherlino

This cheese used to be made from rennet-set goat's milk and was eaten fresh with oil and pepper. Today, it is made using cow's milk. Raw milk is heated to 30-32°C and inoculated with liquid calf's rennet. After coagulation, the curd is divided roughly into four with a cross cut and left to stand for 10-20 minutes. It is then gently lifted out and placed in containers whose shape may vary considerably. For at least 24 hours, the moulds are topped up continually as the whey drains off. The cheeses are then placed on a wooden table or straw matting, and left to drain completely. And at this point, they are ready for the table.

Rennet: liquid, calf's
Body: soft, not very compact, fatty, fresh, brownish-white in colour
Top and bottom: variable
Height/weight: variable
Territory of origin: the Besozzo area and the area around Monte Generoso in the province of Varese

The producers

Achille Arioli
Via Sega, 2-3
Ozzero (Milan)
Tel. +39 02 9407302
Gorgonzola Dop, Taleggio Dop

Associazione Produttori Valli del Bitto
Via Stelvio, 23 a
Morbegno (Sondrio)
Tel. +39 0342 635665
Bitto Valli del Bitto

Oscar Baccanelli
Via Nazionale, 42
Berzo Demo (Brescia)
Tel. +39 0364 630893
Formaggella di Monte, Silter

Giacomo Bazzana
Via San Vigilio, 62
Cevo (Brescia)
Tel. +39 339 7448535
Formaggella di Monte

Rosolino Benatti
Strada Pioppette, 17
Goito (Mantova)
Tel. +39 0376 60219
Grana Padano Dop

Bionatura
Via Cavalier Pietro Rini, 2
Bormio (Sondrio)
Tel. +39 0342 904602
Scimudin

Tilde Bonomelli
Via Androla, 24
Cevo (Brescia)
Tel. +39 0364 634495
Silter

Barbara Bontempi
Località Prestello
Prestine (Brescia)
Tel. +39 0364 300834
Formaggella di Monte

Angelo Carena e Figli
Via Pozzo Bonella, 7
Caselle Lurani (Lodi)
Tel. +39 0371 96054
Pannerone di Lodi

Casa Eden
Via Eden, 1
Località Cornalita
San Giovanni Bianco (Bergamo)
Tel. +39 0345 41733
Gorgonzola Dop, Stracchino

Caseificio Sociale Europeo
Via Buozzi, 2
Bagnolo San Vito (Mantova)
Tel. +39 0376 414191
Grana Padano Dop

Luigi Comelli & C.
Via Cantoni, 8
Groppello Cairoli (Pavia)
Tel. +39 0382 815034
Gorgonzola Dop, Taleggio Dop

Comunità Montana Valle Brembana
Via Don Angelo Tondini, 14
Piazza Brembana (Bergamo)
Tel. +39 0345 81177
Branzi, Formai de Mut, Strachitund, Taleggio Dop

Consorzio Forestale Valvestino
Piazza Madonna Pellegrina, 1
Turano di Valvestino (Brescia)
Tel. +39 0365 745007
Tombea

Cooperativa Agricola Sant'Antonio in Valtaleggio
Località Reggetto
Vedeseta (Bergamo)
Tel. +39 0345 47454
Branzi, Quartirolo Lombardo Dop, Salva, Strachitund, Taleggio Dop

Cooperativa Val Palot
Località Val Palot, 8
Pisogne (Brescia)
Tel. +39 339 4636700
Silter

Cooperativa Valle di Bagolino
c/o Comune di Bagolino
Via Parrocchia, 34
Bagolino (Brescia)
Tel. +39 0365 904011
Bagòss di Bagolino

Croce
Via Cesare Battisti, 73
Casalpusterlengo (Lodi)
Tel. +39 0377 84236
Gorgonzola Dop, Pannerone di Lodi,
Stracchino, Taleggio Dop

Alberto Dedè
Cascina Propio
Borghetto Lodigiano (Lodi)
Tel. +39 0371 80238
Tipico Lodigiano

Domenico e Giacomo Ducoli
Via Fontane, 5
Breno (Brescia)
Tel. +39 0364 21388
Silter

Germano Eggiolini
Località Denai
Magasa (Brescia)
Tel. +39 338 8712919
Tombea

Gianpaolo Garbelli
Cascina Paltinera
Linarolo (Pavia)
Tel. +39 0382 489052
Grana Padano Dop

Carlo Gelmini
Via Papa Giovanni XXIII, 15
Besate (Milan)
Tel. +39 02 9050314
Gorgonzola Dop

Leone Giani
Strada Statale dei Cairoli, 16
Carbonara Ticino (Pavia)
Tel. +39 0382 400655
Grana Padano Dop

Fioravante Gottardi
Via Garibaldi
Magasa (Brescia)
Tel. +39 0365 74166
Tombea

Latteria Agricola Cooperativa Livignese
Via Sant'Anton, 23
Livigno (Sondrio)
Tel. +39 0342 997578
Scimudin

Latteria Agricola di Marmirolo
Via Belbrolo, 32
Marmirolo (Mantova)
Tel. +39 0376 466258
Grana Padano Dop

Latteria Agricola San Pietro
Via Segrada, 36
Goito (Mantova)
Tel. +39 0376 607051
Grana Padano Dop

Latteria Cooperativa San Sebastiano
Strada Rodone, 13
Marmirolo (Mantova)
Tel. +39 0376 466017
Grana Padano Dop

Latteria Sociale Cooperativa di Chiuro
Via Nazionale, 45
Chiuro (Sondrio)
Tel. +39 0342 482113
Scimudin, Valtellina Casera Dop

Latteria Sociale del Mincio
Via Randaccio, 83
Frazione Casale
Roncoferraro (Mantova)
Tel. +39 0376 668138
Grana Padano Dop

Latteria Sociale di Bormio
Via De Simoni, 22
Bormio (Sondrio)
Tel. +39 0342 901437
Valtellina Casera Dop

Latteria Sociale di Mantova
Via Fratelli Kennedy, 48
Località Sant'Antonio
Porto Mantovano (Mantova)
Tel. +39 0376 390808
Grana Padano Dop

Latteria Sociale Pennello
Via Romana Conventino, 23
Bagnolo San Vito (Mantova)
Tel. +39 0376 414224
Grana Padano Dop

Latteria Sociale Valtellina
Strada Statale Stelvio, 139
Delebio (Sondrio)
Tel. +39 0342 685368
Magnocca, Scimudin,
Valtellina Casera Dop

Latteria Soresina
Via IV Novembre, 19-21
Soresina (Cremona)
Tel. +39 0374 341849
Grana Padano Dop

Latteria Vo Grande
Strada Vo, 46
Pegognaga (Mantova)
Tel. +39 0376 558091
Parmigiano Reggiano Dop

Le Frise
Località Rive dei Balti, 12
Artogne (Brescia)
Tel. +39 0364 598298 - +39 0364 598285
Crescenza

Guglielmo Locatelli
Via Reggetto, 84
Vedeseta (Bergamo)
Tel. +39 0345 47166
Strachitund, Taleggio Dop

Bernardino Mora
Località Loritto, 36
Malonno (Brescia)
Tel. +39 0364 65673
Formaggella di Monte

Giacomina Morgani
Via San Marco, 29
Saviore dell'Adamello (Brescia)
Tel. +39 0364 634416
Formaggella di Monte

Pasetti
Via Rismondo, 62
Pavia
Tel. +39 0382 530525
Grana Padano Dop

Fratelli Pedretti
Cascinello Valerio
Località Cascinazza
Robecco sul Naviglio (Milan)
Tel. +39 02 9470601 - +39 02 9470791
Taleggio Dop

Giacomo Romelli
Via Pedena, 1
Breno (Brescia)
Tel. +39 0364 21047
Silter

Alessandro Stefani
Via Cesare Battisti, 23
Valvestino (Brescia)
Tel. +39 0365 74202
Tombea

Silverio Stefani
Via Dosso, 2
Magasa (Brescia)
Tel. +39 0365 74136
Tombea

Tiziano Stefani
Via Rest, 1
Magasa (Brescia)
Tel. +39 0365 74235
Tombea

Tommaso Tognolina
Via Beccaria, 4
Sondrio
Tel. +39 0342 212385
Bitto Dop, Valtellina Casera Dop

Giulio Venturini
Località Cima Rest
Magasa (Brescia)
Tel. +39 0365 74054
Tombea

Giovanni Zeni
Via Roma, 1
Magasa (Brescia)
Tel. +39 0365 74073
Tombea

Zucchelli
Cascina Marmorina
Orio Litta (Lodi)
Tel. +39 0377 804232
Tipico Lodigiano

Trentino Alto Adige

Almkäse

Bergkäse

Caprino di Cavalese

Casolèt

Dolomiti

Graukäse

Hoamatkas

Lagundo or Bauernkäse

Malga Fane

Malga Stagionato
nelle Vinacce

Malga Stelvio

Mattone

Nostrano Fiavè

Nostrano Val di Fassa

Puzzone di Moena ●

Spressa delle Giudicarie DOP

Tosèla

Trentingrana

Vezzena ●

Vorderkas

Ziger or Zigerkäse

Almkäse

Most Almkäse, one of the region's oldest cheeses, is made in mountain dairies. Its name derives from *Alm*, the German word for Alpine pasture. Part-skimmed raw milk is heated to 32°C and inoculated with powdered rennet. After it has coagulated, the soft curd is cut up into granules the size of a pea or grain of sweetcorn. It is then semi-cooked at 38-40°C. If the cheese is made in the mountains, it is cooked over a wood fire. The curd is then removed, cut up into large lumps and transferred to moulds, where it is pressed for 24 hours. The following day, the pressed curd is taken out of the mould and immersed in a brine bath for 48 hours. Next, the rounds are matured in cool, damp rooms where they will remain for at least three months. During maturing, the cheeses are turned over, scraped and brushed every day.

Rennet: powder, calf's
Outer rind: smooth, firm, deep yellow tending to brown in colour
Body: firm, uneven, with variable, unevenly distributed eyes, ivory-white shading into deep straw-yellow in colour
Top and bottom: flat, 35-40 cm in diameter
Height/weight: 8-10 cm / 7-14 kg
Territory of origin: the mountain areas of Alto Adige, in particular Val Venosta

Bergkäse

A relatively new cheese first produced about 25 years ago, Bergkäse is faithful to the cheesemaking tradition of Val Pusteria. It is made only with local milk. Usually pasteurised whole or part-skimmed milk is inoculated with milk enzymes and heated to 32°C. It is inoculated with calf's rennet in powder. About 30 minutes later, the soft curd is cut into pea-sized lumps and then cooked at 40°C for about 50 minutes. The curd is then removed, placed on a table, cut and transferred into moulds. The following day, the rounds are immersed in brine, where they will remain for two days. After salting, the cheeses are stored in a warm environment for three weeks. They then go into a cooler, damper room, where they complete the maturing process in about ten weeks.

Rennet: powder, calf's
Outer rind: hard, firm, smooth, brownish in colour
Body: firm, solid, with irregularly distributed, often large, eyes, straw-yellow in colour
Top and bottom: flat, 40 cm in diameter
Height/weight: 10 cm / 10-12 kg
Territory of origin: Upper Val Pusteria

Caprino di Cavalese

Caprino was once made all over Val di Fiemme. Today, goat's milk produced in the valley is taken to the cheese dairy at Cavalese, which now is only maker of this traditional product. The milk is heated to 31°C and inoculated with rennet. The soft curd is then cut into small pieces and cooked at 44°C until the desired consistency is obtained. Next, the curd is transferred into moulds and dry-salted, the rounds being treated until they no longer absorb salt. After this, the cheeses go on to maturing, which was once carried out in the earth or stone-floored cellars of the mountain farms. Now maturing is done in cool, damp, purpose-built rooms. During the maturing process, the cheeses are turned over and moistened with a brine solution once a week.

Rennet: paste, calf's or lamb's
Outer rind: thin, tending to reddish-yellow with maturing
Body: firm, with sparse or plentiful eyes, ivory-white in colour
Top and bottom: flat, 15-25 cm in diameter
Height/weight: 8-10 cm / 3-4 kg
Territory of origin: the municipalities of Cavalese and Fiavé Pinzolo

Casolèt

Today, it is very difficult to find this soft, uncooked mountain dairy cheese, a traditional product of Valle di Rabbi and Val di Sole. In fact, *casoletti* was once a nickname for the residents of Celentino, an important cheesemaking centre. The name Casolèt has Latin roots and derives from *caseolus*, meaning a small cheese. Today, it continues to be made with whole raw milk from one or two milkings that is left over from making puzzone (see entry) or vezzena (see entry). The curd forms in about 15-20 minutes after the milk is inoculated with liquid calf's rennet, and is then cut up into walnut-sized lumps. As soon as the curd settles on the bottom of the vat, the whey is removed and the curd is transferred to moulds, where it is turned over several times in the same day. Twenty-four hours later, the cheeses are placed in a dilute brine bath for about six hours. Casolèt is generally eaten fresh, or semi-mature after ageing for 20-30 days. More mature versions, aged for three to four months, are unusual nowadays but offer greater sensory complexity.

Rennet: liquid, calf's
Outer rind: smooth, regular, white or pale yellow in colour
Body: uncooked, soft, with a few sparsely distributed eyes, white or straw-yellow in colour
Top and bottom: flat, 10-22 cm in diameter
Height/weight: 7-12 cm / 1-3 kg
Territory of origin: Val di Rabbi and Val di Sole in the province of Trento

COW'S MILK

Dolomiti

Dolomiti, which has been produced since the 1930s, is one of the few cheeses in the region to be matured only briefly. Whole cow's milk from one or two evening or morning milkings is heated to 60-65°C and then cooled to 40-42°C. It is inoculated with a milk-fermented starter culture, or calf's rennet, and coagulates in 10-15 minutes. The curd is stirred with a short-handled *spanarola* ladle, then cut into hazelnut-sized lumps with a *lira* or *spino* curd knife. Most of the whey is drained off and then the soft curd is transferred to plastic or aluminium moulds, which may be doused with hot water at 60-70°C. The cheeses are turned repeatedly and then placed in a dilute brine bath. They are turned again after three hours, and removed after four or five. After drying, the cheeses mature for about 15 days.

Rennet: liquid, calf's
Outer rind: thin, smooth or faintly furrowed
Body: soft, with sparse, small or medium-small eyes, white or pale straw-yellow in colour
Top and bottom: flat, 18-20 cm in diameter
Height/weight: 10-11 cm / 2.8-3 kg
Territory of origin: the entire province of Trento

Graukäse

This is a cheese with a long tradition in the Tyrol. It takes its name from the greyish (*grau*) colour of its body. Graukäse is obtained by acid coagulation only. Nothing is actually added to the milk. The cream is allowed to rise to the top and the milk is then part-skimmed before being heated to 25°C and left to coagulate naturally, a process that may take as long as 36 hours. The soft curd is then stirred slowly and the mixture is cooked briefly at 40°C. It is removed and pressed for about half an hour. It is then crumbled, seasoned with salt and pepper and placed in moulds, where it stands at a temperature of 20°C for 24 hours. Subsequently, the cheese is matured for a week in a cellar with very high humidity. In the mountain dairies of Monte Cavallo near Vipiteno/Sterzing, Graukäse is sometimes matured by hanging the cheese from the ceiling near the fire so that it undergoes light smoking.

Body: grainy, tender, uneven, yellow tending to grey in colour
Top and bottom: irregular, furrowed
Height/weight: varying from 1-1.5 kg
Territory of origin: the eastern part of Alto Adige, especially Valle Aurina

COW'S MILK

Hoamatkas

The name of this cheese derives from the local term for *heimatkäse* (home cheese). The preparation technique is similar in some respects to that of Malga Stelvio (see entry), the main differences being the maturing method and times. Whole morning milk is mixed at 32°C with milk from the evening milking that has been part-skimmed after the cream has been allowed to rise. It is inoculated with milk enzymes and coagulated with calf's rennet. The curd is milled into lumps the size of a grain of wheat. Forty-five minutes later, the soft curd is removed and transferred to steel containers, where it is pressed and cut into rectangles. These are placed in moulds one on top of another. The cheeses, separated by roundels, undergo further pressing in the moulds. They are then placed in a brine bath for 24 hours. After salting, the cheeses mature for four to six months, during which time they are periodically brushed with water and salt. Next, the cheeses spend about one and a half months in wooden barrels under a layer of hay. They are cleaned and dried, then covered again with clean hay before going on sale.

Rennet: liquid, calf's
Outer rind: thin, orange in colour
Body: elastic, firm, with no or very few sparsely distributed eyes, straw-yellow in colour
Top and bottom: flat, 25 cm in diameter
Height/weight: 6-7 cm / 4.5 kg
Territory of origin: Val Venosta

Lagundo or Bauernkäse

Part-skimmed milk is pasteurised, cooled to 32°C and then inoculated with a starter culture and powdered calf's rennet. When it has coagulated, which takes an average of 35 minutes, the curd is cut into cherry-sized lumps and then semi-cooked at 42°C for 20 minutes. It is left to stand for 15 minutes and then transferred to the moulds, where it will remain for eight hours. When it is taken out of the moulds, the firm curd goes into a brine bath for about two days. Subsequently, the cheeses are placed for eight weeks in a cool (13°C) room at 98% humidity, where they are turned over and washed every week.

Rennet: powder, calf's
Outer rind: hard, smooth, dark brown in colour
Body: springy, with close-packed, evenly distributed eyes, straw-white in colour
Top and bottom: flat, 35 cm in diameter
Height/weight: 10 cm / 7 kg
Territory of origin: the mountain dairies of Velloi, Rio Lagundo, Rablà, Parcines, Tablà and Monte Sole

Malga Fane

The cheesemaking tradition of Malga Fane dates back to the seventeenth century, if not earlier. Situated at 1,700 metres above sea level, this venerable mountain dairy has a grazing area that extends as high as 2,600 metres. The fragrances of the many Alpine flowers and herbs found on the pastures can be detected in the sensory profile of Malga Fane cheese. To make it, part-skimmed milk is ripened at 26°C for 45 minutes. The curd forms in 30 minutes at 32°C, after inoculation with liquid calf's rennet. It is then cut up with a *lira* curd knife into sweetcorn-sized granules. The soft curd is heated to 42°C and removed in a cloth for transfer to moulds, where it stays for 24 hours, during which time it is turned over five times. Malga Fane then goes into a brine bath for a day, before being dried and placed on wooden boards to mature for 6-12 months.

Rennet: liquid, calf's
Outer rind: thin, ochre in colour
Body: elastic, with pea or hazelnut-sized eyes, straw-yellow in colour
Top and bottom: flat, 20-25 cm in diameter
Height/weight: 6 cm / 3.5-4.5 kg
Territory of origin: Malga Fane, above Rio di Pusteria in the province of Bolzano

Malga Stagionato nelle Vinacce

Like similar products in other parts of Italy, this cheese was inspired by farmers' perennial need to treat the rind during maturing with something less expensive than oil. In Alto Adige, Lagrein wine and grape pomace are used. Lagrein is a native red variety with an ancient, noble heritage. It is mentioned, for example, in seventeenth-century documents held at the Benedictine monastery of Muri. The mountain dairy cheese is carefully cleaned and then immersed in a mixture of wine and grape pomace. Two or three days later, it is drained before it is left to mature for about eight months. During maturation, the cheeses are turned over and wiped with a wine-soaked cloth every three or four days.

Rennet: liquid, calf's
Outer rind: thin, dark almost black in colour
Body: firm, elastic, cream-yellow in colour
Top and bottom: wrinkled, containing fragments of pomace, 20-25 cm in diameter
Height/weight: 6 cm / 3.5-4.5 kg
Territory of origin: Alto Adige

Malga Stelvio

The *malga*, or mountain dairy, that produces this cheese is one of the oldest in Alto Adige. It originally belonged to the Benedictine Convent of St John at Müstair, today a UN-ESCO world heritage site, and is mentioned in documents dating from 1322. Whole morning milk is mixed with milk from the previous evening's milking, part-skimmed by allowing the cream to rise to the top. It is heated to 32°C in copper vats and inoculated with milk enzymes. The curd is obtained at 39°C with liquid calf's rennet, and then broken up into lumps the size of a grain of wheat. The curd is removed 45 minutes later and transferred to steel tubs, where it is pressed with weights to expel the whey. It is then cut up into rectangles. The cheeses are arranged in hoops one on top of the other, separated by a roundel. They are pressed again. Finally, the cheeses spend 24 hours in a brine bath before maturing for 4-12 months.

Rennet: liquid, calf's
Outer rind: thin, slightly irregular, red tending to brown in colour
Body: elastic, fondant, with pinhead eyes, yellow in colour
Top and bottom: flat, 25 cm in diameter
Height/weight: 6-7 cm / 4.5 kg
Territory of origin: Stelvio

Mattone

Known locally by its German name Ziegel, Mattone is produced 1,600 metres above sea level at the Hochgruberhof
farm. The raw milk used comes exclusively from Pinzgauer
cows. Farmed in Austria and Bavaria as well as in this area, Pinz-
gauers are hardy, adaptable animals that cope very well with
harsh mountain conditions. Whole morning milk is mixed with
the previous evening's milking that has been part-skimmed after
allowing the cream to rise to the top. Milk enzymes are inoculated at 20°C and the mixture is allowed to stand for half an
hour. It is then coagulated at 32°C with liquid calf's rennet, and
the curd is cut up into hazelnut-sized lumps before being
cooked at 39°C. The soft curd is then transferred into moulds.
When it has acquired the desired consistency, the cheese is placed in
a brine bath for 12 hours. It is matured at a temperature of 9-12°C
for eight weeks. During maturing, the rind is periodically
washed with water and salt, first with a cloth and then with a brush.

Rennet: liquid, calf's
Outer rind: thin, brick-red in colour
Body: elastic, with pinhead or barleycorn-sized eyes, straw-yellow in colour
Top and bottom: slightly concave
Height/weight: 5 cm / 0.8-1 kg
Territory of origin: Selva dei Molini in the province of Bolzano

Nostrano Fiavè

This Nostrano (local) belongs to the *de casèl* family, Trentino's most traditional group of cheeses, but Fiavé's flavour and eyes are distinctly reminiscent of Asiago. The cheese is made by heating part-skimmed milk to 32-35°C and inoculating it with powdered rennet. Thirty minutes later, the curd is cut in two stages into sweetcorn-sized lumps. After cutting, it is cooked briefly at 44-46°C. Next, the curd is gathered up in cloths and transferred to moulds, where it stands for six to eight hours, during which time the rounds are turned over. The next stage is salting in a brine bath for three to five days, or dry-salting for eight days. The cheeses are then transferred to a very damp room (90% humidity) where they mature at 12-16°C for about four months. During maturation, the rounds are regularly turned over and washed with brine, or in some cases with whey.

Rennet: powder, calf's
Outer rind: firm, thin, deep yellow or brownish in colour
Body: elastic, with abundant large and small eyes, pale to deep straw-white in colour.
Top and bottom: flat, with a slightly raised edge, 30-35 cm in diameter
Height/weight: 10-11 cm / 7-9 kg
Territory of origin: the area around the Massiccio del Lagorai

Nostrano Val di Fassa

The best Nostrano cheeses are made in mountain dairies during the summer months, using a cheesemaking technique similar to that employed for puzzone. Part-skimmed raw milk is heated to 36°C and inoculated with powdered rennet. After coagulation, which may take 25-30 minutes, the curd is cut into sweetcorn-sized granules and then semi-cooked at a temperature of 43-45°C for 20 minutes. After transfer into moulds, the curd is left to stand and then pressed and salted in a brine bath. Next comes maturing, the most crucial stage in cheesemaking and the procedure that will determine the product's final taste profile. For this, the rounds are placed in a very damp room, where they will be washed with a tepid salt solution several times a week. Nostrano Val di Fassa takes 40 days to mature but ageing is usually extended for as long as five or six months. The resulting product is an ideal complement for the polenta-based dishes of the Trentino kitchen.

Rennet: powder, calf's
Outer rind: smooth, damp, with an oily sheen, brick-red in colour
Body: firm, elastic, with a few eyes, white or straw-white in colour
Top and bottom: flat, 35 cm in diameter
Height/weight: 8-10 cm / 9-10 kg
Territory of origin: Val di Fassa and Conca del Primiero

Puzzone di Moena

Puzzone di Moena is the only washed-rind cheese in this region, although other examples such as fontina (see entry) and taleggio (see entry) can be found elsewhere in Italy. There is no documentary evidence, but it is said that Puzzone di Moena has been made in exactly the same way in Val di Fassa since very ancient times. The name, however, dates back only to the 1970s. Previously, valley residents simply called it *nostrano* (local) in Italian or *spretz tzaorì* (tangy cheese) in the local Ladin language. Raw milk arrives at the cheese dairy twice a day from the mountain dairies of Predazzo in the heart of the Dolomites. Some of these small dairies are located inside the Regional Park of Paneveggio-Pale di San Martino. The milk is heated in copper cauldrons to 34°C and inoculated with a milk-based starter culture made on the farm. Pre-packaged enzymes are not permitted. Coagulation is obtained with calf's rennet and then the curd is cut into sweetcorn-sized granules and cooked at 47°C. When the curd settles on the bottom of the cauldron, it is stirred with a wooden ladle and removed in a cloth. The mass is then cut into pieces and placed in wooden hoops, where it is lightly pressed by hand and left to drain. The cheeses are then pressed again, and finally placed in a brine bath for four days. Maturing lasts for a minimum of 60 days, but may go on for six or seven months, during which time the cheeses are washed.

This is a very labour-intensive task. Each cheese has to be individually turned and washed with a cloth moistened in water. The treatment leaves an oily surface that encourages the formation of the bacteria that give the cheese its intense, penetrating aroma – *puzzone* means "stinky" – and distinctive brick-red crust. When the cheese is sliced, it releases pungent notes of fermentation and damp cellar, deriving from the treatment of the rind, but these give way to meadow aromas of Alpine grass and ripe fruit. Puzzone di Moena is satisfying on the palate and tends to melt in the mouth, suggesting roasted hazelnuts and offering impressive length. The M mark, which stands for *malga* (mountain dairy), tells you the cheese is Puzzone from the Slow Food Presidium. Only cheeses bearing this mark are made with mountain dairy milk, drawn in summer from Alpine pasture-grazed cows. Only first-quality fodder supplements may be used. Silage, industrial by-products and GM fodder are all prohibited by the Presidium.

Rennet: powder, calf's
Outer rind: thin, soft, moist, with an oily sheen, reddish-brown in colour
Body: soft, with a few, evenly distributed eyes, straw-white in colour
Top and bottom: flat, 36 cm in diameter
Height/weight: 10 cm / 9 kg
Territory of origin: the municipalities of Predazzo and Moena in the province of Trento

During maturing, the cheeses are washed once a week with a damp cloth. This encourages the bacterial fermentation that gives Puzzone di Moena its intense aroma – puzzone means "stinky" – and brick-red outer rind.

Spressa delle Giudicarie DOP

Spressa is one of the most ancient Alpine cheeses. The first historical reference to the product is in the 1249 Regola di Spinale and Manez, but the cheese obtained DOP status relatively recently, in December 2003. Its name derives from *Spress*, a local word that indicates pressed curd. Once, this was a very low-fat cheese, as the milk was skimmed several times. Dairy farmers earned much more from butter than from cheese, most of which they made for domestic consumption. Today, Spressa delle Giudicarie DOP contains more fat than it once did, although it is still lower in fat than most other cheeses. Most of the cheese is made at the Pinzolo Fiavè Val di Ledro e Chiese co-operative dairy. Only a small quantity comes from local farmers. Raw milk from the morning and evening milkings is used. It is drawn from Bruno Alpina, Grigio Alpina, Frisian, Red Simmental and the native Rendena cows. After part-skimming by allowing the cream to rise to the top, the milk is heated in a cauldron and inoculated with calf's rennet. Coagulation takes from 20 to 50 minutes at a temperature of 35°C. The curd is broken up into granules the size of a grain of rice. The soft curd is then stirred constantly as it is semi-cooked at a temperature of 42°C. It is allowed to stand in the whey for no more than 65 minutes, and is then removed and placed in special branding hoops. Twenty-four hours later, the cheeses are salted dry or in a brine bath for 8-12 days. Maturing then begins. It will last for three months, in the case of the fresh cheese, or six for the mature version. Ageing is carried out in special rooms at a temperature of 10-20°C and 80-90% humidity. Spressa delle Giudicarie DOP may be enjoyed at table but is also used in the recipes for several Trentino dishes, including the classic *polenta carbonera*.

Rennet: powder, calf's
Outer rind: smooth, thin, brown tending to dark brown in colour as maturing progresses
Body: compact, elastic, with sparse, medium-sized eyes, straw-yellow in colour
Top and bottom: flat, 35 cm in diameter
Height/weight: 8-9 cm / 6-8 kg
Territory of origin: the Giudicarie, Chiese, Rendena and Lero valleys
DOP status awarded on 22 December 2003, regulation no. 2275

Once, this was a very low-fat cheese, as the milk was skimmed several times. Today, Spressa delle Giudicarie DOP still has a low fat content, but not as low as in the past.

Tosèla

Tosèla derives from the verb *tosare* (to shear), used to describe the operation of levelling off the curd before it goes into the mould. The cheese is made by heating fresh-drawn milk to 37-39°C and inoculating it with powdered rennet. Coagulation takes 15-20 minutes. The next stage is to cut the curd into large slices, which are then dried. The slices are left to stand for five to ten minutes and then placed in moulds. No set shape is used for this cheese but the moulds are usually rectangular. Tosèla is neither salted or matured, and should be eaten as fresh as possible. Traditionally, the cheese is sliced and fried in butter with a little salt sprinkled on top.

Rennet: powder, calf's
Body: soft, elastic, very moist, milk-white in colour
Top and bottom: variable but generally flat
Height/weight: variable
Territory of origin: Valle di Primiero, Lower Val Sugana, Val di Tesino, the Asiago plateau and Massiccio del Lagorai

Trentingrana

Grana produced in Trento valley is disciplined by the Grana Cheese Protection Consortium but may carry the Trentino mark on the rind, in compliance with the DPR regulation dated 26 January 1987. The mark guarantees that the round was made in Trentino, but the production method is the same as that used for parmigiano reggiano (see entry). The cream of the evening milking is allowed to rise and is skimmed off the following morning. The morning milk is added and the mixture is heated to 31-33°C. After inoculation with a whey-based starter culture and powdered calf's rennet, the milk coagulates and the soft curd is cut into rice-sized granules before being cooked at 53-55°C. When the curd has become elastic and reached the desired level of acidity, it is divided in two and transferred into moulds. These are then placed in brine baths. This process generally takes 26-28 days, after which the Trentingrana cheeses are ready for their twelve-month stay in the maturing rooms at a temperature of 18-20°C and 85% humidity.

Rennet: powder, calf's
Outer rind: hard, even-textured, smooth, lustrous, brownish yellow in colour
Body: crumbly, grainy, becoming rock hard with maturing, with very faint eyes, straw-yellow in colour
Top and bottom: flat, 35-40 cm in diameter
Height/weight: 8-25 cm / 35-40 kg
Territory of origin: the entire province of Trento

Vezzena

Vezzena is emblematic of the Trentino cheesemaking heritage. It is said that the Austro-Hungarian Emperor Franz Joseph demanded that it should be on his table every day. The cheese-making procedure is the standard one for semi-fat Alpine cheeses, but Vezzena is unique, thanks to leisurely maturing and the Alpine flora on which the cows graze. The co-operative diary at Lavarone is where the best milk from member farmers is selected to be used for the milk-based starter culture. Raw, part-skimmed cow's milk from the evening milking is mixed with milk drawn the following morning. It is slowly heated, inoculated with the starter culture and then with calf's rennet after reaching a temperature of 33-35°C. Coagulation takes 20-25 minutes. The curd, which has sometimes already been stirred with a spoon-shaped *spanarola*, then cut with a *lira* curd knife into sweetcorn-sized granules. After cooking slowly at 45-48°C, the curd is allowed to settle to the bottom of the vat. Part of the whey is drained off and the curd is cut into single cheese-sized portions. These are transferred to wooden hoops and pressed. The weights are re-moved in the evening and the cheeses moved to a warm, damp room known as the *frescura*. The cheeses are then salted dry or in brine. Maturing on wooden boards is the next stage. Once a month, the cheeses are cleaned and brushed with linseed oil. Even when very mature, Vezzena has exceptional appeal and butteriness, releasing distinctive aromas that vary with the changing seasons. For example, Vezzena made with June milk has a subtle note of garlic. After 12-18 months, the eyes disappear and the very yellow body becomes flaky. The aromas acquire complexity and the palate offers a wealth of grassy and spicy notes. The Slow Food Presidium was set up for Vezzena made during the summer months with mountain dairy milk. Presidium cheeses are marked with an M – for *malga* (mountain dairy) – on the rind. Presidium members must comply with strict regulations. Their animals must be grazed and the pasture may only be supplemented with first-quality materials. Silage, industrial by-products and GM fodder are all prohibited by the Presidium regulations.

Rennet: powder, calf's
Outer rind: thin, elastic, straw-yellow in colour tending to brownish
Body: compact, even-textured becoming grainy and suitable for grating with maturing, straw-yellow in colour
Top and bottom: flat, 35-40 cm in diameter
Height/weight: 8-10 cm / 8-12 kg
Territory of origin: the municipalities on the plateau of Lavarone, Vezzena and Folgaria in the province of Trento

The curd is portioned and placed in wooden hoops, where it is pressed. The weights are removed in the evening and the cheeses are moved to a warm, damp room known as the frescura.

Vorderkas

This small, traditional product takes its name from the farm where it is made, some 1,700 metres above sea level in Val Senales, inside the Gruppo di Tessa Park. Whole milk from an evening milking is mixed with milk drawn the following morning and inoculated with milk enzymes at a temperature of 20°C. The curd, obtained by coagulating the milk with calf's rennet at 32°C for half an hour, is cut twice, first into two-centimetre cubes and then into sweetcorn-sized granules. It is stirred continuously and cooked for 45 minutes at 42°C. The soft curd is removed and placed in hoops for 36 hours, during which time it is turned over several times. Next, the cheeses go into a brine bath for 48 hours. Finally, they are matured on wooden boards for about six months. During maturing, the rind is brushed occasionally with salt and water to encourage the formation of mould.

Rennet: liquid, calf's
Outer rind: thin, grey in colour with white patches of mould, occasionally speckled with pink
Body: soft, oily, with tiny, irregular eyes, cream-white tending to pale yellow in colour
Top and bottom: flat, 17 cm in diameter
Height/weight: 10 cm / 3 kg
Territory of origin: Val Senales

Ziger or Zigerkäse

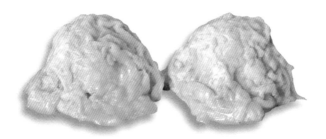

T he name of this cheese may derive from *tsigros*, a Celtic word for cheese, or more probably from the German *Ziege*, meaning "goat". Whatever the case, Ziger is a very ancient cheese that was once made over a vast area of the Alps. Today, very little is produced. The milk is part-skimmed by allowing the fat to rise to the surface. It is then heated to 30°C and inoculated with buttermilk. Acid coagulation is complete after about 48 hours. Some cheesemakers break up the curd into walnut-sized lumps while others pour it directly into cloth bags to drain. The following day, the curd is poured out onto a table and kneaded with chives, salt and pepper. After it has been modelled by hand into a pear shape, Ziger is ready for the table. It may also be matured for six to eight weeks. After maturing, the outer surface is gelatinous and the body is soft and ricotta-like.

Rennet: buttermilk, a by-product of buttermaking
Body: soft, dirty white or yellowish shading into grey in colour
Top and bottom: variable
Height/weight: varying from 0.3-1 kg
Territory of origin: from Val Pusteria and Lower Val d'Isarco to the Belluno Dolomites

The producers

Caseificio Sociale Comprensoriale di Primiero
Via Roma, 179
Mezzano (Trento)
Tel. +39 0439 62941
Dolomiti, Tosèla, Trentingrana

Caseificio Sociale di Lavarone
Via Marconi, 5
Lavarone (Trento)
Tel. +39 0464 783106
Vezzena

Caseificio Sociale di Predazzo e Moena
Via Fiamme Gialle, 34
Predazzo (Trento)
Tel. +39 0462 501287
Puzzone di Moena

Ferruccio Cetto
Via Monte Panarotta, 40
Levico Terme (Trento)
Tel. +39 0461 707126
Vezzena

De Gust
Via Isarco, 1
Varna-Vahrn (Bolzano)
Tel. +39 0472 849873
Hoamatkas, Malga Stagionato nelle Vinacce

Richard Kofler
Val di Fosse, 6
Senales-Schnals (Bolzano)
Tel. +39 0473 679230
Vorderkas

Latteria di Sesto
Via del Bersaglio, 6
Sesto-Sexten (Bolzano)
Tel. +39 0474 710251
Graukäse, Ziger

Latteria Dobbiaco San Candido
Via San Giovanni, 25
Dobbiaco-Toblach (Bolzano)
Tel. +39 0474 972045
Graukäse

Latteria Sociale di Lagundo
Via Plars di Mezzo, 29
Lagundo-Algund (Bolzano)
Tel. +39 0473 448710
Graukäse

Josef Lobis
Maso Ersbaumerhof
Via Gaster, 2
Località Auna di Sotto
Renon-Ritten (Bolzano)
Tel. +39 0471 359117
Graukäse, Ziger

Ferdinand Oberhollenzer
Maso Hochgruberhof
Via Gorner, 100
Selva dei Molini-Mühlwald (Bolzano)
Tel. +39 0474 653325
Mattone

Sergio Panizza
Località Volpaia, 3
Vermiglio (Trento)
Tel. +39 0463 758393
Casolèt

Nilo Pelanda
Via Chiesa
Brione (Trento)
Tel. +39 0465 621277
Spressa delle Giudicarie Dop

Anna Piazzola
Via San Bernardo, 38
Rabbi (Trento)
Tel. +39 0463 985109
Casolèt

Ennio Prandini
Via Lucchi, 10
Roncone (Trento)
Tel. +39 0465 901406
Spressa delle Giudicarie Dop

Ruatti
Frazione Pracorno, 95
Rabbi (Trento)
Tel. +39 0463 901070
Casolèt, Tosèla

Veneto

Asiago d'Allevo DOP

Asiago Pressato DOP

Cansiglio

Carnia

Casalina

Casatella Trevigiana

Comelico

Fodom

Formaggio Agordino
di Malga ●

Formaio Embriago
or Ubriaco

Monte Veronese DOP

Monte Veronese
di Malga DOP ●

Morlacco del Grappa ●

Nostrano di Malga

Pecorino Veneto

Piave

Renaz

Ricotta Affumicata

Schiz

Stravecchio di Malga
dell'Altopiano
dei Sette Comuni ●

Asiago d'Allevo DOP

A cheese that originates from the Asiago plateau it is named after, Altopiano d'Asiago is made in the mountain pastures or larger dairies where it is matured – one might say *allevato* (literally, "raised") – with particular care. Raw milk from Pezzata Nera and Bruno Alpina cows is allowed to stand for 6-12 hours and the cream that rises is skimmed off. Milk from two milkings, only the first of which should be skimmed, can also be used. Coagulation takes place at 35°C in 25-30 minutes. The soft curd is then milled finely and cooked twice, first at 40°C and then at 47°C. After being transferred into moulds, the curd is pressed first in special wooden hoops and then in plastic hoops to stamp the DOP mark on the rind. Next, the rounds are salted either dry or in brine baths before maturing, which takes place on shelving in a temperature-controlled environment. Depending on the maturing period, Asiago may be called *mezzano* (at least three months old) or *vecchio* (nine months old or more). The outer rind is thin and springy, shading into brown in colour as maturing progresses. The body is semi-hard, even-textured and straw-white, with occasional small or medium-sized eyes for the Mezzano version. In the Vecchio or Stravecchio versions, which may also be used for grating, the body becomes hard and grainy. At first, the palate is mild but it gradually becomes fuller and more fragrant as the months pass. Asiago d'Allevo Vecchio and Stravecchio made in the province of

Trento, and especially on the plateaux of Vezzena, Lavarone and Folgaria, is also known as Vezzena. During the Middle Ages, there were many flocks producing exclusively ewe's milk cheese and today, the dialect term used by older mountain-dwellers to indicate Asiago is still *pegorin*, or "sheep's cheese".

Rennet: liquid or powder, calf's
Outer rind: thin, springy, shading into brown with maturing
Body: semi-hard, even-textured, with occasional small or medium-sized eyes for the Mezzano version, hard and grainy for the Vecchio and Stravecchio cheeses, straw-white in colour
Top and bottom: flat or almost flat, 30-36 cm in diameter
Height/weight: 9-12 cm / 8-12 kg
Territory of origin: the provinces of Vicenza and Trento, the hill country and low-lying area beneath to the west of the river Piave in the province of Treviso, and some municipalities in the province of Padua
DOP status awarded on 12 June 1996, regulation no. 1107

Asiago d'Allevo is suitable for prolonged ageing. In this case, the body becomes rock hard, as can be seen from the photograph, and the tangy palate is correspondingly fierce.

Asiago Pressato DOP

In contrast with Asiago d'Allevo, Asiago Pressato is made in low-lying areas, and generally in fairly large dairies. The milk employed is also different, for it is pasteurised, and the salting techniques involves dry-salting the curd as soon as it comes out of the whey, and then a brine bath after pressing. Coagulation takes place at 36°C after inoculation with starter cultures and liquid rennet. The soft curd is broken up and then cooked at 46-48°C, drained and pressed on perforated plates before being cut into pieces and transferred to the moulds where it will be pressed. Asiago Pressato has a mild, delicately milky, flavour. Like Asiago d'Allevo, the Pressato version enjoys DOP status.

Rennet: liquid, calf's
Outer rind: thin, springy
Body: with deep, irregularly distributed eyes, white or faint straw-white in colour
Top and bottom: flat or almost flat, 30-36 cm in diameter
Height/weight: 11-15 cm / 11-15 kg
Territory of origin: the provinces of Vicenza and Trento, the hill country and low-lying area beneath to the west of the river Piave in the province of Treviso, and some municipalities in the province of Padua
DOP status awarded on 12 June 1996, regulation no. 1107

Cansiglio

Produced all year round on the Cansiglio plateau, this venerable cheese type comes from pastures more than 1,000 metres above sea level. It is made with raw milk from Bruno
Alpina cows nourished with fresh grass or hay dried in the
mountains. The milk is heated to 38-40°C and coagulates in
about ten minutes. The soft curd is broken up into rice-sized
granules and cooked again at 45°C for a further ten minutes.
Next, it is transferred into moulds, where it is pressed for a few
hours and then salted in a brine bath. The cheese will be ready
for table after spending a month in a cool (about 10°C), very
damp room. The rounds are turned over periodically and, if
necessary, scraped clean. If maturing goes on for more than six
months, the cheeses are treated with linseed oil. Initially mild,
Cansiglio's flavour acquires fullness and intensity with ageing.

Rennet: liquid, calf's
Outer rind: thin, soft, light-coloured
Body: even-textured, with small, sparse eyes, straw-white in colour
Top and bottom: flat, 30-35 cm in diameter
Height/weight: 7 cm / 6-7 kg
Territory of origin: the Cansiglio plateau in the province of Belluno

Carnia

Carnia cheese has been made at Padola for as long as anyone can remember. Today, part-pasteurised milk is used so a milk-based starter-culture is inoculated to encourage coagulation. The milk comes from Bruno Alpina cows. The soft curd is ready about half an hour later and is cut into rice-sized granules. It is semi-cooked at 42-43°C for about ten minutes and then drained before being transferred to moulds for 48 hours. Next, it is salted in a brine bath. The rounds mature at about 12°C in a room kept at 60% humidity. Every week, they are turned over, and once a fortnight they are scraped. Carnia is mild and delicate on the palate when young, acquiring tangier notes when well matured.

Rennet: powder, calf's
Outer rind: robust, yellowish in colour
Body: round, with close-packed eyes, straw-yellow in colour
Top and bottom: flat, 30 cm in diameter
Height/weight: 8 cm / 6-6.5 kg
Territory of origin: Padola in the municipality of Comelico Superiore, in the province of Belluno

Casalina

Casalina is a characteristic cheese from the Marca Trevigiana area. In the past, it was one way of making use of milk that had soured. Today Casalina, sometimes known as Casalino, is made using pasteurised milk inoculated with a milk-based starter culture and liquid rennet. Coagulation takes only a few minutes and the soft curd is then broken up into hazelnut-sized lumps. After the whey has been drained off, the firm curd is semi-cooked at 45°C and transferred into hoops. The rounds are then dry-salted. Two days later, the Casalina is ready for consumption. It may also be matured for a few months in damp rooms at a low temperature. Since it is a relatively fresh cheese, it has no outer rind. The body is white, firm and fairly soft, becoming crumbly with maturing. On the palate, there is a dominant sourish note.

Rennet: liquid, calf's
Body: compact, soft, becoming crumbly with maturing, white in colour
Top and bottom: flat, 15 cm in diameter
Height/weight: 6 cm / 1 kg
Territory of origin: the province of Treviso

Casatella Trevigiana

The name of this cheese derives from the Latin *caseus*, or "cheese", although some prefer to think of it as coming from the Italian word *casa* (house) because it was once the cheese that was made at home. Whole milk, usually pasteurised, is coagulated at about 4°°C for 15-20 minutes. The curd is cut into large granules and then transferred into moulds for about a day. The hoops are removed and the Casatella is salted in brine. On the second day, it is ready for the table but leaving it to mature for seven days will enhance its fragrance. Casatella has no outer rind. It has a creamy, buttery texture and a milk-white body whose mild flavour reveals a characteristic note of acidity that distinguishes it from other similar products.

Rennet: liquid, calf's
Body: creamy, with a buttery consistency, milk-white in colour
Top and bottom: flat or slightly convex, 8-22 cm in diameter
Height/weight: 4-6 cm / 0.4-2.2 kg
Territory of origin: the province of Treviso and a few municipalities around Pordenone and on the Friulian plain

Comelico

Whole raw milk from Bruno Alpina cows is coagulated for about half an hour at 35-36°C. The soft curd is cut in two stages. The first reduces the pieces to half the size of a walnut, and the second to that of a grain of rice. The curd is then cooked at 45°C for ten minutes. It is pressed for five or six minutes and put into hoops in a cool place for one day. Salting is also carried out in two stages. The rounds go into a brine bath for two days and are then dry-salted on top and bottom for 12 hours each. After 60 days, during which time the cheeses are scraped and turned over every other day, the cheese is ready for consumption. Comelico has a fairly mild flavour.

Rennet: liquid, calf's
Outer rind: soft, light brown in colour
Body: medium-sized, evenly distributed eyes, pale straw-yellow in colour
Top and bottom: flat, 30 cm in diameter
Height/weight: 8 cm / 5 kg
Territory of origin: the municipality of Santo Stefano in Cadore, in the province of Belluno

Fodom

A new type of cheese created in the mid 1980s, Fodom is named after the place where it is produced. Part-skimmed milk from Bruno Alpina cows is coagulated at 36-37°C for 30 minutes. When the curd has formed, it is cut into granules the size of a grain of sweetcorn and then cooked at 45-46°C for 30 minutes. The whey is drained off and the curd transferred to hoops, where it is pressed mechanically. Pressing is carried out in two stages, first for ten minutes and then for one hour. The cheeses are then salted in a brine bath for two days. The Fodom will be ready for the table after maturing for two months, during which time the rounds are turned over every other day and scraped once a month. It has a fairly mild flavour.

Rennet: liquid, calf's
Outer rind: hard, dry, yellow in colour
Body: close packed medium to large eyes, pale straw-yellow shading into brown with maturing
Top and bottom: flat, 30 cm in diameter
Height/weight: 8-10 cm / 5 kg
Territory of origin: the municipality of Livinallongo in the province of Belluno

Formaggio Agordino di Malga

Cheesemakers in the valleys around Agordo have always called their cheese simply *formai* (cheese) or *casél* (local). In January 1872, Fr Antonio Della Lucia founded Italy's first co-operative dairy at Canale d'Agordo. The new initiative was copied all over the province of Belluno, in Trentino and in other Alpine areas. The co-operative system enabled farmers to rationalise production, improve quality and market their cheese and butter more easily. Today, the overriding priority is to protect mountain dairy products, which achieve superb levels of quality thanks to the outstanding pastures on which the animals graze. The Slow Food Presidium was set up to do this. The mountain dairies are located at various altitudes, and are easy to reach. The farmers take their Bruno Alpina and Red Simmenthal cows up to the high-altitude pastures in the early summer. The odd donkey or goat always accompanies them to clear the area of the toughest plants, and the herds return in September, when the summer grazing period is over. Milk from the evening milking is part-skimmed by allowing the cream to rise to the top and mixed with whole milk from the following morning's milking. The mixture is poured into tin-plated copper vats and heated to 33-36°C over a wood fire. The milk is then inoculated with rennet and stirred. The curd is removed from the heat and allowed to stand for 25-40 minutes. The soft curd is broken up twice with a *lira*

curd knife. The first time it is cut up roughly and, 10-15 minutes later, it is milled to barleycorn-sized granules. The curd is constantly stirred while being heated to 38-43°C, and is then allowed to settle to the bottom of the vat before it is removed with cotton or linen cloths. The soft curd is transferred to metal moulds and pressed for 20 minutes. It then spends 48 hours in a brine bath before maturing for two to eight months. Formaggio Agordino di Malga is not sold through normal commercial channels. Most of the cheese produced is sold directly at the mountain dairies, partly because they are easy to reach and partly because the habit of purchasing cheese directly from the cheesemaker continues to thrive in the Veneto, unlike other regions.

Rennet: powder, lamb's and/or kid's
Outer rind: with characteristic mould, straw-yellow tending to dark yellow in colour
Body: compact, with small, irregular, fairly close-packed eyes, varying from white to yellow in colour
Top and bottom: flat, 25-35 cm in diameter
Height/weight: 5-8 cm / 3-4 kg
Territory of origin: the Agordo area in the province of Belluno

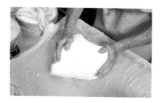

Most Formaggio Agordino di Malga is sold at mountain dairies. The habit of purchasing cheese directly from the cheesemaker continues to thrive in the Veneto, in contrast with other regions.

Formaio Embriago or Ubriaco

This cheese has an ancient tradition, dating back to times when oil to treat the outer rind was scarce and expensive, forcing the cheesemaker to fall back on grape pomace and must. Obviously, the cheese was made in the months that followed the vintage, from the end of September to early November. Curd is obtained by heating the milk at 33-35°C for about half an hour. It is then broken up into granules the size of a grain of rice and cooked for 15 minutes at 45-48°C. After the whey has been drained off, the curd is transferred to hoops. Next, it is salted, either in brine or using a mixed technique of dry-salting and brine baths. Twenty days later, the rounds are placed under fresh pomace from black grapes. The varieties used are Raboso, Cabernet and Merlot. They will stay there for about two days, and are continually sprinkled with wine from the press. After this, the cheese is ready for the table but it may also be matured for one or two months. Rounds of Montasio, Asiago d'Allevo or Latteria may also be "inebriated" in this way.

Rennet: powder, calf's
Outer rind: fairly thick, purplish or wine-red in colour
Body: firm, redolent of milk and wine, white to straw-yellow in colour
Top and bottom: flat, 25-28 cm in diameter
Height/weight: 8 cm / about 5 kg
Territory of origin: the left and right banks of the river Piave in the province of Treviso

Monte Veronese DOP

Whole or full-fat milk Monte Veronese is a relatively recent cheese type which, like Monte Veronese d'Allevo, enjoys DOP status. Milk from Pezzata Nera herds is coagulated unpasteurised at 33-34°C. The curd forms in about 20 minutes and is then cut into lumps the size of half a walnut. The soft curd is cooked for 10-15 minutes at 43-46°C. Next, it is transferred to moulds and either dry-salted or immersed in a brine bath. The cheese matures in 30 days, during which time it is turned over regularly. Monte Veronese has a deliciously mild flavour.

Rennet: powder, calf's
Outer rind: thin, elastic, pale to deep straw-white in colour
Body: with small, evenly distributed eyes, ivory-white or faint straw-white in colour if made in summer
Top and bottom: flat or slightly convex, 25-35 cm in diameter
Height/weight: 7-11 cm / 7-10 kg
Territory of origin: the Monti Lessini range in the province of Verona
DOP status awarded on 1 July 1996, regulation no. 1263

COW'S MILK

Monte Veronese di Malga DOP

Monte Veronese di Malga DOP is made with part-skimmed milk. The cheese is cylindrical with an almost flat side and slightly convex top and bottom. Cheeses weigh from six to nine kilograms on average. Ripening lasts for a minimum of 90 days, if the cheese is to be consumed at table, and for a minimum of six months – although it may go on as long as two years in the Stravecchio version – if the product is for grating. An excellent way to round off a meal, Monte Veronese di Malga DOP is a cheese to nibble in small quantities with one of the red wines of the Breganze DOC, or a Valpolicella. If it is very mature and tangy, Recioto di Soave or Amarone are fine partners. The mountains of the Verona area are ideal grazing country. The Monti Lessini are south-facing, their slopes are not steep and the grass grows abundantly for a long period. It is hardly surprising that the tradition of making cheese from cow's milk is firmly established in the area. Monte Veronese d'Allevo is the classic product, but until today, the version made with mountain dairy milk has not attracted particular attention. In past centuries, there were more than 100 mountain dairies in the Monti Lessini, some built by the Cimbrians in ancient times. Today, about 30 survive. Many have been converted into holiday homes, or byres for mountain-grazed beef cattle. The milk produced by mountain-grazed cows is taken to dairies down in

VENETO

229

the valley, where it is often mixed with milk from barn-reared animals. Only two mountain dairies are still working and making their cheese exclusively with milk from pastures in the Monte Lessini. If this production is not supported, not only will a high-quality cheese be lost, but it will also mean that the Monti Lessini mountain dairies will slowly be abandoned, jeopardising the survival of the mountain ecosystem. The Slow Food Presidium was set up with the help of the Monte Veronese Protection Consortium to act as an umbrella organisation for the mountain dairies willing to produce Monte Veronese d'Allevo with mountain dairy milk. Their cheeses are branded with a distinctive M for *malga* (mountain dairy) on the side, next to the DOP mark.

Rennet: powder or liquid, calf's
Outer rind: hard, dry, fairly dark
Body: compact, with few eyes, slightly more than in the whole-milk version, white if made during the winter, straw-yellow in the summer version
Top and bottom: flat or slightly convex, 25-35 cm in diameter
Height/weight: 6-10 cm / 6-9 kg
Territory of origin: Monti Lessini and Monte Baldo in the province of Verona
DOP status awarded on 1 July 1996, regulation no. 1263

The photograph illustrates three stages of maturing. The colour of the outer rind ranges from greenish straw-yellow to gold and pale brown.

COW'S MILK

Morlacco del Grappa

Known in former times as *murlak*, *murlaco* or *burlacco*, Morlacco was a soft, uncooked, low-fat cheese made from cow's milk. It originates from the tableland of the river Grappa, where farmers and woodsmen from Morlacchia in the Balkans settled during the heyday of the Venetian Republic. The milk used to be skimmed completely, and the fat used to make butter. Burlina cows supplied the raw material, but today the breed is seriously endangered. The cows are small, with a black and white coat. Their hardy constitution made them ideal for the poor grazing of the Grappa pastures, but their yield of milk is limited, and much inferior to that of today's Frisian or Bruno Alpina cows. Today, there are about 270 Burlina cows left, almost all in the province of Treviso. Morlacco is still made today on mountains pastures, using milk from the evening milking, skimmed by allowing the cream to rise to the top, to which whole milk from the following morning's milking is added. The cheesemaking technique has remained the same over the centuries. The milk is heated to 38-42°C and coagulated with liquid calf's rennet. The curd is cut up into walnut-sized lumps, left to stand for a short while and transferred to wicker baskets, where the whey is allowed to drain. The cheeses are salted and carefully turned over several times a day for 12 days. They are ready for the table after about two weeks, but can mature for up to three months. Morlacco is a semi-soft cheese that slices cleanly. It exudes droplets of whey from the eyes and has a very salty flavour. As the cheese matures, the salty sensations fade to reveal meadowland aromas that mingle with hazelnuts. In the tradition of local mountain farmers, Morlacco is eaten with polenta, boiled potatoes or homemade bread as a staple food throughout the day, from breakfast to the evening meal. The Slow Food Presidium was set up to promote Morlacco made from raw mountain milk, and differentiate it from the less interesting product produced by flatland dairies with pasteurised milk. The Presidium brings together farmers who make the cheese in the mountains during the summer on Monte Grappa. It intends to promote excellence in production, restore the mountain dairies (*cason*) and encourage the farmers to keep Burlina cows.

Rennet: liquid, calf's
Outer rind: vestigial, lined, semi-soft, white or straw-yellow in colour
Body: semi-soft, with small, prominent eyes, white in colour
Top and bottom: flat, 25-30 cm in diameter
Height/weight: 8-10 cm / 6-7 kg
Territory of origin: the Monte Grappa massif in the provinces of Treviso, Belluno and Vicenza

The curd is cut into walnut-sized lumps, left to stand for a short while and transferred to wicker baskets, where the whey is allowed to drain.

Nostrano di Malga

This is an ancient type of cheese that once had a very low fat content and was matured for longer than it is today. Now, it is made from June to September using milk from Bruno Alpina cows that have grazed on fresh grass. The raw milk is skimmed by allowing the cream to rise and usually inoculated with a small quantity of whole milk to obtain the fat content desired and prevent the cheese from becoming too dry. It is then coagulated at 32-40°C for 30-50 minutes and the curd is broken up into sweetcorn-sized pieces. The next stage is cooking at about 42-46°C, after which the curd is transferred into moulds and pressed for one day. Then comes salting, which may be either dry or in a brine bath. Nostrano di Malga matures in about 30 days, during which time the rounds are turned over and washed with brine. It has an intense, mild flavour that acquires tanginess after the fourth month of ageing.

Rennet: liquid or powder, calf's
Outer rind: hard, smooth, pinkish yellow or brown in colour in the mature version
Body: firm, with small, evenly distributed, fairly close packed eyes, white to yellow in colour
Top and bottom: flat, 20-30 cm in diameter
Height/weight: 7-12 cm / 2-7 kg
Territory of origin: the mountain and foothill areas of the province of Belluno

Pecorino Veneto

This limited-production cheese has its origins in the past when sheep farms were much more common. Ewe's milk, mostly from Massese sheep, is inoculated with calf's rennet, as lamb's or kid's rennet are difficult to procure. Coagulation is carried out at 37°C and takes about 20 minutes. The curd is broken up into sweetcorn-sized granules and then cooked, if a hard cheese with a long shelf life is desired. Otherwise, it is transferred to moulds raw. The uncooked version yields a soft cheese that is ready for the table much sooner. Generally, the rounds are ripened at 36-38°C for a few hours. Pecorino Veneto has a characteristically mild flavour, free of tanginess.

Rennet: liquid or powder, calf's
Outer rind: thin, fairly hard, straw-yellow in colour
Body: firm, white to straw-white in colour
Top and bottom: flat, 22 cm in diameter
Height/weight: 8 cm / 2-2.5 kg
Territory of origin: the provinces of Padua and Mantua, and the municipality of Anguillara in the province of Padua

Piave

Piave cheese, which was standardised about 1960, used to be made in small quantities at community dairies. Although it is made industrially nowadays, its quality is as high as ever. Raw or heat-treated milk is inoculated with milk enzymes and coagulated with calf's rennet. The curd is portioned and placed in circular containers, where it is left to drain. It is pressed for about 40 minutes, losing more humidity and acquiring the desired degree of firmness. The cheeses are then transferred to hoops which have the name Piave engraved on the inner surface. After branding, the cheeses are left for 12 hours in the *torri di sosta* (resting towers). They are then immersed in a brine bath for at least 48 hours and placed to mature on wooden shelves, where they are periodically cleaned with a brush and turned over. There are three types. Fresh Piave matures for 20-60 days, medium for 60-120 days and mature for more than 120 days. After maturing for 10-12 months, Piave is an excellent cheese for grating, as well as eating at table.

Rennet: paste, calf's
Outer rind: semi-soft, pale in the fresh version, becoming harder and tending to brown in colour as maturing progresses
Body: with no eyes, white tending to straw-yellow in colour
Top and bottom: flat, 31-33 cm in diameter
Height/weight: 7-9 cm / 6-7 kg
Territory of origin: the province of Belluno

Renaz

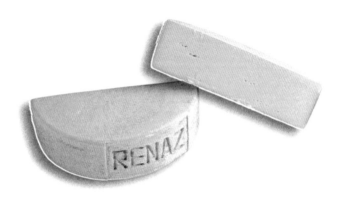

A new type of cheese created in the mid 1980s, Renaz is named after the place where it is produced. Part whole, part skimmed, raw milk is coagulated at 36°C. The process takes about 20 minutes. The curd is broken up into granules the size of half a grain of wheat and cooked at 46°C. It is then transferred to moulds and pressed in two stages, first for ten minutes and then for about one hour. The rounds are then salted in a brine bath for two days. In the following three months, they will be regularly turned over, scraped and treated with linseed oil before finally going on sale. Renaz has a rather tangy flavour.

Rennet: powder, calf's
Outer rind: hard, yellow in colour
Body: with sparse, medium-sized eyes, straw-yellow in colour
Top and bottom: flat, 40 cm in diameter
Height/weight: 8 cm / about 5.5 kg
Territory of origin: the municipality of Livinallongo in the province of Belluno

Ricotta Affumicata

Whey from the milk of Bruno Alpina cows is heated to 90-100°C and inoculated with salt and vinegar. The coagulate rises to the surface, where it is collected and transferred to cloth sacks. The sacks are hung up to drain for a few hours, and then their contents are pressed and dry-salted. The Ricotta takes one week to mature, during which time the cheeses are smoked over green conifer wood fires. Naturally, the product has no outer rind. If matured for at least one month, the body becomes hard and suitable for grating. Ricotta Affumicata from Cansiglio, made in the area's mountain dairies, is particularly well-known. Citric acid is widely used as a fermenting agent and beechwood is popular for smoking. Ricotta Affumicata is ready to go on sale after one week.

Rennet: vinegar or citric acid
Body: soft, with a characteristic smoked flavour, brown in colour
Weight: about 1 kg
Territory of origin: the area of Agordo and Sappada in the province of Belluno, the Cansiglio flatlands and mountain diaries in general

Schiz

W hen fried fresh in butter with salt, this cheese *schizza*, or "spurts", drops of whey all over the hob, a characteristic that has earned it its name. In Alpago, it is also known as *tosella*. Very fresh, whole or skimmed, raw milk is coagulated at 35-36°C in 20-40 minutes. The curd is then broken up into sweet-corn-sized granules and, after being quickly drained, is transferred to moulds with a variety of shapes ranging from circular to rectangular. For the homemade version, a colander is often used. Schiz is eaten almost as soon as it is made. Salt is added the table. The cheese has a milky aroma and very little flavour. Since it is unsalted, it tends to be insipid.

Rennet: liquid or powder, calf's
Body: soft, slightly grainy, whey-rich, white in colour
Top and bottom: flat
Height/weight: varying from 1-2 kg
Territory of origin: the province of Belluno, especially the area around Agordo

Stravecchio di Malga dell'Altopiano dei Sette Comuni

On the tableland of the Altopiano dei Sette Comuni, people know that the best cheese comes from the mountains, where the cows graze on Alpine pastures. Bruno Alpina, Frisian and Rendena cows are all kept, but Rendena is the traditional breed. These hardy cows have a very dark chestnut coat that sometimes verges on a shimmering black. They came here in the late eighteenth century from Val Rendena in Trentino, are ideal for mountain grazing and give the best-quality milk. On this plateau an excellent cheese has been produced for centuries: Stravecchio di Malga, a hard-to-find product, obtained with semi-skimmed milk and ideal for ageing (19 months or more), with an extraordinary complexity of flavour and aromas. The aim of the Slow Food Presidium is to convince cheesemakers to mature as much cheese as possible for as long as possible, and to raise awareness of their increasingly crucial role in the protection of the mountains while safeguarding their ancient traditions and heritage. Stravecchio di Malga has a smooth, even rind that is dark yellow tending to brown in colour. The body is grainy, crumbly and white in colour, with scattered small or medium-sized eyes. A product of outstanding equilibrium, Stravecchio di Malga is free of the shortcomings sometimes presented by low-fat or semi-fat cheeses. Its aromatic profile ranges from freshly scythed grass to ripe fruit and moss. It has a mild, almost sugar-sweet front palate that gradually acquires a tangy note, lifted by hints of roasted hazelnuts and toasted bread. Stravecchio di Malga is an excellent partner for a liqueur-sweet wine such as Verduzzo or Picolit, or a red wine from the Breganze DOC.

Rennet: powder or liquid, calf's
Outer rind: smooth, even, dark yellow tending to brown in colour
Body: grainy, crumbly, with scattered small or medium-sized eyes, pale yellow in colour
Top and bottom: flat or almost flat, 30-36 cm in diameter
Height/weight: 9-12 cm, 7-9 kg
Territory of origin: the municipalities of Asiago, Conco, Enego, Foza, Gallio, Lusiana, Roana and Rotzo in the province of Vicenza, and Grigno in the province of Trento

Stravecchio di Malga, protected by a Slow Food Presidium, ages for 19 months or more. This very hard-to-find product has an extraordinarily complex wealth of flavours and aromas to offer nose and palate.

The producers

Achille
Località Stander, 1
Velo Veronese (Verona)
Tel. +39 045 7835549
Monte Veronese di Malga

Albi
Contrada Viaverde, 9
Velo Veronese (Verona)
Tel. +39 045 7835579
Monte Veronese di Malga

Ivan Andreatta
Malga Campo de Roa
Solagna (Vicenza)
Tel. +39 368 3571201
Morlacco del Grappa

Quinto Andreatta
Malga Coston Da Quinto
Località Val de Foie
Borso del Grappa (Treviso)
Tel. +39 0423 53660
Via Europa, 11
Località Fietta
Paderno del Grappa (Treviso)
Tel. +39 0424 53660
Morlacco del Grappa

Livio Ballis
Via Bosco Verde, 5 a
Rocca Pietore (Belluno)
Tel. +39 0437 722190
Formaggio Agordino di Malga

Antonio Basso
Malga Cason del Sol
Località Val di Mure
Paderno del Grappa (Treviso)
Tel. +39 330 482631
Via Trento e Trieste, 29
Castelcucco (Treviso)
Tel. +39 0423 563368
Morlacco del Grappa

Sergio Basso
Malga Pusterle
Strada della Valdassa
Località Ghertele
Roana (Vicenza)
Tel. +39 0444 660529 - +39 368 3974635
Stravecchio di Malga dell'Altopiano dei
Sette Comuni

Giovanni Battilana
Malga Pat
Località Val di Coston
Borso del Grappa (Treviso)
Tel. +39 336 502274
Via Appo Castello
Borso del Grappa (Treviso)
Tel. +39 0423 542127
Morlacco del Grappa

Ugo Bonafini
Via Prà Bestemà, 21
San Zeno di Montagna (Verona)
Tel. +39 045 7285388
Monte Veronese di Malga

Guido e Franco Boscari
Malga Mazze Superiori
Località Montecorno Lusiana
Conco (Vicenza)
Via Pastoreria, 12
Grossa di Gazzo Padovano (Padova)
Tel. +39 049 5963055
Stravecchio di Malga dell'Altopiano dei
Sette Comuni

Giovanni Bressan
Via Prà Grande, 47
Agordo (Belluno)
Tel. +39 0437 62401
Formaggio Agordino di Malga

Angelo Brotto
Malga Cason Vecio
Località Val Poise
Borso del Grappa (Treviso)
Via Cenghia
Borso del Grappa (Treviso)
Tel. +39 0423 542051
Morlacco del Grappa

Ca' Verde
Località Ca' Verde
Sant'Ambrogio di Valpolicella (Verona)
Tel. +39 045 6888452
Monte Veronese di Malga

Cadelmonte
Contrada Maso di Sotto
Roverè Veronese (Verona)
Tel. +39 045 6518022
Monte Veronese Dop

Agostino Loris Cadorin
Via Foch, 38
Taibon Agordino (Belluno)
Tel. +39 0437 660328
Formaggio Agordino di Malga

Omero Campedelli
Via Degli Alpini
Erbezzo (Verona)
Tel. +39 045 7075009
Monte Veronese di Malga

Canop
Località Fontanelle
Rivamonte Agordino (Belluno)
Tel. +39 0437 69235
Nostrano di Malga, Schiz

Giovanni Carraro
Malga Meda
Località Meda
Borso del Grappa (Treviso)
Via Gorghesana, 36
Maser (Treviso)
Tel. +39 0423 529237
Morlacco del Grappa

Umberto Ceccato
Malga Paradiso
Località Paradiso
Possagno (Treviso)
Tel. +39 0423 538515
Via Molinetto, 62
Crespano del Grappa (Treviso)
Tel. +39 0423 53545
Morlacco del Grappa

Antonio Cenci
Malga Valcoperta
Località Marcesina
Grigno (Trento)
Via Stoner, 45
Enego (Vicenza)
Tel. +39 0424 493938
Stravecchio di Malga dell'Altopiano dei
Sette Comuni

Centro Caseario Allevatori del Cansiglio
Valmenera del Cansiglio
Tambre (Belluno)
Tel. +39 0437 472222
Cansiglio, Ricotta Affumicata

Consorzio Tutela Formaggio Asiago
Corso Fogazzaro, 18
Vicenza
Tel. +39 0444 321758
Asiago d'Allevo Dop

Cooperativa Latteria Tisoi
Via Antonio da Tisoi, 24
Belluno
Tel. +39 0437 294422 - +39 0437 294435
Nostrano di Malga, Schiz

Cooperativa Produttori Latte Schio
Via Vicenza, 20
Schio (Vicenza)
Tel. +39 0445 511168
Asiago d'Allevo Dop, Asiago Pressato
Dop, Grana Padano Dop

Novella De Boni
Via Valle di Lamen, 113
Feltre (Belluno)
Tel. +39 0439 301067
Nostrano di Malga, Schiz

Irno De Cassan
Via Gavaz, 29 b
Zoldo Alto (Belluno)
Tel. +39 347 4755539
Formaggio Agordino di Malga

Andrea Della Lucia
Via Crostolin, 18
Agordo (Belluno)
Tel. +39 0437 63137 - +39 347 2949353
Formaggio Agordino di Malga

Giovanni De Nardin
Via Ronche, 28
La Valle Agordina (Belluno)
Tel. +39 0437 63203
Formaggio Agordino di Malga

Silvano Eros De Nardin
Via Cal de le Mule, 13
Agordo (Belluno)
Tel. +39 0437 63539
Formaggio Agordino di Malga

Ezio e Diego Dorigo
Via Moè - Laste, 1
Rocca Pietore (Belluno)
Tel. +39 0437 529066
Formaggio Agordino di Malga

Antonio Follador
Malga Ostaria Vecia de Poise
Località Val Poise
Borso del Grappa (Treviso)
Via Appo Castello
Borso del Grappa (Treviso)
Tel. 0423 561049
Morlacco del Grappa

Livio Follador
Località Sappade, 43
Falcade (Belluno)
Tel. +39 0437 590544
Formaggio Agordino di Malga

Elido Fornasier
Malga Balbi - Campini
Possagno (Treviso)
Via Sant'Albino, 6
Possagno (Treviso)
Tel. +39 360 583742 - +39 360 461317
Morlacco del Grappa

Roberto Frigo
Malga Larici
Località Larici
Asiago (Vicenza)
Via Dante, 103
Canove di Roana (Vicenza)
Tel. +39 0424 692224
Stravecchio di Malga dell'Altopiano dei
Sette Comuni

Narciso Gasparetto
Malga Mure
Località Val delle Mure
Paderno del Grappa (Treviso)
Tel. 330 334571
Via Palazzo Neville, 2
Castelli di Monfumo (Treviso)
Tel. +39 0423 560062
Morlacco del Grappa

Alfredo Gaz
Via Besarel, 8
Taibon Agordino (Belluno)
Tel. +39 349 1953853
Formaggio Agordino di Malga

Giulia
Via Dalla Bona, 4
Sant'Anna d'Alfaedo (Verona)
Tel. +39 045 7532575
Monte Veronese di Malga

Dario Gugole
Via Cotto, 44
San Giovanni Ilarione (Verona)
Tel. +39 045 6550285
Monte Veronese di Malga

La Casara di Romano Roncolato
Via Nuova, 1
Roncà (Verona)
Tel. +39 045 7460052
Monte Veronese di Malga

Lattebusche
Via Nazionale, 59
Cesiomaggiore (Belluno)
Tel. +39 0439 3191
Nostrano di Malga

Latteria cattolica di Breganze
Via Roma, 100
Breganze (Vicenza)
Tel. +39 0445 873187
Asiago d'Allevo Dop, Asiago Pressato
Dop, Grana Padano Dop

Latteria cooperativa di Sedico
Via San Felice, 4
Sedico (Belluno)
Tel. 0437 83717
Nostrano di Malga, Schiz

Latteria sociale pedemontana del Grappa
Via Valcavasia, 36-38-40
Cavaso del Tomba (Treviso)
Tel. +39 0423 942022
Asiago Pressato Dop, Casatella
Trevigiana

Lessinia
Località Maso di Sotto, 8
Roveré Veronese (Verona)
Tel. +39 045 6516028
Monte Veronese Dop

Tarquinio Marini
Malga Dosso di Sotto
Località Dosso di Sotto
Asiago (Vicenza)
Via Boschi di Camazzole, 1
Carmignano di Brenta (Padova)
Tel. +39 049 5958371
Stravecchio di Malga dell'Altopiano dei
Sette Comuni

Edoardo Martinello
Malga Biancoia
Località Biancoia
Conco (Vicenza)
Via Barche, 27
San Pietro in Gù (Padova)
Tel. +39 049 5991439 - +39 0424 420009
Stravecchio di Malga dell'Altopiano dei
Sette Comuni

Laura Masocco
Malga Domador
Località Val delle Mure
Alano di Piave (Belluno)
Via Montegrappa, 22
Alano di Piave (Belluno)
Tel. +39 0439 779276
Morlacco del Grappa

Alcide Miola
Via Toccol, 94
Agordo (Belluno)
Tel. +39 0437 62611 - +39 348 3041660
Formaggio Agordino di Malga

Morandini
Località Dosso, 1
Erbezzo (Verona)
Tel. 045 7075050
Grana Padano Dop, Monte Veronese
Dop

Silvano e Angelo Nicolin
Malga Campo Rossignolo
Località Monte Corno
Lusiana (Vicenza)
Via Nicolin, 24
San Pietro in Gù (Padova)
Tel. +39 049 9455215 - +39 049 5991447
Stravecchio di Malga dell'Altopiano dei
Sette Comuni

Maria Luisa Pangrazio
Malga Zebio
Località Monte Zebio
Asiago (Vicenza)
Via San Domenico, 212
Asiago (Vicenza)
Tel. +39 0424 463958
Stravecchio di Malga dell'Altopiano dei
Sette Comuni

Afra Panizzon
Malga Archeson
Località Archeson
Possagno (Treviso)
Tel. +39 330 764168
Via Ceccato, 16
Crespano del Grappa (Treviso)
Tel. +39 0423 538470
Morlacco del Grappa

Perenzin
Via Cervano, 85
Località Bagnolo
San Pietro di Feletto (Treviso)
Tel. +39 0438 21355
Casatella Trevigiana

Giovanni Pescosta
Località Sappade, 5 a
Falcade (Belluno)
Tel. +39 0437 592074
Formaggio Agordino di Malga

Pier Giorgio Pescosta
Località Sappade, 5
Falcade (Belluno)
Tel. +39 0437 592119
Formaggio Agordino di Malga

Pian de Levina di Fabio Pra Floriani
Località Cornigian, 2
Forno di Zoldo (Belluno)
Tel. +39 0437 787687
Nostrano di Malga

Luigi Pozza
Malga Mandrielle
Strada per l'Ortigara
Località Marcesina
Gallio (Vicenza)
Via Pernechele, 6
Lusiana (Vicenza)
Tel. +39 0424 407044
Stravecchio di Malga dell'Altopiano dei
Sette Comuni

Armando e Riccardo Rela
Malga Zovetto
Località Cesuna Monte Zovetto
Roana (Vicenza)
Via Cima 12, 6
Canove di Roana (Vicenza)
Tel. +39 0424 450101
Stravecchio di Malga dell'Altopiano dei
Sette Comuni

Antonio Rodeghiero
Malga Porta Manazzo
Strada per i Larici
Località Porta Manazzo
Asiago (Vicenza)
Via Berga, 126
Asiago (Vicenza)
Tel. +39 0424 462591
Stravecchio di Malga dell'Altopiano dei
Sette Comuni

Oscar Rodeghiero
Malga Mandrielle
Rotzo (Vicenza)
Via Berga, 169
Asiago (Vicenza)
Tel. +39 0424 463481
Stravecchio di Malga dell'Altopiano dei
Sette Comuni

San Giorgio
Frazione Sorriva
Sovramonte (Belluno)
Tel. +39 0439 98498
Nostrano di Malga

Girolamo Savio
Malga Monte Asolone
Località Val de la Giara
Pove del Grappa (Treviso)
Via Gherla, 44
Crespano del Grappa (Treviso)
Tel. +39 0423 53778
Morlacco del Grappa

Dario Schievenin
Malga Piz
Alano di Piave (Belluno)
Tel. +39 368 3063410
Via Foba, 3
Alano di Piave (Belluno)
Tel. +39 0439 787613
Morlacco del Grappa

Antonio Spiller
Malga Busa Fonda
Strada per Le Melette Campomulo
Gallio (Vicenza)
Via Santa Lucia, 46
Marano Vicentino (Vicenza)
Tel. +39 0445 621295
Stravecchio di Malga dell'Altopiano dei
Sette Comuni

Benito Toldo
Malga Campo Rosà
Rotzo (Vicenza)
Via Righele, 4 a
Valdastico (Vicenza)
Tel. +39 0445 745254
Stravecchio di Malga dell'Altopiano dei
Sette Comuni

Dino Todesco
Malga Col del Gallo
Solagna (Vicenza)
Tel. 0424 556003
Via Albere, 15
Romano d'Ezzelino (Vicenza)
Tel. +39 0424 510506
Morlacco del Grappa

Ven.Lat.
c/o A.Pro.La.V.
Vicolo Mazzini, 2-4
Fontane di Villorba (Treviso)
Tel. +39 0422 422040
Morlacco del Grappa

Gianni Zanotto
Malga Archeset
Località Archeset
Possagno (Treviso)
Via Barbarigo
San Zenone degli Ezzelini (Treviso)
Tel. +39 0423 567266
Morlacco del Grappa

Luigi Zerbato
Via Mainenti
Vestenanova (Verona)
Tel. +39 045 7470026
Monte Veronese Dop

Friuli Venezia Giulia

Caciotta Caprina

Carnia or Cuc

Cuincîr

Formadi Frant

Formaggio Salato or Asìno

Formai dal Cit

Latteria

Malga

Montasio DOP

Scuete Fumade

Sot la Trape

Caciotta Caprina

The local names for this semi-hard cheese, which is made all over the region, are *formadiele, formaele, formajele, formadeut di cjavre, jama classico* and *vecjo di cjavre* (if matured). Once, making cheese from goat's milk was a family affair, but in recent years, fresh caprino and caciotta have been making a comeback, albeit a timid one. The raw or pasteurised goat's milk is coagulated at 27°C with a milk-based starter culture and calf's rennet. The curd is cut up, first with a larger-gauge *spada* curd knife, then with the smaller *lira*. After cooking at 45°C, the curd is removed and placed in cheese moulds. It drains for 24 hours, and is pressed and turned over repeatedly. After salting in a brine bath for four to five hours, the cheese matures for about 30 days.

Rennet: liquid, calf's
Outer rind: thin, straw-yellow in colour
Body: soft, almost entirely without eyes, white tending to straw-yellow in colour
Top and bottom: flat or slightly uneven, 12-15 cm in diameter
Height/weight: 8-10 cm / 0.8-1.2 kg
Territory of origin: the entire region

Carnia or Cuc

In the Carnian dialect, *cuc* means cheese in general. Today, the term Carnia is preferred as it indicates the product's origin. Carnia is made with a similar technique to that used for Montasio. Whole or part-skimmed raw milk is heated to 33-35°C, inoculated with calf's rennet and left to coagulate for 20-30 minutes. The soft curd is then milled into rice-sized granules, part-cooked at 44-48°C for 15 minutes and the whey is drained off. Finally, the curd is gathered up in a cloth and transferred into hoops. It is pressed and turned over, before going into a brine bath for salting after it has dried. Maturing takes place in a cool, well-ventilated room, where the rind is rubbed regularly with an oil-soaked rag.

Rennet: liquid or powder, calf's
Outer rind: hard, firm, elastic, straw-yellow shading into brown in colour with maturing
Body: elastic, firm, without eyes, straw-yellow in colour
Top and bottom: flat, 30-40 cm in diameter
Height/weight: 6-10 cm / 5-9 kg
Territory of origin: the whole of Carnia

COW'S MILK WHEY

Cuincîr

This simple, ricotta-based dairy product originates in Canal del Ferro and Val Canale, particularly in the municipalities of Chiusaforte, Dogna, Malborghetto, Moggio, Pontebba, Resia, Resiutta and Tarvisio. It is generally made during the summer grazing period, to take advantage of the more flavoursome mountain dairy ricotta, and then conserve the product for use in winter. Salt, pepper and sometimes other seasonings are kneaded into the fresh ricotta, which is left to mature for 45-60 days in large glass or plastic containers. The cheese is kneaded frequently during maturation. The final product is a white cream. Its particularly pungent aroma comes from the souring of the ricotta, which also makes it an excellent product for conserving. Cuincîr is an excellent accompaniment for polenta.

Body: creamy, easy-to-spread, greyish white in colour
Weight: variable
Territory of origin: Canal del Ferro and Val Canale

Formadi Frant

Formadi Frant is a typical dairy product from Carnia. Its origins are humble, and even today it is principally associated with farming families, who made it with cheese considered defective after maturing. Three or four latteria (see entry) cheeses matured for varying periods (40-90 days, more than 100 days, more than seven months) are broken up into flakes. The cheeses are mixed and seasoned with salt and pepper (other seasonings may be added), then milk and/or cream is kneaded in by hand. The quantities of milk and cream may be adjusted to vary the softness and smoothness of the end product. It is gathered up in cloths and placed in cylindrical or rectangular wooden moulds, and then matured for 30-40 days. Formadi Frant has an intense fragrance and a flavour that is mild yet tangy.

Body: soft, crumbly, ivory-white tending to dark yellow in colour
Top and bottom: flat
Height/weight: variable
Territory of origin: Carnia

Formaggio Salato or Asìno

The first documented reference to this cheese dates from 1659. Known in Carnia as *formaggio salato*, or "salt cheese", this version owes its name to its place of origin, Mont d'As in Val d'Arzino. Today, two varieties are made, the traditional one and a soft cheese. The former is obtained exclusively from raw or heat-treated cow's milk, which is inoculated with a natural milk-based starter culture or selected local enzymes. The curd is milled into walnut-sized lumps, and cooked at 45-46°C. The cheeses are pressed, and then immersed in wooden vats called *salmueries* for three to six months. The vats contain a bath of brine with milk and cream that can be used for centuries, if properly maintained. The soft version is made with pasteurised milk. The curd is cut into larger lumps, and is not cooked. The cheeses are not pressed, and stay in the vats for only 20 days.

Rennet: liquid, calf's
Outer rind: soft and smooth for the fresh version, becoming harder with maturing
Body: soft, yielding, chalk-white in colour
Top and bottom: flat, about 20 cm in diameter
Height/weight: 6-10 cm / 2-5 kg
Territory of origin: Carnia, Val d'Arzino, Spilimbergo

Formai dal Cit

Formai dal Cit is an extremely ancient product, and sadly increasingly hard to find. Like formadi frant (see entry), it came into being because of the need to recycle defective latteria cheeses that could not be matured. The name derives from *cit*, the stone tubs in which the product was once conserved. Today, plastic containers are generally used. Latteria cheeses matured for at least six or seven months are ground up in two stages, using a mincer for the second. A little milk, or sometimes cream, is kneaded in to bind the mixture until a thick cream is obtained. Salt, pepper and local herbs may be added. The product is ready for the table at once, and has a tangy flavour.

Body: soft, creamy, white in colour
Height/weight: variable
Territory of origin: Val Tramontina, in the province of Pordenone

COW'S MILK

Latteria

Latteria was once the name for cheese made at the old *latterie turnarie*, or community dairies. Variations in fodder, breeding techniques and the natural microflora mean that its flavour varies from producer to producer. In fact, each dairy identifies its own cheese by name. It should be mentioned, for example, that in May 1987, the dairy in Fagagna registered the town's name as a trademark for its cheese which, like montasio, is also available in a very mature version. The cheesemaking technique is very similar to that used for montasio, although the curd is milled into rather larger pieces that retain a greater proportion of whey.

Rennet: liquid or powder, calf's
Outer rind: straw-yellow in colour
Body: lightly eyed
Top and bottom: flat, 25-30 cm in diameter
Height/weight: 7-8 cm / 5 –7.5 kg
Territory of origin: the entire region

COW'S, EWE'S AND GOAT'S MILK

Malga

Malga is the name given to products made in the mountain dairies of Friuli, where cheeses have been made since ancient times. The cheesemaking technique resembles that used to make montasio and latteria. Malga sometimes has a tangy flavour that is due to, or enhanced by, the goat's milk that may be included in the cheesemaking process. An Alpine cheese, which may on occasion reveal a bitterish note, Malga owes its characteristic taste profile to the unique grazing conditions and fodder available in the region's mountain pastures. Normally, the cheese is aged for about 10-20 days, although it may also be matured for a longer period.

Rennet: liquid or powder, calf's
Outer rind: smooth, thin, straw-yellow in colour
Body: no or very few eyes
Top and bottom: flat, 20-25 cm in diameter
Height/weight: 6-8 cm / 5 -8 kg
Territory of origin: the mountainous area of the provinces of Udine and Pordenone

FRIULI VENEZIA GIULIA

255

Montasio DOP

Montasio originated in Carnia, in the mountains of Friuli Venezia Giulia, and takes its name from a group of mountains in the Julian Alps. It was here, on a broad plateau overlooking the southern slopes of the group, that herds were brought for the summer. Cheesemaking for Montasio is defined and regulated by a special consortium, the Montasio Cheese Protection Consortium, recognised by the Italian Ministry of Agriculture and Forests in 1987. Only milk produced on dairy farms in the territory of origin may be used. Once, raw milk was used, which permitted the conservation of the product's natural bacteria and enzymes and enabled the cheese to express its full potential during the maturing process. Today, the increasingly widespread practice of inoculation with milk-based starter cultures and selected enzymes has prompted most producers to carry out a mild heat treatment on the milk when it arrives at the dairy. Coagulation with powdered or liquid bovine rennet takes 20-25 minutes and the soft curd is then milled into rice-sized granules before being cooked to about 46°C. The curd is placed in the characteristic hoops that impress the mark of origin and date of production on the rind before pressing to drain off the whey. Montasio may be brine-salted in a bath or dry-salted with crystal salt. Sometimes, a mixed system is employed in which the cheese is briefly immersed in brine and the process is subsequently completed by dry-salting.

Rennet: liquid or powder, calf's
Outer rind: barely discernible when fresh, elastic, straw-yellow in colour with maturing.
Body: firm, with sparse, uniformly distributed eyes when fresh, flaky, with very few eyes, when mature.
Top and bottom: flat or slightly convex, 30-40 cm in diameter
Height/weight: 6-8 cm / 6.5 -7.5 kg
Territory of origin: the entire region of Friuli Venezia Giulia, and the provinces of Belluno and Treviso and a small part of the provinces of Padua and Venice in the Veneto region
DOP status awarded on 12 June 1996, regulation no. 1107

Illustrated above are several whole and portioned Montasio cheeses matured for various lengths of time. The Consortium mark, with the date of production and dairy code, may be clearly seen on the sides, tops and bottoms of the cheeses.

Scuete Fumade

To make the basic ricotta, whey separated from the curd during cheesemaking is heated to 95-100°C. When the protein-rich solids rise to the surface, they are worked into finely woven linen bags that are then hung up to drain. Infusions or herbs may be added to the product to obtain an aromatised ricotta for use in sauces for pasta or rice. After light pressing, the mild ricotta is removed from the bags, placed on rush mats and exposed to smoke in the smoking room for two to four days before being left to dry in a special store. It will be ready for the table in about one month. Scuete Fumade for grating should be allowed to mature for a longer period, as this allows more intense flavours and aromas to develop. Together with montasio and latteria, Scuete Fumade – Carnia's traditional smoked ricotta – is one of the region's most popular and characteristic foodstuffs.

Outer rind: thin, tending to brown in colour
Body: no eyes, white
Top and bottom: irregular
Height/weight: varying, up to 1 kg
Territory of origin: the entire region, especially Carnia

Sot la Trape

Traditionally made in Carnia, Val Canale and Canal del Ferro, Sot la Trape is a cheese that matures in grape pomace. Whole latteria (see entry) cheeses, at least two months old, and caciottas matured for at least 20 days, are used. Contact with the pomace varies depending on the size of the individual cheese, but generally lasts from four to ten days. Alternate layers of cheese and pomace are placed in unfermented grape must. The grape varieties used for the purpose are Cabernet, Merlot, Refosco, Sauvignon, Tocai and Verduzzo, and the grapes may be part-dried. After pomace contact, the cheeses are matured for at least one month before going on sale. The rind of Sot la Trape takes on a purplish colour if red grape pomace is used, and is bright yellow if the debris is from white varieties. Sot la Trape has a subtle, slightly tangy flavour.

Rennet: powder or liquid, calf's
Outer rind: purplish or bright yellow in colour
Body: firm, with sparsely distributed or small-diameter eyes in the latteria version, and almost no eyes in the caciotta variety, straw-yellow in colour
Top and bottom: flat, 10-15 cm in the caciotta type, 30-35 cm in the latteria version
Height/weight: 6-8 cm / 1-3 kg (caciotta), 6 kg (latteria)
Territory of origin: Carnia, Val Canale, Canal del Ferro

The producers

Consorzio Carnia
Via Carnia Libera 1944, 29
Tolmezzo (Udine)
Tel. +39 0433 466464
Carnia, Formaggio Salato

Cooperativa Tre valli
Via Roma, 44
Meduno (Pordenone)
Tel. +39 0427 86718
Formaggio Salato

Luciano Floram
Via Coceanzi, 211
Frazione Pegliano
Pulfero (Udine)
Tel. +39 0432 709178
Caciotta Caprina

Renato Gortani
Via Palmanova, 16
Mereto di Capitolo (Udine)
Tel. +39 0432 995365
Formadi Frant

Magrin di Rosa Dorigo
Via Garibaldi, 28
Frazione Molevana di Usago
Travesio (Pordenone)
Tel. +39 0427 90389
Formaggio Salato

Maria Carmen Spironelli
Frazione Studena Bassa, 16
Pontebba (Udine)
Tel. +39 0428 90929
Cuincir

Renato Tosoni
Via Barbeano
Spilimbergo (Pordenone)
Tel. +39 0427 2448
Asìno

Sabatina Varnerin
Località Chiavalir
Tramonti di Sopra (Pordenone)
Tel. +39 0427 869035
Formai dal Cit

Vidali
Località Basovizza, 308
Trieste
Tel. +39 040 226713
Latteria

Liguria

Bruzzu

Bruzzu was long ago identified by the Jacini enquiry as a dairy product made from soured and fermented ricotta. Until 20 or so years ago, it was very popular and produced in large quantities. At that point, output fell dramatically but today there is something of a revival. The cheese is obtained from ewe's milk whey heated to 70-90°C, as is the case with all ricottas. Unlike other cheeses of this type, the solids are put into moulds to drain after being collected, and thereafter into small wooden vats, where they ferment. Salt is added when fermentation takes place but an unsalted version can also be found. The wooden vats are then transferred to the cellar for about a week, during which time the cheeses are turned over every day.

Body: creamy, ivory-white or brownish-white in colour
Height/weight: irregular
Territory of origin: the municipalities of Triora, Molini di Triora and Cosio di Arroscia in the province of Imperia, and Ormea in the province of Cuneo

Caprino della Valbrevenna

This goat's milk cheese is made in the months of September and October. Raw whole goat's milk is inoculated with milk enzymes to encourage souring at a temperature of 20-25°C. Some producers add a little whey from the previous cheesemaking session. A few hours later, the milk is slowly coagulated with calf's rennet, a process that takes 12-16 hours. The rennet may be in paste or preferably liquid form. After salting, the curd is cut up into large lumps. It is then removed from the whey and transferred to moulds. As a lot of whey tends to be expelled, the moulds usually have to be topped up once or twice. Caprino della Valbrevenna is almost invariably eaten fresh. However, it can be matured in the mould for about a month.

Rennet: liquid or paste, calf's
Outer rind: no rind when fresh, milk-white tending to yellow as maturing proceeds
Body: soft, milk-white
Top and bottom: flat, 6 cm in diameter
Height/weight: 6 cm / 100 g
Territory of origin: Valbrevenna in the province of Genoa

Formaggetta della Valle Argentina

Every farmer in the production zone makes this cheese with the milk to hand, taking care to make a separate curd for each round. Some put the rennet into the milk, then divide the mixture up into moulds whereas others put the milk into moulds, and then inoculate it with rennet. The curd is never milled. When the soft curd is transferred from the container to the mould, the whey is delicately drained off and the mould is turned upside down, taking care not to break up the curd. Coagulation takes about 20-22 hours. The flavour of the milk, which is traditionally whole and unpasteurised, depends on the pastures where the herds have grazed. Cheeses from the hinterland are rich in aromatic herbs which imbue the milk, and also the cheese, with a special fragrance. Formaggetta is generally eaten fresh but it may be left to mature, sometimes for long periods. Three months after production, it can be used as a grating cheese to enhance the flavour of pesto sauce or vegetable pies.

Rennet: liquid chemical
Outer rind: rindless when fresh, yellow shading into ochre as maturing proceeds
Body: white, firm, soft when fresh, elastic, fatty, with small, evenly distributed eyes when mature, straw-white in colour
Top and bottom: flat, about 10 cm in diameter
Height/weight: 2-10 cm / 150-300 g
Territory of origin: the hinterland of Savona and Imperia

Formaggetta di Cabannina

Cabannina is a hardy breed that adapts well to the harsh conditions of mountain cattle farming. Since they yield relatively little milk, Cabannina cows are gradually disappearing and have been replaced by more productive breeds. Today, Cabannina cattle can be found chiefly in Liguria in Val d'Aveto and Valbrevenna. It is here that their milk is used to make a cheese with a firmer body than similar products from the Savona area. Raw or pasteurised cow's milk, which may be mixed with a small proportion of goat's milk, is inoculated first with milk enzymes and then with rennet in paste form. It coagulates in one hour at 37°C. The curd is then continuously stirred as it is broken up thoroughly two or three times. When the desired consistency has been achieved, the curd is transferred to the cheese moulds and gently pressed. Formaggetta di Cabannina matures for 7-20 days. During maturing, a white patina of mould may form on the surface.

Rennet: paste, calf's
Outer rind: skin, white in colour
Body: firm, milk-white in colour
Top and bottom: flat, 10-12 cm in diameter
Height/weight: 2-3 cm / 400-500 g
Territory of origin: Valbrevenna in the province of Genoa

Formaggetta Savonese

Low-acidity milk from one or more milkings on the same day is poured into small cylindrical earthenware containers and inoculated with liquid rennet. It is left to coagulate at room temperature for 8-24 hours. After coagulation, each container is slowly turned upside down to tip the contents into a mould without breaking the curd. The whey is allowed to drain and then the top of the curd is hand salted. A few hours later, the round is turned upside down and the bottom is salted. After another 8-12 hours, the cheese can be removed from the mould and eaten, or it may be left to ripen for 30 days. Today, Formaggetta Savonese is produced only in the municipality of Stella, using 90% goat's milk and 10% cow's milk, at the initiative of a local dairy. Predictably enough, it is known as Formaggetta di Stella.

Rennet: liquid, calf's
Outer rind: rindless when fresh, thin, soft, straw-white when mature
Body: firm, soft, with a characteristic, faintly sour aroma, white to straw-yellow in colour, depending on maturing
Top and bottom: flat, 12 cm in diameter
Height/weight: 3 cm / 200-500 g
Territory of origin: the province of Savona

Formaggio d'Alpeggio di Triora

An industrial version of this cheese is made using pasteurised milk but the mountain pasture product involves heating raw milk to 37°C and inoculating it with liquid rennet. About two hours later, the curd is milled into hazelnut-sized pieces and allowed to settle on the bottom of the vat, where is stands for about one hour. It is then removed, salted and transferred to moulds. It is pressed in the moulds for three or four days, after which the hard-pressed curd is moved to a damp, cool room to mature. It ages for about three months, but in many cases maturing goes on for up to a year. It is these more mature cheeses that offer a more complex tasting profile.

Rennet: liquid, calf's
Outer rind: rough, sometimes lined by the basket, straw-yellow shading into brown with maturing
Body: firm, compact, sometimes with a few eyes, golden yellow in colour
Top and bottom: flat, 25-40 cm in diameter
Height/weight: 5 cm / 5-7 kg
Territory of origin: the mountains around the municipality of Triora

Pecorino del Beigua

In 1978, a family of Sardinian shepherds took over an abandoned farm at Stella in the province of Savona. Since then, they have been making this ewe's milk cheese. The raw milk used comes from sheep bred in Sardinia. In early June, the flocks are taken to mountain pastures 1,000 metres above sea level on Mount Beigua, where they stay until the first snows fall. Milk from the morning and evening milkings is mixed and coagulated in 30-35 minutes at 40-42°C, using liquid calf's rennet. In the past, rennet from a lamb's stomach was used. The curd is milled into sweetcorn-sized granules with a curd knife, and scalded for five to seven minutes. It is dry-salted for 12 hours, and subsequently placed in a brine bath for 36 hours. The cheese is left to drain for four to five days, and then matured for at least 45 days, reaching its peak after six months.

Rennet: liquid, calf's
Outer rind: thin, yellow in colour
Body: soft, firm, sometimes with faint eyes when fresh, harder, slightly grainy when mature
Top and bottom: flat, 14-20 cm in diameter
Height/weight: 20-22 cm / 3-5 kg
Territory of origin: The Beigua Park in the provinces of Genoa and Savona

COW'S MILK

Prescinseûa

The derivation of this dialect term is obscure but Prescinseûa is well-known in Genoa. It is a cream cheese obtained by allowing cow's milk to sour and adding milk enzymes if necessary. Once the milk has coagulated, it is filtered through a cloth. In former times, the cream was then placed in small earthenware containers but today plastic or glass jars are used. The flavour is distinctly sourish and reminiscent of yoghurt. Prescinseûa is generally sprinkled with sugar if served at table. However, it is used mainly in the kitchen, where it complements the traditional cuisine of Liguria, for example in local baking and Easter cakes.

Body: creamy, easy-to-spread
Weight: variable
Territory of origin: Genoa and its hinterland

San Sté

San Sté is a name invented to indicate a cheese with a long history in Val d'Aveto but which had become extinct. When the local dairy was set up, the owners decided to revive this traditional cheese. Today, it is made with milk from Bruno Alpina or Cabannina cows grazed in local pastures. Raw milk is heated to 35°C and inoculated with paste or powdered calf's rennet. It is left to coagulate for 35 minutes. The soft curd is milled into rice-sized granules, collected in a cloth and placed on a board, where it is kneaded. Coarse salt is added and the mixture transferred to moulds, which are then pressed to drain off the whey. Next, the rounds are removed and immersed in brine for two days to harden the outer rind. Finally, the cheeses are moved to damp, cool, but unventilated maturing rooms, where they will stay for at least 60 days. During this period, they are regularly turned over and oiled.

Rennet: liquid or paste, calf's
Outer rind: thin, firm, elastic, golden yellow tending to brown in colour
Body: firm, with a few eyes, straw-white in colour
Top and bottom: flat, 30-35 cm in diameter
Height/weight: 10 cm / 12 kg
Territory of origin: Val d'Aveto in the province of Genoa

Stagionato de Vaise

The Cooperativa Casearia Val di Vara, set up in 1978, has restarted production of this classic mature Apennine toma, using only milk from organically farmed herds. The milk is pasteurised, then heated to 38°C and inoculated with a starter culture and powdered calf's rennet. After 32 minutes, the soft curd is milled in three stages, with an interval of five minutes between each milling. In the first phase, the curd is cut into walnut-sized lumps, then into almond-sized, and finally into hazelnut-sized granules. Subsequently, the whey is drained off by heating the curd to 45°C and then semi-cooking it. After ripening at 38°C for four hours, the cheeses are removed, dry-salted and placed in a room at 10-12% humidity, where they mature. They remain there until maturing is complete, after an average of 60 days.

Rennet: powder, calf's
Outer rind: smooth, hard, light to dark brown in colour
Body: elastic, firm, straw-yellow in colour
Top and bottom: flat, 18 cm in diameter
Height/weight: 5-7 cm / 1.5 -2 kg
Territory of origin: Val di Vara in the province of La Spezia

Tome di Pecora Brigasca

Brigasca derives from La Brigue, a village in Val Roya that in the past was the most important sheep farming centre in the border areas of Liguria, Piedmont and Provence. Over the centuries, La Brigue has been part of both France and Italy, but the local dialect derives from Occitan, the ancient *langue d'oc*. In all probability, the Brigasca sheep comes from the same stock as the Frabosana breed. The convex profile of the head, and the backwards-slanting horns, curled on the rams, are similar to the Frabosana. The Brigasca is a little less stocky but its sturdy hooves are ideal for grazing on mountain pastures. The traditional farming cycle includes seven or eight months on high-altitude pastures and about four in the *bandia*, the coastal area where the mild climate permits open-air grazing even in winter. The breed's milk yields three cheeses, made using traditional methods, Sora, Toma and Brus. Sora is made exclusively with ewe's milk from the evening milking mixed with milk drawn the following morning. It is heated to 34°C and coagulated with liquid rennet. The curd is milled with a *rubatà*, the traditional wooden curd knife, and allowed to settle. It is then removed using a rough cloth known as a *raireura*. The cloth is tied into a bundle, and a large stone placed on top. Twelve hours later, the curd is removed from the cloth and cut into symmetrical parts. After maturing for 15 days, the cheeses are washed in running water, dried and matured on wooden boards in a cool room for at least 60 days. Toma production differs from Sora only in that goat's milk may be added, moulds are used to shape the cheeses and the maturing period is shorter. Sadly, the number of Brigasca sheep farmed in the area has fallen dramatically from the early twentieth century's figure of 60,000. Only 1,800 graze the pastures of Liguria, and 800 of those are on farms in Val Roya. The impoverishment of the livestock heritage in these mountain areas has had negative repercussions on the landscape, as well as on the local economy. The Slow Food Presidium, sponsored by the Liguria regional authority, aims to promote raw milk Toma di Pecora Brigasca cheeses made in the few remaining mountain dairies, and to support farmers in protecting the natural environment.

Rennet: kid's in liquid, paste or powder form
Outer rind: generally smooth, cream tending to light brown or pale grey in colour as maturing proceeds
Body: elastic, soft to semi-hard, with a few, evenly distributed eyes, pale or dark straw-yellow in colour
Top and bottom: flat, 15-20 cm in diameter
Height/weight: 3-8 cm / 1-4 kg
Territory of origin: the valleys in the province of Imperia and mountain pastures on the border with France

The Brigasca sheep may come from the same stock as the Frabosana breed. Its robust legs and sturdy hooves are ideal for grazing in mountain pastures.

The producers

Autra
Località Olmi, 13
Savignone (Genoa)
Tel. 010 9690992
Caprino della Valbrevenna, Formaggetta
di Cabannina

Nevio Balbis
Strada Montà Da Lanza, 80
Sanremo (Imperia)
Tel. 333 3302604
Tome di Pecora Brigasca

Caseificio Val d'Aveto
Via Rezzoaglio Inferiore, 35
Rezzoaglio (Genoa)
Tel. 0185 870390
Prescinseûa, San Sté

Enrico Codara
Località Cascina Pasti
Stella (Savona)
Tel. 019 706303
Formaggetta Savonese

Cooperativa Casearia Val di Vara
Località Perazza
Varese Ligure (La Spezia)
Tel. 0187 842108
Stagionato de Vaise

Il Boschetto di Aldo Lo Manto
Regione Boschetto
Albenga (Savona)
Tel. 339 4167938
Tome di Pecora Brigasca

Il Castagno di Tersilia Pelassa
Via San Bernardo, 39
Mendatica (Imperia)
Tel. 0183 328718
Tome di Pecora Brigasca

Pasquale Usai
Località Corona, 177
Stella (Savona)
Tel. 019 703137
Pecorino del Beigua

Emilia Romagna

Casatella Romagnola

Formaggio di Fossa

Parmigiano Reggiano DOP

Pecorino dell'Appennino
Reggiano

Pecorino Dolce
dei Colli Bolognesi

Raviggiolo dell'Appennino
Toscoromagnolo

Squaquarone

Casatella Romagnola

Afresh cheese, whose name reveals its traditional role as a homemade foodstuff (*casatella* is a diminutive of *casa*, meaning "house"), Casatella is made today from pasteurised milk heated to about 37°C and then inoculated with rennet and milk enzymes. The soft curd is milled into walnut-sized pieces and left to stand for a few minutes before it is cut again, this time more finely. The next stage is to transfer the curd into moulds and allow the whey to drain off at a temperature of 20-22°C. The product is then either dry-salted or immersed in a brine bath. Ripening is carried out in a cold store at 4°C.

Rennet: liquid, calf's
Outer rind: rindless when fresh, ivory-white tending to yellow in colour as maturing progresses.
Body: soft, white
Top and bottom: round, even, the top is slightly convex
Height/Weight: 5 cm / 0.2-2 kg
Territory of origin: the whole of Romagna

Formaggio di Fossa

The term *formaggio di fossa* refers to a maturing technique, not a kind of cheese. Rounds of ewe's or cow's milk cheese are placed to age for about three months in the caves at Sogliano, ancient grain stores thought to date from the heyday of the Malatesta family in the fourteenth century. Carved from the tufaceous rock, they are oval in section, two metres wide and two metres high. The cheeses are packed into cloth sacks and "buried" at the end of August, to be "exhumed" in late November. By local tradition, they are taken out on 24 November, the feast of Saint Catherine. The *fosse*, or holes, are closed with wooden covers and sealed with chalk paste to ensure a constant temperature of 21°C, humidity close to 100% and minimum ventilation. As it ferments under these conditions, the cheese develops bitterish flavours and an aroma of autumn leaves, mushrooms and truffle. It is also very easily digestible. Naturally, not all Formaggio di Fossa has the same sensory characteristics, as these will depend on the type of cheese that was originally interred.

Rennet: variable, depending on the original cheese
Outer rind: soft, covered with green, yellowish and white moulds
Body: light, flaky, crumbly, dirty white to straw-yellow or pale hazel in colour
Top and bottom: smooth
Weight: variable
Territory of origin: Sogliano sul Rubicone

Parmigiano Reggiano DOP

Alberto Savinio has written that Parmigiano Reggiano is to cheese what the double bass is to string instruments. In other words, it is Italy's emblematic cheese, and certainly the one that is best-known at home and abroad. The milk for Parmigiano Reggiano is collected and brought to the cheese dairies twice a day. Milk from the evening milking is put into broad, shallow troughs so that the cream rises to the surface. The following morning, the cream is removed and the part-skimmed milk is mixed with whole milk from the morning milking, and transferred to truncated cone-shaped vats. The mixture is then inoculated with milk enzymes obtained by allowing the previous day's whey to sour naturally. Next, the milk is heated to 33-34°C and inoculated with natural calf's rennet. Coagulation takes 10-12 minutes. The soft curd is then milled finely into granules no bigger than a lentil. After cooking, which is carried out at a temperature of about 55°C, the curd is removed and divided into two parts, each of which is placed in a mould known as a *fascera*. The cheesemakers then apply the marking ring that punches onto the side of the cheese the characteristic Parmigiano Reggiano mark, the producer's registration number, and the year and month of production. Since January 2002, each cheese has also carried a casein plaque with a unique alphanumeric identification code. The next stage is salting by immersion in saturated brine at a temperature of 16-

18°C for about 24 days. Maturing, which lasts for a minimum of 12 months, comes next, after which each cheese undergoes an expertisation examination. Cheeses that present an appropriate appearance, structure and other characteristics are branded with the well-known mark. The selection examination identifies two categories: Parmigiano Reggiano for extended maturing of 12-24 months or longer; and Parmigiano Reggiano Prima Stagionatura, which is released for consumption after branding (12 months) and indelibly marked with parallel grooves on the side.

Rennet: natural calf's
Outer rind: about 6 mm thick, slightly oily, natural straw-yellow in colour
Body: flaky, fine-grained, yellow to straw-yellow in colour
Top and bottom: flat, 35-45 cm in diameter
Height/Weight: 20-26 cm / average weight 38 kg (minimum 30 kg)
Territory of origin: the provinces of Parma, Reggio Emilia and Modena, the municipalities on the left bank of the river Reno in the province of Bologna and the municipalities on the right bank of the river Po in the province of Mantua
DOP status awarded on 12 June 1996, regulation no. 1107

Parmigiano cheeses weigh more than 30 kilograms. Note the mark of the Consortium on the side of the round.

This is the cheese's ID, printed on the outer rind. It shows the code number of the dairy where it was made, the Consortium mark and the date of production.

Pecorino dell'Appennino Reggiano

Sheep have been farmed in the Reggio Emilia Apennines since time immemorial. Various historic documents mention *cacio*, *caseus* or *giuncata* ewe's milk cheeses which, until the nineteenth century, were more expensive than cow's milk products. At the turn of the century, there were more than 60,000 sheep and about 160 farmers. The most common breed was the now almost extinct Cornella. A medium to large animal with a white coat, the Cornella can be bred for milk and meat. In the twentieth century, the trend shifted and farmers went over to breeding cows for milk to make parmigiano reggiano (see entry). Fewer and fewer farmers took their flocks to summer pastures. Currently, about 5,000 sheep remain on the Reggio Emilia Apennine, in about 30 flocks. Most of the animals are Massese sheep. Only one farmer still takes his flock to summer pastures. Production of pecorino cheese is restricted to a small number of farms, only one of which uses raw milk. Traditionally, only whole raw ewe's milk is used, and the cheeses are matured for three to four months, although this can be extended to eight or ten months, often with excellent results. Cheeses weigh about two kilograms but they are not easy to find. Old-style Pecorino Reggiano, matured for several months, is almost a thing of the past. Pecorino dell'Appennino Reggiano is sweeter than ewe's milk cheeses from neighbouring Tuscany. Its flavour is less intense but it has excellent balance and outstanding elegance. Consumers are advised to accompany it with a wine that bring out its elegance, and will not overwhelm its flavour. A dried-grape Albana Passito is excellent with more mature versions whereas a mid-bodied red, for example Sangiovese or Merlot, will successfully partner younger cheeses. The Slow Food Presidium was created to safeguard and encourage production of the increasingly marginalised Pecorino dell'Appennino Reggiano in the mountain area between Tuscany and the Upper Apennines of Modena and Parma. Flocks and farmers constitute an effective defence of the territory against abandonment and consequent hydrogeological disruption.

Rennet: liquid or powder, kid's or lamb's
Outer rind: varying shades of yellowish-white in the semi-hard version, tending to become browner as maturing progresses
Body: compact, moderately difficult to slice, sometimes with moderately close-packed and often irregular eyes in the soft version; compact, very difficult to slice, sometimes with tiny, irregularly distributed eyes in the semi-hard version
Top and bottom: flat, with slightly convex side, 15-22 cm in diameter
Height/Weight: 6-10 cm / 2 kg
Territory of origin: the municipalities of Baiso, Buana, Canossa, Carpiteti, Casina, Castelnovo ne' Monti, Collagna, Ligonchio, Ramiseto, Toano, Vetto, Viano and Villa Minozzo in the province of Reggio Emilia

Currently, there are about 5,000 mainly Massese sheep left in the Reggio Emilia Apennines. Only one farmer still takes his flock to summer pastures. Production of ewe's milk cheese is restricted to a very small number of farms.

Pecorino Dolce dei Colli Bolognesi

The milk is pasteurised at 72-74°C and then cooled to 30-35°C before it is inoculated with rennet and milk enzymes. After coagulation, the curd is broken up and then reheated to 42°C. At this point, the now firm curd is transferred into plastic moulds to drain. The process is encouraged by heating. Next, the rounds are dry-salted and subsequently matured for a minimum of 20 days or up to four months.

Rennet: liquid, calf's
Outer rind: lustrous, elastic, ochre-yellow in colour with darker tinges
Body: semi-hard, firm, mild-flavoured
Top and bottom: flat, 12-14 cm in diameter
Height/Weight: 5 cm / 1-2 kg
Territory of origin: the Colli Bolognesi

Raviggiolo
dell'Appennino Toscoromagnolo

A relatively hard to find fresh cheese, Raviggiolo is made in a number of valleys in the Romagna Apennines, where it has a centuries-long pedigree. It is mentioned in documents dating from the Renaissance. As long ago as 1515, the Magistrato Comunitativo of Terra di Bibbiena made a gift to Leo X of a basket of fern-covered Raviggiolo cheeses. Pellegrino Artusi, in his landmark *La Scienza in Cucina e l'Arte di Mangiar Bene* (Science in the Kitchen and the Art of Eating Well), indicates *cacio raviggiolo* as an ingredient for a pasta dish, *cappelletti all'uso di Romagna*. Raviggiolo is made with raw cow's milk and rennet. The curd is not milled, but merely drained and salted on the surface. Today, Raviggiolo is made in the valleys of the province of Forlì of Montone, Rabbi, Bidente and Savio, part of the production area falling inside the National Park of the Casentino Forests, Monte Falterona and Campigna. Some cheesemakers continue to use raw milk but since raw milk cheese can be kept for no more than four days, it is only found from October to March. Slightly buttery in texture, Raviggiolo has a soft, white body and a very delicate, almost sweet, flavour. The cheese is circular in shape and about 20-25 centimetres in diameter. It varies in height from two to four centimetres. The cheese is presented on fronds of fern (*Pteridium aquilinum*), which give it its characteristic shape. Freshness is the distinguishing feature of Raviggiolo's sensory profile, which reveals notes of milk and hazelnuts on the palate. This means that over-assertive food matchings should be avoided. The Slow Food Presidium was set up to protect production of raw cow's milk Raviggiolo, and to distinguish it from the Tuscan cheese of the same name (see entry). On the Casentino slopes of the Apennines, and all over Tuscany, Raviggiolo is made with ewe's milk, usually to order.

Rennet: liquid, calf's
Body: soft, tender, white
Top and bottom: smooth, cream-white in colour
Height/Weight: 2-4 cm / 1-2 kg
Territory of origin: the valleys in the province of Forlì-Cesena

Raviggiolo is a circular cheese with a slightly buttery texture. The cheese is presented on fronds of fern that give it its characteristic shape.

Squaquarone

What shape should Squaquarone be? The Italian name suggests the amorphous consistency of this super-fresh cheese, which is usually spread onto unleavened *piadina* pancakes or flat rolls. Made all year round, Squaquarone has a mild, delicate flavour. The cheesemaking process involves heating pasteurised milk to 37°C and inoculating it with a milk-based starter culture and liquid rennet. After about 25 minutes, the curd is milled in two stages with an interval of about 20 minutes. It is left to settle and the whey is drained off. Next, the curd is placed in moulds and the ripening process begins. The cheeses are turned over regularly at this stage. They are then salted in 20% brine for about two hours. A few days later, the Squaquarone is ready for the table.

Rennet: liquid, calf's
Body: soft, fresh, cream-white in colour
Height/Weight: varying from 1-3 kg
Territory of origin: the whole of Romagna, but Squaquarone from Castel San Pietro is especially prized

The producers

Pietro e Luigi Araldi
Via Venturini, 16
Località San Michelino Gatti
Felino (Parma)
Tel. +39 0521 806162
Parmigiano Reggiano Dop

Ottorino Barani
Via Emilio Lepido, 291
Parma
Tel. +39 0521 645148
Parmigiano Reggiano Dop

Pierpaolo Baratta
Piazzale Pincolini, 14
Fontanellato (Parma)
Tel. +39 0521 821570
Parmigiano Reggiano Dop

Bergonzano
Via Sedignano, 20
San Polo d'Enza (Reggio Emilia)
Tel. +39 0522 887273
Parmigiano Reggiano delle Vacche
Rosse

Bertozzi
Via Nazionale, 15
Ozzano Taro (Parma)
Tel. +39 0521 257611
Parmigiano Reggiano Dop

Leonida e Francesco Bocchi
Via Taro, 1
Collecchio (Parma)
Tel. +39 0521 800428
Parmigiano Reggiano Dop

Roberto Boscherini
Via Collina di Pondo, 194
Santa Sofia (Forlì Cesena)
Tel. +39 0543 971143
Raviggiolo dell'Appennino Toscoro-
magnolo

Bottega di Fattoria Ghetti Rondanini
Via Monte Mauro, 17
Frazione Zattaglia
Brisighella (Ravenna)
Tel. +39 0546 71470 - +39 0546 84521
Formaggio di Fossa

Germano Bresciani
Via Case Nuove di Pezzolo, 59
Località Monteguidi
Bagno di Romagna (Forlì Cesena)
Tel. +39 0543 913042
Raviggiolo dell'Appennino Toscoro-
magnolo

**Caseificio Cooperativo Intercomunale
Castellettese**
Via Castello, 573
Castello di Serravalle (Bologna)
Tel. +39 051 6704808
Parmigiano Reggiano Dop

**Caseificio Sociale Cooperativo
San Mauro**
Via Scondoncello, 35 b
Collecchio (Parma)
Tel. +39 0521 805767
Parmigiano Reggiano Dop

Caseificio Sociale La Medesanese
Via Carnevala
Medesano (Parma)
Tel. +39 0525 420607
Parmigiano Reggiano Dop

Caseificio Sociale Querciola
Località Querciola
Lizzano in Belvedere (Bologna)
Tel. +39 0534 56064
Parmigiano Reggiano Dop

Caseificio Sociale San Nicomede
Località San Nicomede
Salsomaggiore Terme (Parma)
Tel. +39 0524 572089
Parmigiano Reggiano Dop

Caseificio Sociale Superchina Canevare
Via Cà Frati, 200
Località Canevare
Fanano (Modena)
Tel. +39 0536 68031
Parmigiano Reggiano Dop

Cooperativa Casearia della Selva Romanesca
Via Radici, 5
Località Piandelagotti
Frassinoro (Modena)
Tel. +39 0536 967119
Parmigiano Reggiano Dop

Cooperativa Casearia Val del Dolo
Via Chiesa, 36
Località Romanoro
Frassinoro (Modena)
Tel. +39 0536 963062
Parmigiano Reggiano Dop

Dall'Aglio
Località Rio Corto di Bacedasco Basso
Vernasca (Piacenza)
Tel. +39 0523 895231
Grana Padano Dop

Flavio Dall'Aglio
Via Cabriolo, 3
Fidenza (Parma)
Tel. +39 0524 524086
Parmigiano Reggiano Dop

Angiolino Dieci
Strada Sarturano, 9
Agazzano (Piacenza)
Tel. +39 0523 975271
Grana Padano Dop

Fanticini
Via Anna Frank, 73
Località Villa Sabbione
Reggio Emilia
Tel. +39 0522 344126
Parmigiano Reggiano delle Vacche Rosse

Fior di Latte
Via Torretta, 128
Gaggio Montano (Bologna)
Tel. +39 0534 31126
Parmigiano Reggiano Dop

Formaggio di Fossa
Via Pascoli, 4-8
Sogliano al Rubicone (Forlì Cesena)
Tel. +39 0541 948687
Formaggio di Fossa

Gennari
Via Varra Superiore, 14
Collecchio (Parma)
Tel. +39 0521 805947
Parmigiano Reggiano Dop

Davide Gigli e Barbara Masini
Via Benedetti
Località Gazzano
Villa Minozzo (Reggio Emilia)
Tel +39 0522 803310
Pecorino dell'Appennino Reggiano

La Madonnina
Via Scipione Ponte, 19
Salsomaggiore Terme (Parma)
Tel. +39 0524 570905
Parmigiano Reggiano Dop

La Pelata
Via Scipione Ponte
Salsomaggiore Terme (Parma)
Tel. +39 0524 570928
Parmigiano Reggiano Dop

Latteria Sociale Asta Febbio Cervarolo
Via Casa Balocchi, 19 a
Località Asta
Villa Minozzo (Reggio Emilia)
Tel. +39 0522 800121
Parmigiano Reggiano Dop

Latteria Sociale di Quara
Via Crocetta, 1
Località Quara
Toano (Reggio Emilia)
Tel. +39 0522 808402 - +39 0522 808101
Parmigiano Reggiano Dop

Latteria Sociale Pieve San Vincenzo
Via Fornolo
Ramiseto (Reggio Emilia)
Tel. +39 0522 892187
Parmigiano Reggiano Dop

Latteria Sociale Salsese
Via Laurano, 94
Salsomaggiore Terme (Parma)
Tel. +39 0524 574868
Parmigiano Reggiano Dop

Montauro
Via Montauro, 220
Salsomaggiore Terme (Parma)
Tel. +39 0524 572151
Parmigiano Reggiano Dop

Notari
Via Fratelli Rosselli, 41/1
Località Coviolo
Reggio Emilia
Tel. +39 0522 294655
Parmigiano Reggiano delle Vacche Rosse

Piazza Di Sabbione
Via Cantù, 28
Località Sabbione
Reggio Emilia
Tel. +39 0522 344169
Parmigiano Reggiano delle Vacche Rosse

San Girolamo
Via Peroggio, 8
Guastalla (Reggio Emilia)
Tel. +39 0522 820173
Parmigiano Reggiano delle Vacche Rosse

Santa Elisabetta
Via Bergamino, 10
Collecchio (Parma)
Tel. +39 0521 806083
Parmigiano Reggiano Dop

Società Minozzo
Corso Don Verio Fontana, 10 a
Località Minozzo
Villa Minozzo (Reggio Emilia)
Tel. +39 0522 801101
Parmigiano Reggiano Dop

Valline
Via Montecoppe Sopra, 3
Collecchio (Parma)
Tel. +39 0521 805942
Parmigiano Reggiano Dop

Zabo Form
Via Langhirano, 264
Frazione Fontanini
Parma
Tel. +39 0521 649003
Parmigiano Reggiano Dop

Tuscany

Accasciato

Caciotta Toscana

Marzolino del Chianti

Pecorino Baccellone

Pecorino della Garfagnana

Pecorino della Montagna
    Pistoiese ●

Pecorino di Garfagnina

Pecorino di Montagna

Pecorino di Pienza

Pecorino Senese

Pecorino Toscano DOP

Raviggiolo di Pecora

Tendaio

Accasciato

Accasciato means "collapsed", a name that derives from the shape the cheese assumes when it comes out of the mould. It also used to be called *formaggio del piatto* (plate cheese) because it took the shape of the plate it was placed on. The best Accasciato is made with ewe's milk only, in the period from January to late spring. In summer, most producers make the cheese from a mixture of ewe's milk and cow's milk. Coagulation, which used to be induced by inoculating the milk with vegetable rennet extracted from the cardoon, a wild thistle, is achieved at the relatively low temperature of 28°C. The curd is cut into walnut-sized lumps and transferred into moulds, where it is left to drain at about 30°C for a whole day. It is turned over several times during this period. When it has acquired the desired degree of acidity, the mass is salted and placed in a cool room. In some cases, it is matured at very high humidity. Each cheese weighs about one and a half kilograms and is about 20 centimetres in diameter, although smaller examples are also made. Accasciato is eaten fresh but is still delicious 40-60 days after production.

Rennet: natural calf's
Outer rind: slightly furrowed, soft, cream in colour
Body: moist, milk-white in colour
Top and bottom: flat, irregular
Height/weight: 3-5 cm / 1-1.5 kg
Territory of origin: the Garfagnana area and the Apuan Alps

Caciotta Toscana

Caciotta is one of the most popular cheeses in Tuscany. Generally, it is made with pasteurised milk for immediate consumption. When the milk has been heated to about 40°C, calf's rennet is added and about 20 minutes later, the soft curd is broken up into walnut-sized lumps. It is then placed in moulds and the whey is drained off. To encourage draining, the rounds are heated to 45-50°C for about an hour. Salting is carried out in a brine bath, where the rounds remain for 8-16 hours. Caciotta is ready for the table after maturing for about 20 days at a temperature ranging from 8-19°C, in rooms with humidity as high as 60%. The rounds are turned over and washed frequently during maturing.

Rennet: liquid, calf's
Outer rind: slightly dimpled, pale to dark yellow
Body: fatty, firm, straw-yellow in colour
Top and bottom: flat, 14-20 cm in diameter
Height/weight: 5-8 cm / 0.8 –1.5 kg
Territory of origin: the whole of Tuscany, particularly Maremma

Marzolino del Chianti

Warm, raw milk from the morning milking is mixed with milk drawn the previous evening. It is heated to 30-32°C and inoculated with vegetable rennet. After a period of one to three hours, the soft curd is ready to be broken up into granules the size of a grain of sweetcorn. It is then removed from the whey, pressed and shaped into ovals. Next, the curd is transferred into concave moulds to drain off the whey. Draining is completed by pressing the rounds. The firm curd is dry-salted and then inserted into a *saccola*, or cloth bag, and hung for about two days, during which time the rounds are turned every eight hours or so. Marzolino ripens for a further seven days in the cellar, where the rounds are again regularly turned and washed. Finally, the cheese is matured, a process that can last for up to six months. During maturing, the forms are brushed with oil or oil dregs.

Rennet: vegetable, from the flower of the cardoon (*Cynara cardunculus silvestris*) in powder or infusion
Outer rind: faint to marked "orange-peel" effect, depending on maturing, yellow to reddish in colour
Body: white, tending to straw-white in colour
Top and bottom: curved
Height/weight: 9-13 cm / 0.5 –1.5 kg
Territory of origin: the area of the provinces of Florence and Siena crossed by the steep valleys of the Greve, Pesa and Arbia

Pecorino Baccellone

The milk, usually pasteurised, is heated to about 36°C, salted and inoculated with calf's rennet. About half an hour later, the soft curd can be cut into walnut-sized lumps. The whey is then removed and the curd transferred to special moulds to drain. More whey may expelled by placing the moulds for two hours in a room warmed to 30°C and lightly pressing them. Next, the rounds are salted in a brine bath for 24 hours. After salting, they are ripened for two to five days in a cool (8°C), damp (90% humidity) environment. They are regularly turned over and washed during this period. At this point, the Pecorino Baccellone is ready for the table.

Rennet: liquid, calf's
Body: white, creamy
Top and bottom: flat, 15-20 cm in diameter
Height/weight: 7-15 cm / 1-3 kg
Territory of origin: the entire region

Pecorino della Garfagnana

The milk used for this Pecorino comes from Massese cattle that are raised in the wild. It is heated to 38°C and allowed to coagulate for about 20 minutes after inoculation with calf's rennet. The soft curd is then broken up into very small pieces, about the size of a grain of rice, and transferred to moulds after the whey has been drained off. Draining is completed in the moulds, although the curd may also be pressed or, very occasionally, heated in a warm room or wooden boxes. Once the firm curd is perfectly dry, the rounds are dry-salted and then left to mature for about 30 days in a cool, well-ventilated room, where they are regularly turned over and washed. Pecorino della Garfagnana is usually sold fresh, since output is very limited, but in rare cases, the cheeses are matured for about three months.

Rennet: liquid, calf's or kid's
Outer rind: firm, smooth, varying in texture, golden yellow to brown in colour
Body: firm, with faint or distinct eyes, pale to deep straw-white in colour
Top and bottom: flat, 18-22 cm in diameter
Height/weight: 7-12 cm / 1.8-3 kg
Territory of origin: the entire Garfagnana area in the province of Lucca

Pecorino della Montagna Pistoiese

This is the least famous of the many ewe's milk cheeses made in Tuscany. That may well be why it has remained faithful to the traditional technique. Crucially, Pecorino della Montagna Pistoiese is made with raw milk, which makes it a rare gem on the Tuscan cheesemaking scene. Today in the mountains of Pistoia, this ewe's milk cheese is still made the way it was a century ago. The sheep graze on high-altitude pastures, vegetable or liquid lamb's rennet is used for curdling and above all, no one has ever dreamed of pasteurising the milk. Raw milk, which is also used to make raviggiolo and ricotta, is drawn, sometimes by hand, from Massese sheep. These animals have a distinctive shiny black coat, a slightly convex head and dark, curled horns. Three types are produced. The Fresco (fresh) version matures for only 7-20 days, Abbucciato, which means "with a wrinkly skin", matures for at least 35 days and da serbo (for conserving), is aged for two or three months, and in some cases for up to year. All three are round, the first two weighing 1-1.8 kilograms while the da Asserbo version may weigh three kilograms. The rind is smooth, with a faint or marked skin, depending on maturing, and ranges from straw-yellow to grey-brown in colour. The body is ivory-white. Fresh Pecorino della Montagna Pistoiese has a marked milky note on the nose, sometimes accompanied by grassy nuances. The palate is mild, doughy in texture and reveals a faint twist of bitter honey in the finish. Abbucciato has a more intense aromatic profile veined with feral notes. Richer on the palate, it has greater complexity and a hint of chestnut in the finish. Mature Pecorino della Montagna Pistoiese has a slightly pungent aroma reminiscent of well-aged grana cheese. The nose is echoed on the palate, where a slightly tangy note emerges in the finish with attractive meadow and hay-like sensations. Pecorino della Montagna Pistoiese can be enjoyed with unsalted Tuscan bread, polenta, boiled potatoes or the traditional *necci*, chestnut fritters cooked on an open fire in terracotta dishes. The Slow Food Presidium has brought together about 20 cheesemakers to promote their products, protect the mountain pastures and ensure fair remuneration for the families that have decided to stay in, or return to, the mountains.

Rennet: liquid, lamb's or vegetable
Outer rind: smooth, with a slightly or very wrinkled skin, depending on maturing, straw-yellow to grey-brown in colour.
Body: soft, ivory-white in colour
Top and bottom: flat, 18-20 cm in diameter
Height/weight: variable / 1-3 kg
Territory of origin: the municipalities of Borgo a Bussiano, Cutigliano, Lamporecchio, Montale, Pescia, Pistoia, Piteglio, Quarrata, Sambuca Pistoiese and San Marcello Pistoiese in the province of Pistoia

Three types are produced. The Fresco (fresh) version matures for only 7-20 days, Abbucciato, which means "with a wrinkly skin", matures for at least 35 days and da Serbo (for conserving), is aged for two or three months, and in some cases for up to year.

Pecorino di Garfagnina

Currently, only two farms make cheese with milk from Garfagnina ewes. One is at Cerasa, in the municipality of Pieve Fosciana, where it is taking part in an experimental project set up by the Garfagnana Montain Community, and the other is further south, in the municipality of Fosciandora. Production is extremely limited and the cheese is sold directly at the farms. Whole raw milk is heated to 36-39°C and coagulated with sheep's or goat's rennet. After 40 minutes, the curd is milled into very small lumps, during which time it may be re-heated. The soft curd is allowed to stand for a few minutes and then kneaded by hand, pressing and stroking it to expel the whey. It is then transferred to moulds. There is a one-day interval between salting of the top and bottom. Maturing takes place on poplar wood boards in special rooms, and may last 60-180 days. In the early part of maturation, it is crucial for the cheeses to be carefully washed and dried, every day if necessary.

Rennet: powder or liquid, lamb's or kid's
Outer rind: hard, straw-yellow to golden yellow in colour
Body: compact, cream tending to straw-yellow in colour
Top and bottom: flat
Height/weight: 10 cm / 2 kg
Territory of origin: the Garfagnana area in the province of Lucca

Pecorino di Montagna

The milk, which today is invariably pasteurised and therefore needs a starter culture, is heated to 32-34°C and inoculated with calf's rennet. The soft curd is cut into small lumps, walnut-sized for cheese to be eaten fresh and rice-sized for the mature version. It is then separated from the whey and transferred to moulds to drain. The draining process is encouraged by placing the moulds in a warm room, at a temperature of no more than 35°C, for two to six hours, and pressing them lightly. Salting is carried out by immersion in a brine bath for 12-24 hours. Pecorino di Montagna then matures for 20-40 days in a cool (8°C) room at 90% humidity.

Rennet: liquid, calf's
Outer rind: faint to marked "orange-peel" effect, depending on maturing, dark brown to blackish in colour if ash is used for ageing
Body: soft, floury, white
Top and bottom: flat, 18-20 cm in diameter
Height/weight: 8-10 cm / 1.2 –2.5 kg
Territory of origin: the upper slopes and mountains of southern and central Tuscany at Amiata, Pratomagno, Colline Metallifere and Mugello

EWE'S MILK

Pecorino di Pienza

Regrettably, Pecorino di Pienza is another traditional cheese that is now almost always made with pasteurised milk. The milk is heated to between 30 and 40°C and inoculated with calf's rennet. After about half an hour, the soft curd is cut into hazelnut-sized lumps and transferred into moulds. Further draining of the whey is encouraged by placing the rounds in a room heated to about 35°C for two hours. Next comes salting, which may be either dry or in a brine bath. Pecorino di Pienza requires a ripening period of 20 days, during which time the rounds are regularly turned over and washed. Ripening takes place in a cool (10-14°C) room at 80% humidity. The last stage is maturing, which may continue for 40-60 months. During maturing, the cheeses are treated with oil and tomato.

Rennet: liquid, calf's
Outer rind: faint to marked "orange-peel" effect, depending on maturing, deep yellow tinged with pink from oil and tomato treatment during maturing
Body: firm, elastic, white tending to straw-white in colour
Top and bottom: flat, 14-20 cm in diameter
Height/weight: 4-8 cm / 0.8 –1.8 kg
Territory of origin: the southern part of the province of Siena, including the municipalities of Pienza, Montepulciano, San Quirico d'Orcia, Radicofani, Castiglion d'Orcia, Torrita di Siena, Trequanda, San Giovanni d'Asso and Montalcino

Pecorino Senese

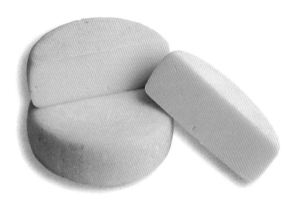

The milk is heated to 36-37°C and inoculated with calf's rennet. After 20-30 minutes, the soft curd is cut into hazelnut-sized lumps, separated from the whey, and then placed in moulds to drain. Further draining is carried out by placing the curd in wooden boxes for half an hour, in the case of fresh Pecorino Senese, and for about two hours for the mature version. Salting is normally done in a brine bath for about 12 hours but dry-salting is sometimes preferred. After ripening for 20 days at a humidity of 80-90% and a temperature of 8-10°C, the fresh cheese is ready to go on sale. Otherwise, Pecorino Senese may be matured for a moderate length of time. During maturing, it is treated with olive oil, oil dregs and tomato, and regularly turned over.

Rennet: liquid, calf's
Outer rind: yellow, tinged with other shades
Body: firm, soft, buttery, white, tending to straw-yellow in colour
Top and bottom: flat, 12-18 cm in diameter
Height/weight: 5-8 cm / 0.8 –1.2 kg
Territory of origin: Siena, neighbouring municipalities and the Sienese part of Val d'Elsa

Pecorino Toscano DOP

The name *pecorino* is a recent invention. Until the end of the Second World War, every area in Tuscany had its own name for the local *cacio* (cheese), even though the cheesemaking techniques used were very similar. Today, ewe's milk produced in the area defined by the DOP regulations is usually pasteurised to make Pecorino Toscano DOP, although there is a movement among small-scale cheesemakers to revert to using raw milk. It is coagulated by inoculation with calf's rennet at a temperature of 35-38°C, which takes about 25 minutes. If a soft cheese is required, the curd is cut into hazelnut-sized lumps. For cheese destined for longer maturing, which will have a semi-hard texture, the curd is broken into smaller pieces, and may also be reheated to 40-44°C. It is then transferred to hoops to allow the whey to drain. This is encouraged by pressing the rounds manually or by steam-treatment – a procedure that causes a rapid drop in the cheese's pH – for half an hour to three and a half hours. Salting is carried out by immersing the cheese in a brine bath for at least eight hours, in the case of the soft version, and 12-14 hours for the firm cheese. Dry-salting is also sometimes employed. The soft version matures for at least 20 days whereas semi-hard Pecorino remains in the cellar for at least four months at 8-10°C and a humidity of 80-90%. Fat in dry matter is never less that 45% in the fresh cheese, or 40% in the mature version. Pecorino Toscano DOP is made all over Tuscany, as well as in a few municipalities in Umbria (Allerona and Castiglion del Lago) and Lazio (Acquapendente, Onano, San Lorenzo Nuovo, Grotte di Castro, Gradoli, Valentano, Farnese, Ischia di Castro, Montefiascone, Bolsena and Capodimonte).

Rennet: liquid, calf's
Outer rind: yellow
Body: firm, supple
Top and bottom: flat, 15-22 cm in diameter
Height/weight: 7-11 cm / 1-3 kg
Territory of origin: the entire region, and a few municipalities in Umbria and Lazio
DOP status awarded on 1 July 1996, regulation no. 1263

The designation Pecorino Toscano embraces the whole of the region's production of this type of cheese. It includes many varieties that differ in the characteristics of the grazing territory, the breed of sheep from which the milk is drawn and the cheesemaking technique used.

Raviggiolo di Pecora

Pasteurised milk is heated to 36-37°C, salted and inoculated with calf's rennet. After about one hour, the soft curd is cut into large lumps, which are carefully removed from the whey without breaking them. These are then placed in moulds to drain. The process may be encouraged by placing the moulds in a warm room for an hour. Raviggiolo ripens at 5°C and 100% humidity for two days, after which it is ready for the table.

Rennet: liquid, calf's
Body: white with straw-white highlights
Top and bottom: flat, 12-20 cm in diameter
Height/weight: 3-6 cm / 0.5-1.2 kg
Territory of origin: the entire region

Tendaio

An ancient, uncooked, pressed curd cheese with a soft texture, Tendaio is made in limited quantities from November to April by a single craft cheesemaker. The farm is located 1,500 metres above sea level in the municipality of Castiglione di Garfagnana, in the province of Lucca. The milk is heated to 37-38°C and coagulated in 30 minutes with calf's rennet in paste form. The curd is milled into lumps the size of a grain of rice, and then extracted a few minutes later to be transferred to a mould known as a *cassina*. After being pressed down to the desired height by hand, it is left to stand for 24 hours before the surface is salted. A few days later, the cheese is removed from the mould and salted on the other surface. The cheese is placed on poplar boards for maturing and is washed carefully every day during the first fortnight of ageing. Tendaio can go on sale after maturing for 60 days, but longer maturation can coax an astonishing range of sensory perceptions from this intriguing cheese.

Rennet: paste, calf's
Outer rind: yellow tending to golden yellow in colour
Body: soft, compact, cream tending to bright yellow in colour
Top and bottom: flat
Height/weight: 8-25 cm / 2.5-3 kg
Territory of origin: the municipality of Castiglione di Garfagnana in the province of Lucca

The producers

Bacciotti
Via Campagna, 27
Località Sant'Agata
Scarperia (Firenze)
Tel. +39 055 8406905
Pecorino Toscano Dop

Bertagni
Via Provinciale
Località Pantaline, 9
Pieve Fosciana (Lucca)
Tel. +39 0583 62723 - +39 335 373463
Accasciato, Pecorino della Garfagnana

Busti
Via Marconi, 10
Località Acciaiolo
Fauglia (Pisa)
Tel. +39 050 650565
Marzolino, Pecorino Toscano Dop

Carlucci
Località Cretacci
Frazione Pomonte
Scansano (Grosseto)
Tel. +39 0564 599088
Pecorino Toscano Dop

Casa del Formaggio
Via San Nicolao
Località Metra
Minucciano (Lucca)
Tel. +39 0583 611079
Pecorino Toscano Dop

Casalfava
Località Casalfava, 68
Chiusi della Verna (Arezzo)
Tel. +39 0575 511310
Pecorino Toscano Dop

Caseificio Seggiano
Viale Trento e Trieste, 50
Seggiano (Grosseto)
Tel. +39 0564 950991 - +39 0564 950459
Marzolino, Pecorino Toscano Dop

Caseificio Sociale Cooperativo
Località La Fratta, 54
Sorano (Grosseto)
Tel. +39 0564 633002
Pecorino Toscano Dop

Caseificio Sociale Manciano
Podere Fedeletto
Località Piano di Cirignano
Manciano (Grosseto)
Tel. +39 0564 609137
Marzolino, Pecorino Toscano Dop,
Raviggiolo di Pecora

Giannetto Casula
Via Arcoveggio, 80
Quarrata (Pistoia)
Tel. +39 0573 72995
Pecorino della Montagna Pistoiese

Cerasa
Località Cerasa
Pieve Fosciana (Lucca)
Tel. +39 0583 644911
Pecorino di Garfagnina

Ciolo
Località Cellane, 6
Zona Artigianale
Castel del Piano (Grosseto)
Tel. +39 0564 956225
Marzolino, Pecorino Toscano Dop,
Raviggiolo di pPcora

Santi Cipriani
Località Lonnano Calcinaia, 95
Pratovecchio (Arezzo)
Tel. +39 0575 558137
Pecorino Toscano Dop

Damiano Corrieri
Via Goraio, 22
Località Olmi
Quarrata (Pistoia)
Tel. +39 0573 744314
Pecorino della Montagna Pistoiese

Marco Corrieri
Via della Buca, 22
Pontelungo (Pistoia)
Tel. +39 0573 911216
Pecorino della Montagna Pistoiese

Fattoria Corzano e Paterno
Via Paterno, 10
Località San Pancrazio
San Casciano in Val di Pesa (Firenze)
Tel. +39 055 8248179
Raviggiolo di Pecora

Silvana Cugusi
Via della Boccia, 8
Pienza (Siena)
Tel. +39 0578 757558
Pecorino di Pienza, Raviggiolo di Pecora

Fattoria dei Barbi
Località Podernovi, 170
Montalcino (Siena)
Tel. +39 0577 848277
Pecorino Toscano Dop

Fattoria Lischeto
Località San Giusto
Volterra (Pisa)
Tel. +39 0588 30403
Pecorino Toscano Dop, Raviggiolo di Pecora

Duilio Ferrari
Via Camogna, 21
Spignana (Pistoia)
Tel. +39 0573 677832
Pecorino della Montagna Pistoiese

Romolo Fini
Via della Cava, 6
Pontelungo (Pistoia)
Tel. +39 0573 911104
Pecorino della Montagna Pistoiese

Enrico Gaggini
Via Ponte di Sorana, 44
Pescia (Pistoia)
Tel. +39 0572 407000
Pecorino della Montagna Pistoiese

Vasco Giani
Via Panoramica, 53
San Marcello Pistoiese (Pistoia)
Tel. +39 0573 630934
Pecorino della Montagna Pistoiese

Gabriele Giannini
Podere Mavigliana, 59
Spignana (Pistoia)
Tel. +39 0573 677702
Pecorino della Montagna Pistoiese

Giuseppe Giusti
Via Capitano E. Maraviglia
Località Speri
Pescia (Pistoia)
Tel. +39 0572 476994
Pecorino della Montagna Pistoiese

Il Fiorino di Duilio Fiorini
Località Paiolaio
Roccalbegna (Grosseto)
Tel. +39 0564 989059
Pecorino Toscano Dop

Il Forteto
Strada Statale 551, km 19
Località Rossoio, 6
Vicchio (Firenze)
Tel. +39 055 8448183
Pecorino Toscano Dop

Il Tendaio
Località Tendaio - San Pellegrino in Alpe
Castiglione Garfagnana (Lucca)
Tel. +39 0583 649103
Tendaio

Renzo Innocenti
Podere La Fornace
Piteglio (Pistoia)
Tel. +39 0573 69034 - +39 0573 69051
Pecorino della Montagna Pistoiese

Marco Iori
Podere Poggio, 1887
Gavinana (Pistoia)
Tel. +39 0573 718427
Pecorino della Montagna Pistoiese

Paolo Iori
Via Croce di Vizzano, 60
Montale (Pistoia)
Tel. +39 0573 558015
Pecorino della Montagna Pistoiese

La parrina
Località Parrina
Orbetello (Grosseto)
Tel. +39 0564 862636
Caciotta Toscana, Pecorino Toscano Dop

Angelo e Fabio Lenzini
Via Ficocchio, 43
Borgo a Buggiano (Pistoia)
Tel. +39 0572 770318
Pecorino della Montagna Pistoiese

Lozzole di Francesco Lecca
Località Quadalto, 76
Palazzuolo sul Senio (Firenze)
Tel. +39 055 8046505
Pecorino Toscano Dop

Marovelli
Via della Chiesa, 14
Località Vibbiana
San Romano Garfagnana (Lucca)
Tel. +39 0583 613212
Pecorino della Garfagnana

Gabriele Matteucci
Località Canvecchio, 26
Chiusi della Verna (Arezzo)
Tel. +39 0575 599261
Pecorino Toscano Dop, Raviggiolo di
Pecora

Mauro Matteucci
Località Canvecchio, 26
Chiusi della Verna (Arezzo)
Tel. +39 0575 599262
Pecorino Toscano Dop, Raviggiolo di
Pecora

Montaione
Via del Montaione, 7
Soprana Pescia (Pistoia)
Tel. +39 0572 407031
Pecorino della Montagna Pistoiese

Valentino Nesti
Via Livogni Alto, 10
Cutigliano (Pistoia)
Tel. +39 0573 68335
Pecorino della Montagna Pistoiese

Remo Paccagnini
Via del Falchero, 82
Località Olmi
Quarrata (Pistoia)
Tel. +39 0573 718672
Pecorino della Montagna Pistoiese

Franco Pagliai
Podere Uffiziatura, 156
Frazione La Lima
San Marcello Pistoiese (Pistoia)
Tel. +39 0573 68490
Pecorino della Montagna Pistoiese

Luana Pagliai
Via della Buca, 1
Cutigliano (Pistoia)
Tel. +39 0573 68185
Pecorino della Montagna Pistoiese

Claudio Petrucci
Podere Paradiso, 116
Melo di Cutigliano (Pistoia)
Tel. +39 0573 68069
Pecorino della Montagna Pistoiese

Cavalier Emilio Pinzani
Località Castel San Gimignano
Colle Val d'Elsa (Siena)
Tel. +39 0577 953005
Marzolino, Pecorino Senese

Podere Campriano
Podere Campriano, 129
Frazione Rosia
Sovicille (Siena)
Tel. +39 0577 345560
Pecorino Toscano Dop

Podere Montapertaccio
Località Montapertaccio, 6
Castelnuovo Berardenga (Siena)
Tel. +39 0577 369044
Pecorino Toscano Dop

Fratelli Putzulu
Località Fattoria Imposto, 7
Torrita (Siena)
Tel. +39 0577 669744
Pecorino di Pienza

Riservo
Località San Quirico
Sorano (Grosseto)
Tel. +39 0564 619023
Pecorino Toscano Dop, Raviggiolo di
Pecora

Stefano Rossi
Località Gualdo, 29 a
Pratovecchio (Arezzo)
Tel. +39 0575 554033
Pecorino Toscano Dop, Raviggiolo di
Pecora

San Polo
Località San Polo, 1
Pienza (Siena)
Tel. +39 0577 665321
Pecorino di Pienza

Giuseppe Tondini
Via Di Baggio, 3
Mengarone (Pistoia)
Tel. +39 0573 46424
Pecorino della Montagna Pistoiese

Franco Torra
Via Pradarola, 2
Filattiera (Ms)
Tel. +39 0187 458526
Pecorino della Garfagnana

Vallolmo
Località Vallolmo
Pratovecchio (Arezzo)
Tel. +39 0575 558155 - +39 0575 560714
Pecorino Toscano Dop, Raviggiolo di
Pecora

Dalmazio Venturi
Via Colle e Doccia, 37
Località Iano
Pistoia
Tel. +39 0573 46739
Pecorino della Montagna Pistoiese

Catia Verdetti
Via del Guaime, 868
Gavinana (Pistoia)
Tel. +39 0573 629312
Pecorino della Montagna Pistoiese

Umbria

Pecorino di Norcia

Pecorino di Norcia

Pasteurised milk is inoculated with a thermophilic starter culture and heated to 40°C. Rennet is then added. After 20 minutes, the soft curd is cut into sweetcorn-sized granules and then placed in moulds to allow the whey to drain. Further draining is encouraged by ripening the product in large chests for three hours. Salting for 48 hours is carried out in brine baths. Pecorino di Norcia matures over 30 days in rooms at 80-90% humidity, and is then aged for up to six months, during which time the cheeses are treated with olive oil.

Rennet: paste, lamb's or kid's
Outer rind: slightly or heavily wrinkled, depending on the maturing period
Body: white tending to straw-white in colour
Top and bottom: flat, 15-25 cm in diameter
Height/weight: 8-14 cm / 3 -5 kg
Territory of origin: Upper Val Nerina, including the municipalities of Norcia, Cascia, Preci, Monteleone di Spoleto and Poggiodomo

The producers

Giustino Graziosi
Via dei Casali, 43
Località Campi
Norcia (Perugia)
Tel. +39 0743 820082
Pecorino dei Monti Sibillini

Il Quadrifoglio di Ernesto Tiberi
Località Madonna del Quattrino
Norcia (Perugia)
Tel. +39 0743 817218
Pecorino dei Monti Sibillini, Pecorino
di Norcia

Duilio Pasqua
Località Case Sparse, 307 b
Norcia (Perugia)
Tel. +39 0743 816723
Pecorino dei Monti Sibillini

Marche

Ambra di Talamello

Cacio in Forma di Limone

Caciotta del Fermano

Casciotta d'Urbino DOP

Casecc

Pecorino
  dei Monti Sibillini

Pecorino di Montagna

Ambra di Talamello

Ambra di Talamello is a formaggio di fossa, made by leaving pecorino and soft caciotta cheeses from Montefeltro to mature in the pits at Talamello. The name was invented by Tonino Guerra and refers to the colour the product acquires during the maturing process. Pecorino, caprino and caciotta cheeses a couple of months old are packed into natural fibre (cotton or hemp) sacks between mid July and the end of August, then buried in large straw-lined pits dug into the tufaceous rock. The openings are closed with wooden covers and then sealed with chalk paste. The pits are re-opened at the end of November. The product that emerges is distinctly tangy, especially if made from goat's milk, and has an intensely aromatic nose.

Rennet: variable, depending on the original cheese
Outer rind: soft, covered with green, yellowish and white mould
Body: light, flaky, crumbly, dirty white to straw-yellow or pale hazel in colour
Top and bottom: irregular
Weight: 0.8-2 kg
Territory of origin: the municipality of Talamello

Cacio in Forma di Limone

Cacio in Forma di Limone, the characteristic cheese of the Metauro valley, is made by combining two apparently incompatible components – milk and lemon. It is made only with ewe's milk from the local area, inoculated with natural rennet, again local, and involves a relatively fast cheesemaking process. The soft curd is broken up very carefully, either by hand or with special tools, into medium-sized granules and then left to stand in the whey for a few minutes before being transferred into lemon-shaped moulds. It is dry-salted with a mixture of salt and grated zest of lemon. The excess salt is removed and the cheese is washed. The next stage is to brush the cheeses with flour and water to enable the lemon rind to adhere to the surface. The product is then matured in a cool, damp room for a period of four to ten days.

Rennet: paste, lamb's
Outer rind: the outer surface of the cheeses is covered in grated lemon zest
Body: fresh, with a lemony flavour, white in colour
Top and bottom: smooth, curved
Height/weight: variable / 100-150 g
Territory of origin: the Metauro valley

Caciotta del Fermano

Caciotta del Fermano is made using varying proportions of local cow's and/or ewe's milk. The production technique is the one typically used for fresh cheeses. The milk coagulates after inoculation with rennet at 35°C. The curd is milled into large lumps, and then may be cooked again at about 45°C, or scalded in the whey. It is then removed and pressed into moulds to drain the whey, after which it is dry-salted. After ripening for 10-15 days in a cool room at average humidity, the cheese is ready for the table. Fresh Caciotta del Fermano is redolent of milk and yoghurt, with faint grassy hints. In the mouth, it is fresh, slightly acidulous, and mild. The mature version, aged for about one and a half months, has a more intense aroma of sun-dried hay. It is tangier in flavour than the fresh cheese and sometimes reveals a bitterish note in the finish.

Rennet: liquid, calf's
Outer rind: soft skin, milk-white in colour tending to straw-yellow in the fresh version, intense yellow with faint white mould when mature
Body: firm, with few eyes, white in colour
Top and bottom: flat, smooth or slightly wrinkled, 15-18 cm in diameter
Height/weight: 4-6 cm / 0.8-1.5 kg
Territory of origin: the hill country of the municipality of Fermo

Casciotta di Urbino DOP

The origins of Casciotta di Urbino are extremely ancient. It has had many famous admirers, including Clement XIV and Michelangelo. There is a sort of folk legend that attributes the product's curious name not to a dialect term but to an error of transcription committed by some faceless ministerial bureaucrat, who was misled by the local pronunciation of the word *caciotta*, or soft cheese. Whatever the truth of the matter, it is a welcome oddity as it helps to distinguish Urbino Caciotta from Montefeltro Caciotta, a very similar product although it differs in the salting and maturing techniques employed. Raw, filtered milk from two milkings (70-80% ewe's milk and the rest cow's milk) is inoculated with liquid rennet. Half an hour later, the soft curd is finely milled. It is then reheated to a temperature of 43-44°C and placed in hoops, where it is pressed with the palm of the hand to encourage draining of the whey. Salting may be either dry or in brine baths. Finally, the cheeses are matured for 15-30 days at a temperature of 10-14°C in rooms with 80-90% humidity. The resulting product has a mild, lingering flavour, a fatty, soft, straw-white texture and a thin, yellowish outer rind. Casciotta is produced all over the province of Pesaro and excellent examples may be found at Urbino, Urbania, Mercatelli, Sant'Angelo in Vado, Pioggico, Fermignano and Caglio.

Rennet: liquid, calf's
Outer rind: fairly thin, soft, springy, beige yellow in colour.
Body: firm, very crumbly, with a few eyes, straw-yellow in colour
Top and bottom: flat, round, 12-16 cm in diameter
Height/weight: 5-7 cm / 0.8-1.2 kg
Territory of origin: the province of Pesaro
DOP status awarded on 12 June 1996, regulation no. 1107

Currently, most Casciotta d'Urbino is made from pasteurised milk but experiments have shown that raw milk gives the cheese a superior sensory profile.

Casecc

Casecc is made from October to March. A typical product of the province of Pesaro and Urbino, and the Montefeltro area in particular, it is also made in the municipality of Belmonte Piceno near Fermo. The milk is inoculated with rennet and coagulated in 30 minutes. The curd is milled into rice-sized granules and then transferred to moulds. After dry-salting, the cheese ripens for ten days on wooden shelves in cool, moist rooms before maturing in the cellar, a process that last for anything from a month to a year. The cheeses are first placed on walnut leaves, and then transferred to traditional terracotta jars. Casecc is squarish in shape, has a creamy body with only a few eyes, and tends to be runny when sliced. The nose is reminiscent of grass, walnut-skin, hazelnuts, topsoil and field mushrooms. On the palate, it is mild and only faintly savoury, with an intense, lingering finish.

Rennet: liquid, calf's
Outer rind: smooth, translucent, intense straw-yellow in colour, sometimes with orangey tinges
Body: creamy, with few eyes, yellow in colour
Top and bottom: flat, rectangular 20-22 cm
Height/weight: 2.5-3 cm / 1.3 kg
Territory of origin: the province of Pesaro and Urbino, in particular the Montefeltro area, and the municipality of Belmonte Piceno near Fermo

Pecorino dei Monti Sibillini

Pecorino is made in almost every part of the National Park. Both the park and the ewe's milk cheese take their name from Monte Sibilla (2,173 metres). There are two versions of the cheese, a fresh ewe's milk product that is available all year round, and is made from pasteurised milk by industrial dairies, and the semi-cooked, raw milk mature version. Only the second type is protected by the Slow Food Presidium. It has survived solely thanks to the efforts of one or two enthusiasts who still breed the rare local Sopravvissane sheep and employ the traditional cheese-making technique. The Presidium's goal is to recover the breed, restore the cheesemaking and maturing facilities, coordinate the producers, some of whom make cheese for domestic consumption, and promote their product. The traditional procedure involves putting freshly drawn milk in a copper cauldron and heating it to 37-38°C. It is then inoculated with natural rennet. The local women still make rennet by drying a lamb's stomach full of curdled milk and then mixing the finely ground contents with a little salt and milk. Every household has its own recipe. Wild thyme, marjoram, basil, bramble shoots, pepper, oil, cloves or even figs, honey or egg yolk may be added to the mixture. After 20-30 minutes, the curd is broken up and heated to 45-48°C by increasing the heat under the cauldron. It is then transferred to moulds. After pressing, the cheese is dry-salted for a couple of days, washed, dried and then placed to mature in a cool, slightly damp environment. Every two or three days, the cheeses are turned over to encourage the rind to form. At about 30 days, the cheese is known as *barzotto*, and is ready for the table, but it is at its peak after several months. The rind acquires a golden, ochre or hazelnut colour. The bright yellow body is compact and slightly fatty, with a rock-hard, flaky texture. On the nose, it is lingering and aromatic, often redolent of mushrooms and truffles, with a full, tangy flavour good complexity and lingering persistence. Whey left over from the curdling of the milk is used to make an excellent ricotta, either fresh or salted for maturing. Traditionally, the firm-textured, tangy salted ricotta is used as a grating cheese in a number of traditional local pasta dishes.

Rennet: liquid, lamb's, aromatised in various ways
Outer rind: soft, straw-yellow in colour when fresh, hard, golden yellow, dappled with rust-coloured patches when mature
Body: firm, with few eyes, white in colour
Top and bottom: flat, 14-20 cm in diameter
Height/weight: 4-9 cm / 0.8-2.5 kg
Territory of origin: the Monti Sibillini area in the provinces of Ascoli Piceno, Macerata and Perugia

This semi-cooked, mature ewe's milk cheese is supported by a Slow Food Presidium. Pecorino dei Monti Sibillini is made with raw milk from the rare local Sopravvissane sheep.

Pecorino di Montagna

To make Pecorino di Montagna, freshly drawn milk heated to a temperature of 36-37°C is inoculated with rennet in paste. After coagulation, the soft curd is broken up by hand or with a *spino* (curd knife) into hazelnut-sized pieces for the fresh cheese, and rice-sized granules for the mature product. The curd may be semi-cooked by reheating it to 45-48°C, after which is transferred into moulds where it is lightly pressed by hand. When the cheese is dry, it is dry-salted by covering it completely and allowing it to absorb the salt naturally. Two days later, the cheeses go into a cool, moderately humid room, where they will remain for a minimum of 20 days. During maturing, the cheeses are turned over daily and washed every other day with water and warm whey.

Rennet: paste, kid's or lamb's, the rennet may be aromatised with local herbs
Outer rind: hard, firm, smooth, yellowish in colour
Body: firm, with a few eyes, ivory or straw-white in colour
Top and bottom: flat, 15-20 cm in diameter
Height/weight: 6-10 cm / 1-2.5 kg
Territory of origin: the mountainous areas of the region

The producers

Agriturismo degli Alti Pascoli
Contrada Sant'Ilario, 10
Fiastra (Macerata)
Tel. +39 0737 52588 - +39 0737 52151
Pecorino dei Monti Sibillini

Cooperativa Agricola del Petrano
Via Gucci, 7
Cagli (Pesaro Urbino)
Tel. +39 0721 782825
Casciotta d'Urbino Dop

Fattoria della Ripa
Via Tre Ponti, 21
Orciano (Pesaro Urbino)
Tel. +39 0721 977605
Cacio in Forma di Limone, Pecorino di
Montagna

Fattoria Lucarini
Frazione Casavecchia
Pieve Torina (Macerata)
Tel. +39 0737 510145
Pecorino dei Monti Sibillini

Fattorie Marchigiane
Via Cerbara, 81
Montemaggiore al Metauro
(Pesaro Urbino)
Tel. +39 0721 87981
Casciotta d'Urbino Dop

Fontegranne
Via Castellarso Ete, 11
Belmonte Piceno (Ascoli Piceno)
Tel. +39 0734 771192
Caciotta del Fermano, Raviggiolo,
Squaquarone

Lina Lambertucci e Erolo Ossoli
Località Pagliano, 395
Matelica (Macerata)
Tel. +39 0737 84777
Pecorino di Montagna

Antonio Ruggi
Via Madonna di Piana, 5
Amandola (Ascoli Piceno)
Tel. +39 360 9182600
Pecorino dei Monti Sibillini

Società Pettacci
Via XXIV Maggio, 5
Visso (Macerata)
Tel. +39 0737 9282
Pecorino dei Monti Sibillini

Val Senatello
Via Lamone
Casteldelci (Pesaro Urbino)
Tel. +39 0541 915465
Pecorino di Montagna

Lazio

Caciofiore della
  Campagna Romana ●

Caciotta di Bufala
  di Amaseno

Caciotta Romana

Marzolina ●

Pecorino del Pastore

Ricotta Romana

Scacione or Caprone

Caciofiore della Campagna Romana

It is the proteolytic action of the enzymes from a flower, the cardoon that grows in the Roman countryside, that produces Caciofiore della Campagna Romana. It is one of the world's most characteristic ewe's milk cheeses, and a product protected by a Slow Food Presidium. The yellowish rind protects a heart of soft cheese. Its unexpected creaminess reveals an intense, slightly bitter flavour that is not salty. The purplish blue flowers of the cardoon are picked during the summer, and left to dry in the dark for four or five days. The dried petals are then steeped in water for a day, and filtered with a cloth. The resulting rennet is usually prepared the day before cheesemaking. A vat containing ewe's milk at a constant temperature of 38°C is inoculated with the vegetable rennet and then allowed to sour for about an hour. The curd is cut for the first time, with a long, smooth blade, into chunky cubes with a base of about six centimetres. It is milled for a second time, with a strainer, 20 minutes later. Since the texture of the curd is blancmange-like, the pieces are fairly large and irregularly shaped. The curd is then placed in moulds for 24 hours to allow the whey to drain, and the cheese to acquire its traditional brick shape. After dry-salting, the cheese is transferred to the maturing room, where it stays for 35-40 days at a temperature of 7-10°C and 90-95% humidity. With its balanced, mouthfilling flavour, Caciofiore della Campagna Romana has a very distinctive personality. The body is moist, soft, firm and crumbly. It is slightly paler in colour than the rind, and the eyes are sparse and irregular. On the nose, there are notes of damp hay and cooked country greens, lifted by a harmonious barnyardy note. The creamy, melt-in-the-mouth palate offers vegetal nuances, an attractively clean, fattiness and a discreetly pungent astringency in the finish.

Rennet: cardoon
Outer rind: thin, straw-yellow in colour
Body: soft, firm, flaky, occasionally creamy, slightly paler than the rind, with irregular, sparsely distributed eyes
Top and bottom: flat, with a few faint cracks, 20 cm long
Height/weight: 3 cm / 600 g
Territory of origin: the countryside around Rome

The yellowish rind protects a heart of almost liquid cheese. Its unexpected creaminess reveals an intense, slightly bitter flavour that is not salty.

Caciotta di Bufala di Amaseno

A maseno is a small village in the province of Frosinone that falls within the production zone of mozzarella di bufala DOP (see entry). A small caciotta producer is active in the village. Raw, whole milk is heated to 35°C and coagulated with kid's rennet. After 50 minutes, the curd is milled and the semi-solid mass is transferred to moulds. Half an hour later, the cheeses are dry-salted. They will mature for up to 24 months in glass containers in cool, dark cellars. During this period, they are brushed periodically with olive oil and vinegar. The flavour is mild when the cheese is fresh but as maturing progresses, it acquires complexity and pungency.

Rennet: paste, kid's
Outer rind: skin white tending to straw-yellow in colour
Body: firm, white in colour
Top and bottom: faintly lined, about 8 cm in diameter
Height/weight: 8 cm / 250-300 g
Territory of origin: the municipality of Amaseno, in the province of Frosinone

Caciotta Romana

This cheese is usually made with pasteurised milk, heated to 36°C and inoculated with lamb's rennet. The soft curd is milled first into walnut-sized lumps. The temperature is then raised to 38°C, when it is cut again into smaller pieces. At this point, the curd is left to ripen in the whey for a short while before it is drained for four or five hours in a warm room. Subsequently, the firm curd is pressed and left to stand for 12-18 hours. Salting is carried out either in a brine bath (eight hours per kilogram), or dry using coarse salt. At this stage, the Caciotta is ready for sale as Primo Sale (first salting), or it may be left to mature for 15 days and sold as a fresh cheese. Alternatively, it may be matured in cool rooms, at 10°C, where the cheeses are washed approximately once a month.

Rennet: paste, lamb's
Outer rind: rindless when fresh, straw-yellow in colour with greenish tinges when mature
Body: white, with very few, large eyes
Top and bottom: flat, 15-25 cm in diameter
Height/weight: 7 cm / 1.5-3 kg
Territory of origin: the Agro Romano countryside

Marzolina

A small cheese, Marzolina takes its name from the month of March, the earliest period of goat lactation, as it was once only produced at that time. The historic production zone is on the slopes of the Monti Ausoni, especially Esperia. With the increase in goat farming in the north of the province of Frosinone, production of the cheese has spread to Val di Comino. Milk from two milkings is inoculated with kid's rennet. The curd is cut up and put into moulds to drain. The cheeses are hand-pressed and salted either dry or in brine. Marzolina may be eaten fresh but traditionally it is left to ripen for a few days on wooden racks, and then matured for several months in glass jars. Some producers mature their cheeses dry, whereas others top up the jars with olive oil. The dry-matured version has more markedly tangy notes. The olive oil-steeped product matures more slowly and stays softer. The cheese is elongated and cylindrical in shape. It has no rind but does present a hard, dry skin. The body is white, firm and flaky, with a few eyes. Milk-white in colour when fresh, it becomes ivory-white after maturing for seven or eight months in olive oil. Marzolina is dry and hard in texture, and is rendered only slightly doughy by steeping in olive oil. The nose has the feral note typical of goat's milk cheeses. The fresh version of Marzolina is fairly mild, rich and oily. Long maturing gives it a stronger flavour and a tangy, but not pungent, finish.

Marzolina had disappeared almost entirely. Then after a period in the doldrums, it was rediscovered by a young cheesemakers, who started to farm goats again. A modest level of production has now been resumed, thanks to a far-sighted cheesemaker in Esperia, who passed the technique on this producer. There is no native local breed of goat. Most producers farm Camosciata delle Alpi animals. The production regulations of the Slow Food Presidium set up to protect and promote Marzolina stipulate that goats should be free-range farmed throughout the grazing period.

Rennet: paste, kid's
Outer rind: skin, pale yellow in colour
Body: white, firm, slightly grainy
Top and bottom: flat, 7-8 cm in diameter
Height/weight: 7-8 cm (if cylindrical) / 70-250 g
Territory of origin: the Lazio side of the National Park of Abruzzo, Lazio and Molise, particularly the municipalities of Campoli Appennino, Gallinaro and Villa Latina in the province of Frosinone

Marzolina may be eaten fresh but traditionally, it is ripened on wooden racks and then put into glass jars, on its own or in olive oil, to mature.

Pecorino del Pastore

The milk is filtered and heated to a temperature of 27-35°C, when it is inoculated with lamb's rennet in paste. The curd forms in about 20 minutes and is left to stand for a further 20 minutes. It is then transferred to moulds and perforated through the middle to allow the whey to drain. Next, it is kneaded by hand in the moulds for 20 minutes. Salting is carried out either dry with coarse or white salt, or in a brine bath, for about 12 hours. The cheese must ripen for 20-30 days before it is ready for consumption, after which maturing may take place in the cellar for up to four or five months. During this procedure, the cheeses are kept under oil.

Rennet: paste, lamb's
Outer rind: golden-yellow in colour
Body: white, almost or completely free of eyes and edged with oil-derived "tears"
Top and bottom: flat, 12 cm in diameter
Height/weight: 10 cm / 1-5 kg
Territory of origin: the provinces of Rieti, Frosinone and Latina

Ricotta Romana

True Ricotta Romana is produced only in the Agro Romano area, even though the term has now come to indicate almost any kind of ricotta, including industrial products. The traditional ricotta technique is employed. The milk is heated to 85-90°C, until the solids rise to the surface. Cheesemakers still strike the bottom of the cheese vat with a stick and listen to the sound to decide when to remove the mass of protein. The froth is skimmed off and the ricotta is taken out, to be placed in rush baskets. The addition of acidity regulators is strictly forbidden.

Body: soft, easy-to-spread, slightly grainy, chalk-white in colour with brown highlights
Top and bottom: irregular
Height/weight: varying, up to 2 kg
Territory of origin: the Agro Romano countryside

Scacione or Caprone

Once, only goat's milk was used to make this cheese and that is why some people even today refer to it as Caprone (literally, "billy goat"). A versatile cheese to be eaten soon after purchase, Scacione is generally served in salads, but it may also be fried or used as a pizza topping. Today, only cow's milk pasteurised at 72°C is used. The milk is cooled to 36°C and inoculated with calf's rennet in pellets. After 20 minutes, the soft curd is milled roughly for the first time and left to stand for a few minutes in the warm whey. It is then milled again into smaller, walnut-sized lumps. The firm curd is now left in the moulds to drain. Salting is carried out while the product is in this form. After draining for about one and a half hours, the Scacione is ready to go on sale.

Rennet: paste, lamb's
Outer rind: vestigial skin
Body: white, soft
Top and bottom: flat, irregular
Height/weight: 12 cm / 1.5 kg
Territory of origin: the Agro Pontino countryside

The producers

Agricola zootecnica Roana
Via Migliara 46-9
Sezze (Latina)
Tel. +39 0773 899402
Mozzarella di Bufala Campana Dop,
Provola Affumicata di Bufala

Acquaranda
Via Provinciale km 6,300
Trevignano Romano (Rome)
Tel. +39 06 9985301
Caciofiore della Campagna Romana

Loris Benacquista
Via Capranica, 11
Campoli Appennino (Frosinone)
Tel. +39 0776 884085
Marzolina

Brunelli
Via della Stazione di Prima Porta, 20
Rome
Tel. +39 06 33610144
Caciotta Romana

Buonanno
Via Mola della Corte, 7-9
Fondi (Latina)
Tel. +39 0771 513011
Mozzarella di Bufala Campana Dop

Casabianca
Via Sant'Anastasia, 3
Fondi (Latina)
Tel. +39 0771 556203
Mozzarella di Bufala Campana Dop

Cesarina
Riserva Naturale della Marcigliana
Via della Cesarina, 212
Rome
Tel. +39 06 41400685
Fior di Latte, Ricotta di Latte Vaccino

Cooperativa Agricola Stella
Via Selvina, 1
Amaseno (Frosinone)
Tel. +39 0775 658365
Caciotta di bufala di Amaseno,
Mozzarella di Bufala Campana Dop

Cooperativa La Collinetta
Via della Falcognana, 30
Località Divino Amore
Rome
Tel. +39 06 7138084
Caciotta Romana

Cooperativa Agricoltura Nuova
Riserva Naturale di Decima Malafede
Via Valle di Perna, 315
Rome
Tel. +39 06 5070453
Caciofiore della Campagna Romana,
Ricotta Romana

Cooperativa Produttori Latte Amatrice
Località Ponte Sommati
Amatrice (Rieti)
Tel. +39 0746 826471
Caciotta Romana, Ricotta Romana

Carla D'Eramo
Via Casale, 2
San Donato Val di Comino (Frosinone)
Tel. +39 0776 508852 - +39 349 3706167
Marzolina

De Juliis
Via Giovanni Gregorio Mendel, 151
Rome
Tel. +39 06 7139146
Caciofiore della Campagna Romana,
Ricotta Romana

Il Pino di Domenico Stocchi
Via Andreassi, 30
Rome
Tel. +39 337 560560 - +39 333 7036380
Caciofiore della Campagna Romana

La Pisana
Strada Provinciale Marittima II
Località Fossanova
Priverno (Latina)
Tel. +39 0773 939054
Mozzarella di Bufala Campana Dop

Lopez
Via di Boccea, 472
Rome
Tel. +39 06 6144724
Ricotta Romana

Piccola Cooperativa San Fedele
Via San Fedele
San Donato Val di Comino (Frosinone)
Tel. +39 349 1236714
Pecorino del Parco

Sergio Pitzalis
Via Settevene Palo, 39
Bracciano (Rome)
Tel. +39 06 9987072
Caciofiore della Campagna Romana

Tor San Giovanni
Riserva Naturale della Marcigliana
Via di Tor San Giovanni, 301
Rome
Tel. +39 06 87122260
Ricotta Romana

Abruzzo and Molise

Cacio in Asse

Caciocavallo di Agnone

Caciofiore Aquilano

Canestrato
di Castel del Monte ●

Caprino di Montefalcone
del Sannio

Formaggella del Sannio

Formaggio di Pietracatella

Marcetto

Pecorino Abruzzese

Pecorino del Matese

Pecorino del Parco

Pecorino del Sannio

Pecorino di Atri

Pecorino di Capracotta

Pecorino di Farindola ●

Ricotta al Fumo di Ginepro

Scamorza Molisana

Stracciata

Treccia di Santa Croce
di Magliano

Cacio in Asse

Made from raw Bruna Alpina cow's milk, Cacio in Asse is a recently invented cheese that has already won first prize at the 2003 Formaggi d'Autore national cheese competition, held at Saint Vincent. The stretched curd technique is used. First, the milk is coagulated with a paste of kid's rennet in a copper container called a *caccavo*. The cheese is hung to mature in natural caves for more than a year. Since the cheeses are large, they are not only tied at the top. A stout cord is used to support the considerable weight, which leaves a clearly visible mark on the surface and gives the cheese its characteristic shape. The body has few eyes and oozes fat. The nose presents attractive contrasting vegetal and feral notes, its milk and cooked butter aromas mingling with tangy sensations. The palate has a grainy mouth-feel and a deliciously melt-in-the-mouth texture.

Rennet: paste, kid's
Outer rind: smooth, hard, brownish in colour
Body: firm, fatty, with uniform flakes, ivory-white in colour
Top and bottom: curved, 25-30 cm high
Height/weight: 18-24 cm / 6-10 kg
Territory of origin: the municipality of Casacalenda, in the province of Campobasso

Caciocavallo di Agnone

The milk is heated to a temperature of 37°C and inoculated with a paste of lamb's or kid's rennet, according to the degree of piquancy desired. Coagulation takes about 50 minutes. The resulting soft curd is cut into rough lumps and the whey is partially extracted. The curd is then milled into tiny granules and left to ripen in warm whey (45-50°C) for several hours. Next, it is extracted from the remaining whey, cut into slices, and placed in water heated to a temperature of 80°C, where the stretching process begins. When the now firm curd has become sufficiently elastic to be modelled into a large pear shape, it is immersed in a brine bath for a period that can vary from 12-20 hours. The cheeses are then tied together in pairs and put in a cool, well-aired room to mature for approximately 20 days. This is the first step in the ageing process, which traditionally takes place in caves at a constant temperature, and lasts anywhere from three months to a year.

Rennet: paste, lamb's or kid's
Outer rind: smooth, thin, hard, light brown in colour
Body: solid, occasional cracks, straw-coloured varying in intensity
Top and bottom: curved, 16-22 cm in diameter
Height/weight: 18-28 cm / 1.5-3 kg
Territory of origin: the entire region, notably Upper Molise

Caciofiore Aquilano

This fresh, delicate cheese is traditionally associated with the province of L'Aquila, where it has always been made using vegetable rennet obtained from an infusion of the flowers of the wild artichoke (*Carlina acaulis*). Production was abandoned for about 60 years before a tenacious Castel del Monte cheesemaker revived the tradition. Whole raw milk is filtered and brought to a temperature of 36-37°C. A whey or milk starter culture may be added to encourage souring. After coagulation with the cardoon rennet, the curd is left to stand for 30-40 minutes. It is then cut up twice, roughly the first time, then into smaller sweetcorn-sized lumps. The curd is then removed by hand and transferred into the baskets that give it its characteristic shape. The Caciofiore then drains on an inclined board for two days, during which time it is turned over at least four times. It matures for 20-40 days.

Rennet: wild artichoke
Body: soft, creamy, cream white in colour with no eyes
Top and bottom: 13-15 cm in diameter
Height/weight: 7-8 cm / 0.5-1 kg
Territory of origin: the province of L'Aquila

EWE'S MILK
Canestrato di Castel del Monte

More than 300 different fodder plants have been identified on the pastures of Gran Sasso. Over the centuries, this rich grazing and the dry, high-altitude climate have encouraged sheep farming, and the seasonal transfer of flocks here from other areas. The symbol of traditional Abruzzo sheep farming is Campo Imperatore, in the Gran Sasso and Monti della Laga National Park, where thousands of animals are taken every year to graze on a 19 kilometre-long plateau 1,800 metres above sea level. For at least 2,000 years, shepherds have been bringing their flocks here along the grassy tracks that lead up and down the mountainside. Local farmers also use these pastures, moving their flocks from other parts of the national park to ensure their sheep have seven to nine months' grazing in the open air. Much of Campo Imperatore lies in the municipal territory of Castel del Monte, which boasts a fine tradition of high-quality cheesemaking. Milk from the locally grazed animals, most of which are Sopravvissana or Gentile di Puglia sheep, is used on its own for cheesemaking. All the farmers have their own personal technique but broadly speaking, the raw milk is filtered, heated to 35-40°C for 15-25 minutes and inoculated with natural lamb's rennet. The curd is broken up into sweetcorn-sized lumps, and then usually cooked at 40-45°C for about 15 minutes before being transferred into baskets and pressed to expel any remaining whey. After salting, the cheeses are placed on wooden boards in a cool, well-ventilated room. Maturing can last for anything from two months to a year, during which time the cheeses are periodically brushed with olive oil. The mature cheese is sold in rounds of varying sizes. It is hard, with a sharp, tangy flavour, making it excellent for the table or for grating. The tradition of moving flocks to summer pastures is gradually disappearing. Fewer and fewer shepherds make the journey to the pastures of the Gran Sasso, partly because of the difficulties associated with making raw-milk cheese in poorly equipped, unlicensed mountain diaries. The Slow Food Presidium was set up to draw attention to the cheesemakers' predicament. In collaboration with the Gran Sasso and Monti della Laga National Park, the Presidium aims to support cheesemaking and turn it into an opportunity for employment and growth.

Rennet: paste, lamb's
Outer rind: hard, with the characteristic furrows left by the rush baskets, dark hazel in colour with patches of mould
Body: firm, with sparsely distributed eyes, creamy shading into straw yellow in colour as the cheese matures
Top and bottom: flat or convex
Height/weight: 0.5-2.5 kg
Territory of origin: the municipalities of Barisciano, Calascio, Carapelle Calvisio, Castel del Monte, Castelvecchio Calvisio, Filetto, Paganica, Camarda e Assergi, Ofena, San Pio delle Camere, Santo Stefano di Sessanio, Villa Santa Lucia in the province of L'Aquila

Maturing can last for anything from two months to a year, during which time the cheeses are periodically brushed with olive oil.

Caprino di Montefalcone del Sannio

Molise has many goat farmers, most with free-range flocks, so caprino cheeses are made all over the region. One particularly well-known example is Caprino di Montefalcone del Sannio, made from April to September with raw milk from the native local breed of goat. Rennet is added to the milk after it has been heated to 38°C. After about 30 minutes, the now firm curd is milled into small pieces. It is allowed to settle on the bottom of the recipient as the temperature is raised to 42°C. When the soft curd has solidified, it is removed from the vat and pressed into rush baskets. The baskets are then immersed in the hot whey from ricotta making. The cheeses are dry-salted for 24 hours before maturing for at least two months in cool, well-ventilated cellars, where they are hung from the ceiling in traditional wooden holders known as *cascere*.

Rennet: kid's
Outer rind: slightly wrinkled, straw-yellow in colour
Body: soft, moist, chalk-white in colour
Top and bottom: flat, 15-17 cm in diameter
Height/weight: 6-8 cm / 500-600 g
Territory of origin: the entire region, in particular the municipality of Montefalcone del Sannio

Formaggella del Sannio

This is essentially a new type of cheese that follows the traditional pecorino production process of the area. The producer came up with idea of using a small dose of rennet to coagulate the ewe's milk so that it retains as far as possible the characteristic aromas of the grazing pastures. The milk is heated to a temperature of no more than 30°C, a small amount of rennet is added and the mixture is left to coagulate for several hours until the curd sours. When it has reached the required level of acidity, the curd is cut up into fairly large lumps to ensure that the cheese will remain relatively moist. It is then put into moulds, lightly pressed and immersed briefly in brine. Finally, the cheese is placed in damp, cold stone cellars where the remaining whey drains off and the outer rind forms.

Rennet: liquid, lamb's or kid's
Outer rind: slightly wrinkled as a result of the whey naturally draining off, greyish-brown in colour
Body: soft, moist, chalk-white in colour
Top and bottom: flat, 15-20 cm in diameter
Height/weight: 4-6 cm / 500-700 g
Territory of origin: Sannio

Formaggio di Pietracatella

This cheese is made with raw milk from grazing animals and is a typical product of the Fortore area of Molise, particularly the municipality of Pietracatella in the province of Campobasso. The milk is heated to 37°C. Rennet is added, and the milk is left to coagulate for about 30 minutes. The curd is cut up with a curd knife and allowed to settle on the bottom of the vat as the temperature is raised to more than 40°C. The curd is then removed from the vat and pressed into rush baskets. The cheeses are dry-salted and left to ripen for at least two months in the traditional tufa caves, known as *mogie*, which are situated under the homes in the historic centre of Pietracella. Cheese-making continues all year round.

Rennet: kid's, calf's or lamb's
Outer rind: slightly wrinkled, straw-yellow in colour
Body: soft, moist, white tending to yellow in colour with maturing
Top and bottom: flat, 15-20 cm in diameter
Height/weight: 6-8 cm / 500 g-4 kg
Territory of origin: the Fortore area of Molise, in particular the municipality of Pietracatella

Marcetto

The basic ingredient of Marcetto is over-ripe pecorino cheese and the cheesemaking process consists solely of the steps necessary to salvage the "bad" pecorino. Marcetto is produced throughout the region of Abruzzo, but the version from the Upper Teramo area is particularly prized. The ageing process lasts for about a year. Inside, the cheese is pale pink and has an extremely tangy flavour while the aroma is strong and pungent. Marcetto, also known as Formaggio Puntato (pitted cheese), is characterised by the presence of *saltarelli*, or "hoppers". These are maggots, the larvae of the cheese fly, *Piophila casei*, which grow inside the cheese.

Body: creamy, variable in consistency, pinkish-white in colour
Territory of origin: the entire region

Pecorino Abruzzese

Rennet is added to raw ewe's milk that has been heated to 38°C, and the mixture is left to coagulate for about one hour. The resulting curd is broken up by hand into fairly large lumps and allowed to stand for a few minutes. This firm curd is then pressed by hand, placed in rush baskets and pressed again. After pressing, the curd is cooked by immersion in boiling whey for a few minutes. It is then dried for two days and salted, usually in a brine bath. After 20 days, during which time it is left in a warm, well-ventilated room, the cheese is mature. To ensure that the rounds are aged to perfection, they are left for a further month and then rubbed with olive oil.

Rennet: liquid, lamb's or kid's
Outer rind: hard, wrinkled, in various shades of brown, sometimes with a slight bloom
Body: solid, open, straw-coloured
Top and bottom: flat, 14-22 cm in diameter
Height/weight: 4-10 cm / 1-3 kg
Territory of origin: the entire region

Pecorino del Matese

This cheese is made from April to September with milk from Pagliarola ewes (75%) mixed with goat's milk (25%). The milk used generally comes from grazing animals. Milk from two milkings is heated to a temperature of 38-40°C in a copper vat. Rennet is added, and the mixture reaches the desired consistency in about 30 minutes. The soft curd is then broken into very small pieces and pushed to help it to settle on the bottom of the vat. When the soft curd has settled, it is removed and placed in baskets to acquire its final shape. It is pressed to expel the whey. The cheeses are dry-salted for two days. Maturing in cool, well-ventilated rooms takes from a minimum of three months to more than a year. As they mature, the cheeses are periodically washed with oil and vinegar, and turned over for at least two months.

Rennet: paste, lamb's or kid's
Outer rind: hard, lined, acquiring a hazelnut colour with maturing
Body: with sparsely distributed eyes, white tending to straw-yellow in colour
Top and bottom: flat, 14-22 cm in diameter
Height/weight: 4-9 cm / 0.8-3 kg
Territory of origin: the Matese massif

Pecorino del Parco

The method used to produce this pecorino is little different from the technique used to make the classic ewe's milk cheeses of Abruzzo. In the National Park area, three young producers have "gone green" and are producing an organically farmed pecorino. Raw milk is heated to 38°C, liquid rennet is added and the mixture is left to coagulate for 20 minutes. When it has coagulated, the curd is divided into nuggets and left to stand for a few minutes. It is then semi-cooked briefly at a temperature of 42°C, wrapped in cloths, pressed by hand and transferred to rush baskets. At this point, there is a variation on the classic procedure in that the firm curd is not cooked so that the product will retain its natural aroma. It is then salted in a brine bath and subsequently matured for a minimum of 60 days.

Rennet: liquid, lamb's
Outer rind: hard, solid, smooth or wrinkled, brown tending to dark brown in colour
Body: solid, slightly open, straw-white in colour
Top and bottom: flat, 14-20 cm in diameter
Height/weight: 4-8 cm / 1-3 kg
Territory of origin: the National Park area of Abruzzo

Pecorino del Sannio

Pecorino del Sannio is made from Comisana ewe's milk using a production process that differs considerably from classic Italian methods. First, the raw milk is filtered and then heated to a temperature of only 30°C. A very small amount of rennet is added, so the milk may take up to six hours to coagulate. The process is, in fact, rennet-assisted lactic acid coagulation. The soft curd is milled into pieces the size of a grain of rice, poured into moulds, pressed by hand and turned over several times in its moulds. When it has dried out, it is dry-salted. The cheeses are then placed in a damp, well-ventilated cave where they are left for 50-90 days. During maturation, the rind is oiled regularly.

Rennet: paste, lamb's
Outer rind: hard, slightly wrinkled, very dark brown to black
Body: firm, fine, rather crumbly, lustrous ivory white in colour
Top and bottom: flat, 18-25 cm in diameter
Height/weight: 4-6 cm / 1.3-1.7 kg
Territory of origin: the Molise side of the Sannio area

Ewe's milk

Pecorino di Atri

Pecorino di Atri is made in spring and summer. The milk is heated to 38°C and coagulated with liquid rennet obtained from a dried, chopped pig's stomach steeped in white wine with chilli peppers, herbs and spices. After about one hour, the curd is cut and left to stand for five minutes at a constant temperature. The mass is removed, transferred to rush baskets and pressed by hand. It is then scalded for a few minutes in hot whey and left to stand for 48 hours, during which time it is turned three or four times a day. After salting, dry or in a brine bath, Pecorino di Atri is matured for a period that can vary from 40 days to two years. It can be aromatised with spices and conserved in the dark for eight months, under olive oil, in glass containers. Pecorino di Atri is also sometimes aged under bran. For this procedure, the outer rind is first washed with a mixture of olive oil and vinegar every fortnight for about two months.

Rennet: liquid, pig's
Outer rind: hard, lined, pale to dark straw-yellow in colour
Body: firm, with variously shaped eyes, cream tending to straw-yellow in colour, slightly pinkish if the cheese is conserved in oil
Top and bottom: flat
Height/weight: variable / 0.5-3 kg
Territory of origin: the municipality of Atri in the province of Teramo

Pecorino di Capracotta

Pecorino di Capracotta has been produced since the times of the ancient Samnites, who originally colonised this territory. The milk is first heated to a temperature of 37°C. Then rennet is added and after approximately 20-30 minutes, when coagulation has taken place, the soft curd is broken up into tiny granules the size of a grain of rice. These granules are wrapped in a cloth and part-cooked at a temperature of 42-45°C for a few minutes, then put into moulds. The firm curd is then cooked and dry-salted. This cheese has an extremely pungent smell and a very tangy flavour when aged. It is particularly delicious when dipped in egg and fried.

Rennet: paste or liquid, lamb's or kid's
Outer rind: hard, solid, yellow-brown in colour
Body: fatty, hard, semi-cooked, straw-white in colour
Top and bottom: flat, 14-22 cm in diameter
Height/weight: 4-9 cm / 1-2.5 kg
Territory of origin: the municipalities of Capracotta, Agnone, Carovilli, Vastogirardi, San Pietro Avellana and Pescopennataro

EWE'S MILK

Pecorino di Farindola

This pecorino is made in a limited area on the eastern side of the Gran Sasso massif. Pecorino di Farindola is a very special cheese because it is coagulated with pig's rennet, which gives it its characteristic aroma and flavour. Pig's rennet has been produced since classical times, and making it remains today, as it was in the past, a task that is carried out exclusively by women, who pass the recipe from mother to daughter. The milk comes from hand-milked sheep from the Pagliarola breed native to the Apennines. The sheep graze freely in their pastures and yield a very limited quantity of milk. The raw milk is heated to 35°C and the curd is milled into sweetcorn-sized lumps. The soft curd is then removed from the vat and placed in wicker baskets that leave the character-istic lines on the cheese's surface. After dry-salting, which is car-ried out within 48 hours, the cheeses are left to mature in old wooden kneading troughs for a period ranging from 40 days to more than a year. The rind is periodically brushed with a mixture of extra virgin olive oil and vinegar, or sometimes with tomato conserve, and acquires a colour that varies from pale yellow to saf-fron, depending on how long it has aged. The body of the cheese is grainy, straw-yellow in colour and slightly moist, even when it has matured for a long time. This is due to the rennet and the method of cheesemaking. The moisture gives the product a slight-ly musty aroma of mushrooms, noble rot and dry wood. On the palate, it has an amazingly doughy texture and excellent balance, the tangy sensations complementing the delicious flavour of sheep's milk. Pecorino di Farindola is produced by only a few families, who make it almost exclusively for their own consumption and pass the recipe from one generation to the next. The Slow Food Presidium aims to safeguard and support the production of this unique cheese, thus promoting its territory of origin.

Rennet: liquid, pig's
Outer rind: smooth, varying in colour from yellow-brown to reddish
Body: solid, slightly open, from light to dark straw-yellow in colour
Top and bottom: flat, 14-22 cm in diameter
Height/weight: 4-8 cm / 1-3 kg
Territory of origin: the municipalities of Farindola, Montebello di Bertona, Villa Celiera, Carpineto della Nora, Civitella Casanova and Penne in the province of Pescara, and Arsita, Bisenti and Castelli in the province of Teramo

Pig's rennet has been produced since classical times. Making pig's rennet remains today, as it was in the past, a task that is carried out exclusively by women, who pass the recipe from mother to daughter.

Ricotta al Fumo di Ginepro

This very strong-flavoured, juniper-aromatised ricotta is made with whey left over from pecorino production. The classic ricotta technique is used. The whey is heated, sometimes after the addition of a small amount of ewe's milk, to a temperature of 80-90°C, taking care not to let it boil. The proteins that rise to the surface are strained off and placed in rush baskets, where the mass is left to drain. When it has dried completely, it is dry-salted and left to ripen for about a week. The cheese is then placed in a closed room in which juniper wood is burned. It remains there for about 24 hours, until it has acquired its characteristic smoky aroma, with notes of balsamic juniper. Ricotta al Fumo di Ginepro is produced with whey from organically farmed milk.

Body: solid, brownish white in colour
Weight: 300-400 g
Territory of origin: the National Park area of Abruzzo

Scamorza Molisana

Scamorza is made in nearly all parts of the region. Versions from Upper Molise are particularly sought-after. The milk used comes from Bruna Alpina cows, generally raised in open pastures, and the cheesemaking procedure is similar to that employed for caciocavallo. In the case of Scamorza, however, rennet is added at a lower temperature (32-36°C) and the temperature of the water for stretching is slightly higher. After being stretched in the usual manner, the cheeses are shaped by hand into pears with truncated tops. They are then salted in brine for 20 minutes. The cheeses are then tied in pairs and left to dry. Scamorza should be eaten within a few days of production. When it is very fresh, it will release a few drops of buttermilk when sliced. Scamorza is excellent broiled.

Rennet: paste, calf's or kid's
Body: plastic, soft and firm, straw-yellow in colour
Top and bottom: smooth
Height/weight: 6-7 cm / 150-200 g
Territory of origin: the entire region

Stracciata

Raw cow's milk is heated to a temperature of 37°C and then coagulated in about 20-30 minutes by inoculation with calf's rennet. The soft curd is milled into sweetcorn-sized granules and allowed to cool for one or two hours. When ready, it is cut and stretched into ribbons that are cooled in water, salted in brine, folded and divided into lumps weighing approximately half a kilogram. Fresh Stracciata should be consumed as soon as possible after it is made. It can be served with salami, ham or other cold meats, or with fresh vegetables such as green salads, tomatoes or rocket. When kept for a few days, Stracciata changes consistency and becomes an appetising spreading cheese.

Rennet: liquid or paste, calf's
Body: elastic, soft, ivory white in colour
Top and bottom: smooth, flat
Height/weight: 2 cm / 400-500 g
Territory of origin: the municipality of Agnone and the Upper Molise area

Treccia di Santa Croce di Magliano

This twist cheese is traditionally made at the end of April. Even today, some shepherds wear it round their necks to share with friends and relatives on the feast of the Madonna dell'Incoronata, on the last Saturday in April. Today, however, it is available all year. Raw milk is coagulated with whey from the previous day's cheesemaking, heated to 35-40°C, and calf's rennet. The curd is cut up after 35 minutes with a curd knife. It is left to stand for a few minutes, then removed and drained in a smaller container. It is covered in whey and brought to boiling point, then left to stand for a few hours. The paste obtained is cut into strips and stretched with boiling water. When they have acquired the desired consistency and are about two centimetres thick, the strips are firmed in cold water, and then placed in brine for 20 minutes. They are laid on a cotton cloth, and finally plaited with great care. Treccia di Santa Croce can be eaten at once, or conserved for up to a week in a cotton cloth. In this case, it will acquire a yellowish colour.

Rennet: paste, calf's
Body: plastic, soft, ivory-white tending to straw-yellow in colour
Height/weight: 2 cm / 1-1.5 kg
Territory of origin: the municipality of Santa Croce di Magliano in the province of Campobasso

The producers

A.R.P.O.
Piazza Roma, 3
Anversa degli Abruzzi (L'Aquila)
Tel. +39 0864 49492
Pecorino del Parco, Ricotta al Fumo di Ginepro

Aromatario
Via San Donato, 2
Castel del Monte (L'Aquila)
Tel. +39 0862 938179 - +39 338 7125156
Caciofiore Aquilano, Canestrato di Castel del Monte, Pecorino Abruzzese

Liborio Carfagnini
Via Napoli, 129 d
Scanno (L'Aquila)
Tel. +39 0864 74657
Pecorino del Parco

Antonio Cherubini
Via Castel del Monte, 24
Villa Santa Lucia (L'Aquila)
Tel. +39 0862 956180
Canestrato di Castel del Monte

Berardino Cipicchia
Via Sotto la Chiesa
Assergi (L'Aquila)
Tel. +39 0862 606107
Pecorino Abruzzese

Colavecchio Borraro
Contrada Selva, 20
Castropignano (Campobasso)
Tel. +39 0874 503495 - +39 330 738055
Pecorino

Salvatore Colella
Via Colle, 136
Pizzoli (L'Aquila)
Tel. +39 0862 977919
Pecorino Abruzzese

Consorzio per la Tutela del Pecorino di Farindola
Via San Rocco, 1
Farindola (Pescara)
Tel. +39 085 823133
Pecorino di Farindola

Conti
Contrada Guastra
Capracotta (Isernia)
Tel. +39 328 5451304
Pecorino di Capracotta

Cooperativa di Campo Imperatore
Strada Provinciale, 1
Calascio (L'Aquila)
Tel. +39 0862 930345
Canestrato di Castel del Monte

Isabella Costantini
Via Provinciale, 3
Rocchetta a Volturno (Isernia)
Tel. +39 0865 955056
Scamorza Molisana

Cusano
Contrada Cusano, 5
Roccamorice (Pescara)
Tel. +39 0858 572208
Pecorino Abruzzese

Giovanni De Santis
Viale Cavalieri di Vittorio Veneto, 15
Goriano Sicoli (L'Aquila)
Tel. +39 0864 720133
Pecorino Abruzzese

Domenico Di Giandomenico
Contrada Castellana
Guglionesi (Campobasso)
Tel. +39 0875 705967 - +39 0875 689757
Pecorino

Di Nucci
Area Artigianale Giovanni Paolo II, 8
Agnone (Isernia)
Tel. +39 0865 77288
Caciocavallo di Agnone, Scamorza Molisana, Stracciata

Di Vaira
Contrada Collecalcioni
Petacciato (Campobasso)
Tel. +39 0875 678112 - +39 0875 67304
Pecorino

Fonte Luna
Località Sterparo
Vastogirardi (Isernia)
Tel. +39 0865 836363
Scamorza Molisana, Stracciata

Michele Forcella
Via Forcella
Pescocostanzo (L'Aquila)
Tel. +39 0864 641196
Pecorino Abruzzese

Gran Sasso di Giulio Petronio
Piazzale del Lago
Castel del Monte (L'Aquila)
Tel. +39 0862 938107 - +39 333 5814030
Canestrato di Castel del Monte,
Marcetto, Pecorino Abruzzese

La Fonte Nuova
Via Di Blasio, 53
Casacalenda (Campobasso)
Tel. +39 0874 844112
Cacio in Asse

La Treccia
Via Colle Morello
Frosolone (Isernia)
Tel. +39 0874 899447 - +39 336 532253
Scamorza Molisana

Le morre
Stazione Palena
Località Vaccareccia
Palena (Ch)
Tel. +39 0864 641796
Pecorino Abruzzese

Berardino Leli
Via Roma, 5
Località Mascioni
Campotosto (L'Aquila)
Tel. +39 0862 909393
Pecorino Abruzzese

Domenico Leli
Località Mascioni
Campotosto (L'Aquila)
Tel. +39 0862 904764
Pecorino Abruzzese

Monica Macino
Via Vulpes, 25
Contrada Pedicagna
Pescocostanzo (L'Aquila)
Tel. +39 0864 641127
Pecorino Abruzzese

Fratelli Mancini
Villa Ilii
Colledara (Te)
Tel. +39 0861 699038
Pecorino Abruzzese

Fratelli Marronaro
Località Marruci
Pizzoli (L'Aquila)
Tel. +39 0862 977348
Pecorino Abruzzese

Pallotta
Via Nicola Falconi
Capracotta (Isernia)
Tel. +39 0865 94262
Scamorza Molisana, Stracciata

Pecorino Hat Atri di Lino Rocini
Contrada San Martino
Atri (Te)
Tel. +39 085 87563 - +39 085 8700222
Pecorino di Atri

Pingue
Via Lamaccio, 2
Sulmona (L'Aquila)
Tel. +39 0864 33580
Pecorino Abruzzese

Ponte Corvo
Contrada Santo Padre
Popoli (Pescara)
Tel. +39 085 986883
Pecorino Abruzzese

Gregorio Rotolo
Via Pescatore, 6
Località La Prata
Scanno (L'Aquila)
Tel. +39 0864 747923 - +39 0864 74318
Pecorino del Parco

Sergio Santilli e Figli
Via Nazionale, 4
Castel di Ieri (L'Aquila)
Tel. +39 0864 79396
Pecorino Abruzzese

Santo Stefano
Via Roma
Carovilli (Isernia)
Tel. +39 0865 838032
Scamorza Molisana, Stracciata

Voltigno Morretti
Contrada Fratte
Carpineto della Nora (Pescara)
Tel. +39 085 849309
Pecorino Abruzzese

Puglia

Burrata

Caciocavallo Podolico
  del Gargano ●

Caciofiore

Cacioricotta

Canestrato Pugliese DOP

Fallone di Gravina

Giuncata

Ricotta Forte

Scamorza

Burrata

The method used to make Burrata is very similar to that used for mozzarella, differing only in the stretching technique employed and, of course, the fact that Burrata has a filling. The main difference lies in the method used to form the "bag". A layer of plastic curd about one centimetre thick is moulded and formed into the desired envelope shape. The bag is then filled with strings of stretchy curd that have been amalgamated with cream from the whey, obtained by separating left-over whey from mozzarella production in a centrifuge. The still-warm bags are knotted at the neck as they lie in the water where the curd was stretched. The Burrata is then dipped in brine for a few minutes to salt it. After salting, the cheeses are packed into bags, plastic tubs or film, and are then ready to go on sale. When it reaches the table, Burrata is smooth on the outside, lustrous white in colour and has a mild, buttery taste.

Rennet: liquid, calf's
Body: composite, comprising a stretched cheese envelope filled with cream of whey
Top and bottom: smooth, 10-20 cm in diameter
Weight: 0.5-1 kg
Territory of origin: the municipalities of Andria and Martina Franca

Caciocavallo Podolico del Gargano

Podolica cows have a straight profile, keen eyes, broad, imposing horns and a grey coat. Their milk makes wonderful cheeses, the most celebrated being Caciocavallo Podolico, but the cows yield very little, and only at certain times of year. It is easy, then, to understand why a breed that once dominated the pastures of Italy is today confined to a few areas of southern Italy, where grazing is poor, water scarce and survival a constant challenge. There is still a relatively substantial population in the Gargano, but the Caciocavallo Podolico produced is consumed by the makers, or sold locally. The aims of the Slow Food Presidium are to promote the production of Podolica milk and cheese, to recover the local traditions that ensure top quality, especially natural cave maturing, and to lobby the authorities so that milk from endangered native breeds of cattle is excluded from the calculation of Italy's milk quotas. To make Caciocavallo Podolico del Gargano, the curd is milled into lumps the size of a grain of rice. The soft curd ripens in whey in a tub, and is then placed to drain for a varying length of time on an inclined wooden board. It is sliced and stretched with boiling water, then worked by hand into a round-bellied flask shape with a head on top, for which each cheesemaker has a personal design. After this skilled operation, the Caciocavallo Podolico is placed in cold water, and then a brine bath. Finally, the cheese matures for a period ranging from a few months up to three years. Caciocavallo is an extraordinary product with outstanding maturing potential. Some cheeses can be matured for as long as eight to ten years. It acquires its distinctive sensory profile only after several months' maturing, revealing notes of freshly scythed grass, bitter flowers, vanilla and spice that make if one of Italy's most aromatic matured cheeses.

Rennet: kid's or lamb's in paste or calf's in liquid form
Outer rind: smooth, golden yellow tending to amber in colour
Body: with a few eyes, straw-yellow tending to bright yellow in colour with maturing
Top and bottom: smooth, 20 cm in diameter
Height/Weight: 25-30 cm / 1.8-2.5 kg
Territory of origin: the Gargano area of the province of Foggia

The curd is stretched in boiling water and then worked into a round-bellied flask shape with a head on top. Each cheesemaker has a personal design for the head.

Caciofiore

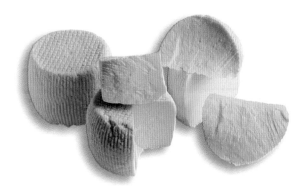

Caciofiore does not have an established tradition as it has only been produced for the last 40 years or so. To make it, pasteurised ewe's milk is inoculated with rennet and a starter culture. The soft curd obtained is broken up, worked together in the bottom of the cheese vat, shaped and, on the following day, salted in a brine bath. Its outer rind is very thin while the body of the cheese is soft and has a sweetish, buttery smell. Caciofiore is allowed to ripen for a short time and is marketed as a table cheese.

Rennet: liquid, calf's
Outer rind: smooth or wrinkled, straw-white in colour
Body: uncooked, soft, ivory-white or cream-white in colour
Top and bottom: flat, varying in diameter
Height/Weight: 3-4 cm / 0.4-1.5 kg
Territory of origin: the entire province of Foggia

Cacioricotta

Cacioricotta is the only cheese made in summertime in the Ceglie area. The milk comes from goats that fed on stubble and the leaves of the small Macedonian oak. After it is heated to 45-48°C, the milk is inoculated with rennet obtained from the rennet bags of suckling kids. The curd is milled slowly at first, and then milling is gradually intensified until the lumps settle to the bottom of the recipient. The whey is removed and the curd is transferred to hoops 8-12 centimetres across and 10-12 centimetres high. The mass is gently pressed by hand to encourage draining. The top is dry-salted, and then the bottom 24 hours later. The following day, the cheeses are removed from the hoops and placed on nets or wooden boards arranged on several levels inside a cage. This is hung outside the farmhouse in the open air. The cheeses are turned over daily. After five or six days, the Cacioricotta cheeses are washed and are now ready to be eaten in flakes or grated.

Rennet: paste, kid's
Outer rind: thin, brownish white in colour
Body: firm, white in colour
Top and bottom: flat, 8-12 cm in diameter
Height/weight: 6 cm / 250 g
Territory of origin: the Ceglie Messapica area

Canestrato Pugliese DOP

Canestrato Pugliese is a fundamental part of Puglia's cheese-making heritage, as it is closely bound up with the traditional movement of flocks to summer pastures, which took place right up to the end of the 1950s. The DOP territory covers the entire province of Foggia and the municipalities of Canosa, Cassano, Altamura, Minervino, Ruvo di Puglia, Bitonto, Andria, Murge, Terlizzi, Toritto, Poggiorsini, Grumo Appuale, Coroto, Gravina di Puglia, Santeramo and Spinazzola. Raw milk from two milkings, drawn from sheep fed with fodder grown in the DOP zone, is heated to a temperature of 37°C and inoculated with liquid rennet. After about 20 minutes, the soft curd is cut and then usually semi-cooked at a temperature of 42°C. It is put in rush baskets, pressed by hand, cooked in boiling whey and dry-salted on the following day by sprinkling it with coarse sea salt. Canestrato Pugliese can be aged for up to ten months on wooden boards in caves or cool, dry cellars. During the ageing process, the outer rind is treated with olive oil and, in some cases, with wine vinegar. Gold in colour on the outside, the cheese is straw-yellow inside. The body is firm in texture with small eyes and has a fairly tangy taste. Canestrato Pugliese is used predominantly for grating over a variety of first courses, including *orecchiette, capunti,* and other traditional types of pasta from the region. It is also an ingredient in a range of typical regional dishes, including artichokes, *lampas-cioni in umido* (stewed small, bitterish onions), *involtini* (rolled slices) of lamb and many others.

Rennet: liquid, calf's or lamb's
Outer rind: firm-textured, hard, wrinkled, yellow or brown in colour
Body: crumbly, hard, with very small eyes, straw-yellow shading into bright yellow in colour
Top and bottom: flat, 14-34 cm in diameter
Height/Weight: 10-14 cm / 2-14 kg
Territory of origin: the entire province of Foggia and many other neighbouring municipalities
DOP status awarded on 12 June 1996, regulation no. 1107

Canestrato Pugliese takes it name from the traditional practice of shaping the cheese in rush baskets. These "canestri" are responsible for the marks on the outer rind.

Fallone di Gravina

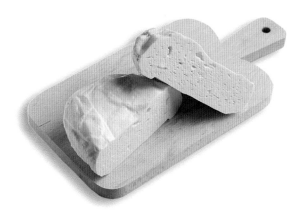

I n the local dialect, the term *fallone* means a worthless, in-significant person. The extremely good fresh cheese called Fallone may owe its name to the fact that it lasts only a very short time and has to be eaten on the day it is made. Shepherds and cheesemakers have been using raw milk to make Fallone for centuries but small-scale producers today have adopted pasteurised milk. Nevertheless, they continue to use the mixture of ewe's milk with 10-15% goat's milk that gives Fallone its slightly tangy taste. When the milk has been heated up to about 40°C, it is inoculated with rennet. The rennet should, if possible, be at least one year old, and is dissolved in tepid water before going into the milk. After about 15 minutes, the soft curd is cut into small pieces, separated from the whey and pressed firmly by hand. It is then divided into lumps of the required size and placed in moulds that used to be made of rushes but nowadays are plastic. At Gravina, Fallone is made by all the small local dairies but only to order, as it deteriorates so quickly.

Rennet: liquid, calf's
Body: white, soft, fatty, firm
Top and bottom: flat, 15-20 cm in diameter
Height/Weight: 10 cm / 0.5-2 kg
Territory of origin: Gravina di Puglia and the surrounding area

Giuncata

A fresh, soft cheese that is sold today in rectangular blocks, Giuncata Leccese was once wrapped in rush leaves, in which it acquired a spherical or elongated roundish shape. Pasteurised milk is heated to a temperature of about 35°C and coagulated with natural or artificial rennet. The curd is cut and left to drain. It is then removed and placed in plastic containers, where it continues to drain for a further two or three hours. The Giuncata Leccese is then plunged into cold water. When it emerges, it is ready for the table. The surface is smooth and uniformly white, with a faint orange-peel effect. The body is white in colour and free of streaking, patches or eyes. The aroma and flavour are characteristically mild and attractive.

Rennet: natural or artificial
Outer rind: skin, white in colour
Body: with no eyes, white in colour
Top and bottom: smooth and flat
Height/Weight: variable / 0.3-1.5 kg
Territory of origin: the province of Lecce

Ricotta Forte

Ricotta Forte, known locally as *ricotta ascquante* (fiery ricotta), is obtained from leftover fresh goat's, ewe's and cow's milk ricotta made in wintertime, from November to March. The leftover ricotta is collected in *capase*, large clay containers that can hold about 50 kilograms each. The mass is kneaded on wooden boards and transferred periodically from one *capasa* to another. This procedure breaks up the lumps that form during fermentation. In early June, the Ricotta Forte is ready for the tasting. The initial sampling takes place on the farms on harvest day. If the product passes this taste test, revealing an aroma of fresh grass and a slightly tangy flavour, it is transferred into smaller *capase* that hold about 20 kilograms. It will stay in these containers for about a year. Ricotta Forte from the hills near Brindisi, which contains a higher proportion of goat's milk, is particularly sought-after.

Body: fatty, soft, creamy, brownish-white in colour
Height/weight: variable
Territory of origin: the hills around Brindisi, the province of Lecce and some areas in the provinces of Taranto and Bari

Scamorza

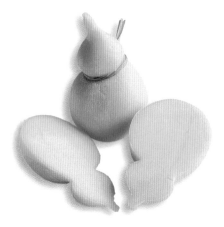

Ewe's milk is inoculated with rennet to coagulate it and the soft curd is broken down into small pieces before being reheated to a temperature of 40-45°C for 10-15 minutes. After about 24 hours, when the curd has ripened sufficiently, it is stretched and moulded. The future Scamorza cheeses are then cooled in cold water and placed in a brine bath for a period that varies according to the weight of the individual cheese. Scamorza can be eaten fresh or it may be aged for a short time. The mature cheese has a fine outer rind and a less elastic, firmer body. It can be used for grating, as an ingredient in a typical traditional local dish called *quagghiaridde*, or in a wide range of vegetable-based recipes.

Rennet: liquid, calf's
Outer rind: smooth, thin skin, brownish-white or straw-white in colour
Body: plastic, elastic or firm, semi-cooked, buttery in texture, with no eyes, ivory-white in colour
Top and bottom: smooth, 10-16 cm high
Height/Weight: 6-12 cm / 300-700 g
Territory of origin: the entire province of Bari

The producers

Antica Masseria Monti del Duca
Località Monti del Duca
Crispiano (Taranto)
Tel. +39 099 5635674 - +39 347 6101383
Fior di Latte

Riccardo Asseliti di Domenico & C.
Via Bisceglie, 13
Andria (Bari)
Tel. +39 0883 541513
Burrata, Manteca

Baffone
Via Sant'Andrea, 2
Andria (Bari)
Tel. +39 0883 594413
Burrata, Manteca, Scamorza

Giuseppe Bramante
Corso Umberto I, 36
San Giovanni Rotondo (Foggia)
Tel. +39 0882 456288 - +39 368 3800207
Caciocavallo Podolico del Gargano

Vito Cicala
Via Montanara, 3
Gravina in Puglia (Bari)
Tel. +39 080 3251893
Scamorza

Cooperativa Allevatori Putignano
Via De Rossi, 178
Bari
Tel. +39 080 5212614
Burrata

Cooperativa Allevatori Valle d'Itria
Via Fasano, 126
Cisternino (Brindisi)
Tel. +39 080 4448984
Burrata, Cacioricotta, Scamorza

Cooperativa Caseificio Pugliese
Strada Provinciale 231 km 34.900
Corato (Bari)
Tel. +39 080 8721567
Burrata, Caciocavallo Silano Dop,
Cacioricotta, Canestrato Pugliese Dop,
Giuncata, Manteca, Scamorza

Consorzio Biogargano
Piazza Marconi
Foggia
Tel. +39 0881 580086
Caciocavallo Podolico del Gargano

Coppa di Vincenzo Caputo
Strada Statale 372 Trani-Gravina km 31
Ruvo di Puglia (Bari)
Tel. +39 330 783257
Fior di Latte

Antonio Cordisco
Via Teanum km 0,300
San Paolo di Civitate (Foggia)
Tel. +39 0882 552113
Cacioricotta

Curci
Via Giovanni XXIII, 73-75
Gioia Del Colle (Bari)
Tel. +39 080 3430722
Burrata, Fior di Latte

Debernardis
Strada Provinciale Ruvo-Altamura c.s. 287
Altamura (Bari)
Tel. +39 328 8671424
Cacioricotta

Francesco Demajo
Contrada Palagano
Rignano Garganico (Foggia)
Tel. +39 0882 820881 - +39 0882 820005
Caciocavallo podolico del Gargano

Mimmo Forte
Piazza Vittorio Emanuele II, 21
Vieste (Foggia)
Tel. +39 0884 708412
Cacioricotta, Manteca, Scamorza

Fragnelli
Via Enrico Toti, 5
Martina Franca (Taranto)
Tel. +39 080 4807241
Burrata, Cacioricotta, Ricotta Forte

Fragnite
Via Ceglie-Ostuni, 102
Ceglie Messapica (Brindisi)
Tel. +39 0831 376365
Burrata, Cacioricotta, Giuncata, Ricotta
Forte

Il Bocconcino di Giuseppe Ferrari
Via Sammichele, 61
Acquaviva delle Fonti (Bari)
Tel. +39 080 7810068
Burrata, Fior di Latte

L'Aia Vecchia
Località Margette
Frazione Pisignano
Vernole (Lecce)
Tel. +39 0832 891154
Ricotta Forte

La Murgetta
Strada Provinciale Corato-Castel del
Monte, 7
Corato (Bari)
Tel. +39 080 8980936 - +39 337 251158
Canestrato Pugliese Dop, Fior di Latte,
Ricotta Forte

Lanzillotti
Via Vito Oronzo Enrico, 33
San Vito dei Normanni (Brindisi)
Tel. +39 0831 981568 - +39 328 6160548
Cacioricotta, Giuncata

Mansueto Arte Casearia
Via Di Vittorio
Noci (Bari)
Tel. +39 080 4949147 - +39 340 4060174
Burrata, Canestrato Pugliese Dop, Fior
di Latte

Anna e Francesco Marra
Via Arnesano
Lecce
Tel. +39 0832 350542 - +39 0832 638490
Cacioricotta, Giuncata

Masi
Corso Mazzini, 195
Ostuni (Brindisi)
Tel. +39 0831 303344
Burrata, Giuncata, Scamorza

Masseria Sgarrazza di Pietro De Vita
Località Sgarrazza San Salvatore
Vieste (Foggia)
Tel. +39 347 7545180
Caciocavallo Podolico del Gargano

Masseria Venere
Strada Statale San Vito-Francavilla
Contrada Venere
San Vito dei Normanni (Brindisi)
Tel. +39 0831 986290
Cacioricotta, Ricotta Forte

Molino a vento
Contrada Molino a Vento
Biccari (Foggia)
Tel. +39 0881 593246 - +39 349 8750915
Cacioricotta

Fratelli Nuzzi
Via Montegrappa, 101
Andria (Bari)
Tel. +39 0883 590359
Burrata, Manteca, Scamorza

Paradiso di Nicola Flace
Via Annunziata, 73 a
Sant'Eramo in Colle (Bari)
Tel. +39 080 3039763
Burrata, Fior di Latte

Pietraficcata di Maria Panaro
Via Canale di Pilo, 1
Località Coreggia
Alberobello (Bari)
Tel. +39 080 4324616 - +39 328 3640945
Fior di Latte

Fratelli Pizzo
Contrada Ciardi
Deliceto (Foggia)
Tel. +39 0881 963054 - +39 339 4240236
Fior di Latte

Sanguedolce
Via Apuleio, 25
Andria (Bari)
Tel. +39 0883 599587
Burrata, Scamorza

Matteo Taronna
Contrada Purgatorio
Monte Sant'Angelo (Foggia)
Tel. +39 0884 562331
Caciocavallo Podolico del Gargano

Campania

Bocconcini di Bufala
alla Panna

Burrino di Bufala

Caciocavallo Affumicato

Caciocavallo di Bufala

Caciocavallo di Castelfranco
in Miscano

Caciocavallo Podolico
Alburni

Caciocavallo Podolico
picentino

Cacioricotta di Capra
Cilentana ●

Caciottina Canestrata
di Sorrento

Casoperuto

Conciato Romano ●

Fior di Latte

Fior di Latte di Agerola

Manteca

Mozzarella di Bufala
Campana DOP

Mozzarella nella Mortella ●

Pecorino Bagnolese ●

Pecorino di Carmasciano

Pecorino Laticauda

Pecorino Salaprese

Provola Affumicata

Provola Affumicata di Bufala

Provolone del Monaco ●

Riavulilli

Scamorza

Scamorza di Bufala

Bocconcini di Bufala alla Panna

This dairy product is made by covering in cream small pieces of mozzarella di bufala campana DOP (see entry). The cream is obtained by centrifuging buffalo or cow's milk. It is pasteurised and then mixed with the cherry-sized pieces of mozzarella. The product is packed in the classic amphora-shaped glazed terracotta food containers, or in transparent plastic trays. Bocconcini alla Panna di Bufala are best enjoyed at a temperature of 15-18°C. Glazed terracotta containers have a practical function, as well as an aesthetic one. The container plays a crucial role in conserving the sensory characteristics of this traditional product.

Rennet: liquid, calf's
Body: plastic, soft, elastic, with evident signs of leafing, porcelain-white in colour
Height/weight: 3 cm / 60 g
Territory of origin: the area defined by the regulations for mozzarella di bufala campana DOP

BUFFALO'S MILK

Burrino di Bufala

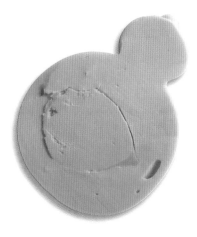

This product comprises a sheet of cheese, made in a similar fashion to scamorza (see entry), inside which is a knob of butter. Raw or heat-treated local buffalo's milk is inoculated with a whey-based starter culture from a previous cheesemaking session and coagulated at 38-39°C. The curd is milled with wooden curd knives and the whey expelled. The firm curd is cut into strips with steel knives, then left to ripen for 24 hours before being stretched with wooden spoons at 94°C. Butter is made by centrifuging or churning milk. The butter is then covered with a layer of stretched curd and placed in brine for about 12 hours. The product may be smoked using wheat straw only. Burrino can be conserved for no more than a week after the date of production.

Rennet: liquid, calf's
Outer rind: thin, straw-yellow in colour tending to brownish
Body: elastic, uniform, straw-yellow in colour darkening towards the centre
Top and bottom: smooth
Height/weight: 6-10 cm / 300-350 g
Territory of origin: the area defined by the regulations for mozzarella di bufala campana DOP

Caciocavallo Affumicato

A classic stretched curd cheese made with local cow's milk all over the region, particularly inland. The shape is the typical caciocavallo globe with a head tied with vegetable fibre. Cheeses can range in weight from 500 grams to two kilograms. The curd is milled with wooden curd knives and the whey expelled. It is then left to ripen. The next step is portioning the curd with steel knives and hand-stretching it using wooden spoons, with the addition of boiling whey. Salting is in brine baths. Once they are tied, the cheeses are smoked in traditional well-ventilated rooms using wood or straw smoke. Maturing lasts for more than 60 days.

Rennet: paste, kid's or lamb's
Outer rind: hard, yellowish in colour
Body: firm, flaky, tending to bright yellow in colour as maturing progresses
Top and bottom: curved
Height/weight: 8-16 cm / 0.5-2 kg
Territory of origin: inland areas of the region

Caciocavallo di Bufala

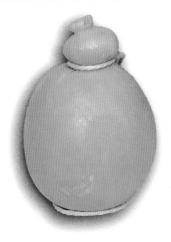

Caciocavallo di Bufala is made mainly in winter, when mozzarella consumption drops and there are small surpluses of milk. Raw or heat-treated local buffalo's milk is inoculated with whey-based starter culture and coagulated at 38-39°C. The curd is milled using wooden curd knives and the whey expelled. It is then cut into strips with steel knives. After ripening for 24 hours, the curd is hand-stretched using wooden spoons at 94°C. It is shaped, salted in brine baths and tied. Caciocavallo di Bufala may be smoked, using wheat straw only, a process that gives it a stronger flavour and enhances the sensory characteristics of the milk. It is matured at 4°C for up to 60 days, or even longer. Extended maturing gives the product a slightly tangy flavour, especially if kid's rennet is used to coagulate the milk. The finished caciocavallo is soft and globular or spherical in appearance, and usually has a head. The body is mild, with an intense mossy aroma.

Rennet: kid's in paste or calf's in liquid form
Outer rind: hard, pale in colour
Body: firm, doughy, white in colour, without eyes
Top and bottom: smooth
Height/weight: 12-18 cm / 1.5-3 kg
Territory of origin: the area defined by the regulations for mozzarella di bufala campana DOP

Caciocavallo di Castelfranco in Miscano

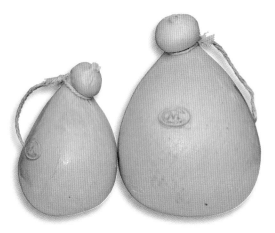

This cheese is produced all year round in the Benevento area, particularly at Castelfranco in Miscano. Milk from Podolica cows is used. The best caciocavallo is made in the spring, when the animals are at pasture. The distinguishing characteristic of this cheese is in its preparation technique, which has several important differences from the way other caciocavallo products are made. First of all, the curd is ripened in the boiling whey from which ricotta has been extracted. A very rudimentary whey-based starter culture is used, comprising the residual acid whey left in the cauldron and wooden vats, which are not washed between batches. Caciocavallo di Castelfranco matures for three months. It is spherical in shape, with a very small head. The smooth, thin rind is straw-yellow in colour. The ivory-white colour of the body is tinged with yellow, and presents very few eyes. Doughy in texture, the cheese has a mild, subtle flavour and delicate aroma.

Rennet: paste, calf's
Outer rind: thin, straw-yellow in colour
Body: ivory-white faintly tinged with yellow, with very few eyes
Top and bottom: smooth
Height/weight: 20 cm / 1.2-1.5 kg
Territory of origin: Castelfranco in Miscano and neighbouring areas in the province of Benevento

Caciocavallo Podolico Alburni

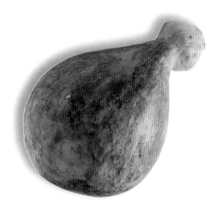

A cheese with a very ancient tradition, Caciocavallo Podolico Alburni is made using a production technique that has been handed down from one generation to the next. The milk is heated to a temperature of 36-37°C and liquid calf's rennet, or a paste of kid's rennet is added. When it has coagulated, which takes 25-40 minutes, the soft curd is milled into rice-sized granules. These are wrapped in a cloth and squeezed to extract as much whey as possible. The curd is then poured into whey that has been heated to about 60°C to maintain a suitable temperature for ripening. This process is repeated two or three times. Several hours later, the firm curd is cut, stretched in hot (80-85°C) water, divided into portions and moulded into shape. The resulting cheeses are cooled in water and then salted in a brine bath. Caciocavallo Podolico Alburni is eaten as a table cheese, either fresh or mature.

Rennet: liquid or paste, lamb's or kid's
Outer rind: hard, ochre in colour
Body: plastic, uncooked, tending to straw-yellow in colour
Top and bottom: smooth, 10-20 cm in diameter
Height/weight: 20-25 cm / 1-3 kg
Territory of origin: the municipalities of Corleto Monforte, Rosciano, Sacco, Acquara, Piaggine, Petina, San Rufo, Ottati, Vallo, Stio and Orria Cilento in the province of Salerno

Caciocavallo Podolico Picentino

Whole milk from Podolica cows is heated to a temperature of about 37°C and inoculated with calf's or kid's rennet. Coagulation takes about 30 minutes. The soft curd is milled fairly finely and wrapped in cloths, the whey is allowed to drain off and then warm whey is poured over it to encourage ripening. The curd is milled a second time and more warm whey is added. After several hours, the now firm curd is extracted, cut into small slices and stretched in hot water. It is then shaped and salted in a brine bath. The cheeses have a smooth, thin, ochre-yellow outer rind while the body is white or straw-yellow when fresh and deep straw-yellow when aged. When fresh, or coagulated with calf's rennet, Caciocavallo Podolocio Picentino has a milder flavour whereas the mature version, and cheese made with kid's rennet, is tangier. The product is consumed exclusively as a table cheese.

Rennet: liquid or paste, calf's or kid's
Outer rind: thin, ochre-yellow in colour
Body: plastic, uncooked, tending to straw-yellow in colour
Top and bottom: smooth, 10-20 cm in diameter
Height/weight: 20-30 cm / 1-3 kg
Territory of origin: the municipalities of Montella, Bagnoli Irpino, Ariano Irpino, Chiusano San Domenico, Volturara Irpina, Vallata, Aquilonia, Zungoli and Lacedonia in the province of Avellino

Cacioricotta di Capra Cilentana

Cilentana goats fall into three different sub-breeds, distinguished by the colour of their coats, which can be grey, tawny or black. They are bred in medium to large-sized herds in a semi-wild state for at least eight months of the year, or are kept as domestic animals. Cilentana goats have always been bred for meat, but the quality of their milk is outstanding. It gains significant aromatic content from the essential oils in the plants of the Mediterranean scrubland. It is also high in unsaturated fatty acids, low in cholesterol and has a good antioxidant content. This milk is used to make cheeses that offer outstanding aromatic complexity, including cacioricotta, made with a technique also found in Puglia (see entry) and Basilicata. The name derives from its special way it is coagulated, partly by acid, the method used in cheesemaking, and partly by heat, typical of ricotta making. Milk from one or more milkings is filtered and heated in a tin-plated copper cauldron called a *caccavo*, or a steel vat, to a temperature of 85-90°C. Coagulation takes place at 36-38°C by inoculation with kid's or lamb's rennet made on the farm. After 15-20 minutes, the curd is broken up vigorously into sweetcorn-sized lumps using a wooden stick known as a *ruocciolo* or *rotolo*. When the curd has settled to the bottom of the vat, it is removed and squeezed by hand to expel the whey and then placed in moulds. It is dry-salted the following day. After 24-36 hours, the cheeses are removed from the moulds, washed and placed on wooden or steel racks. Cacioricotta can be eaten fresh within two or three days of production, or matured for up to 30-40 days. When mature, it is hard, compact in texture, flaky and slightly tangy, and may be used for grating. It is conserved in terracotta jars, glass containers or more traditionally in extra virgin olive oil. The Slow Food Presidium was created to promote cacioricotta, especially the semi-mature version, to offer a valid alternative to selling off the flocks, often the only option left to Cilento goat farmers.

Rennet: paste, kid's or lamb's
Outer rind: very thin, with no inner rind, if the cheese is fresh, hard and yellowish if mature.
Body: firm, chalky, tending to flake, white in colour shading into yellow with grey-white patches
Top and bottom: wrinkled, flat or convex
Height/weight: variable / 250-500 g
Territory of origin: Cilento

The name derives from the special way the milk is coagulated, partly by rennet, the method used in cheesemaking, and partly by heat, which is typical of ricotta making.

Caciottina Canestrata di Sorrento

What makes Caciottina Canestrata di Sorrento stand out from similar cheeses is its very small size. Each cheese weighs no more than 20-50 grams. A typical product of the Sorrento peninsula, it is a soft, cylindrical cheese made from cow's milk, and should be eaten fresh. Raw local cow's milk is heated to 36-37°C and inoculated with rennet. The curd is milled and transferred to characteristic wicker moulds. When they have dried, the cheeses are removed from the baskets and are ready to go on sale after being wrapped in the traditional parchment paper.

Rennet: liquid, calf's
Body: firm, soft, doughy, white in colour, without eyes
Top and bottom: flat
Height/weight: 2-4 cm / 20-50 g
Territory of origin: the Sorrento peninsula

Casoperuto

The literal meaning of *caso peruto* is "wrinkly cheese". A firm-bodied, mature goat's milk cheese, it has been made since classical times. The production period is from January to July. Goat's milk is inoculated with dried vegetable rennet. The curd is milled and then removed, washed and squeezed by hand. It is transferred into plastic moulds, which are left to dry and salted. After salting, the cheeses are moistened with vinegar and a little oil aromatised with thyme leaves. They are then placed in a clay or glass container. Casoperuto matures for 10-12 months in the cellar, where it is periodically moistened with vinegar. The rind and body are grey in colour. The cheese has a strongly aromatic nose and a tangy flavour.

Rennet: vegetable, cardoon
Outer rind: thin, grey in colour
Body: firm, grey in colour
Top and bottom: smooth
Height/weight: 4-9 cm / 150-400 g
Territory of origin: Monte Santa Croce in the province of Caserta

Conciato Romano

Ewe's, goat's or cow's milk is inoculated with kid's rennet and coagulated. The rounds are pressed by hand and then top and bottom are each salted, again by hand, with a 12-hour interval. After a further 12 hours, the rounds are removed from their rush baskets and transferred to a traditional open wooden *casale*, a structure protected by a mosquito net, where they will stay out of doors in the shade until they have dried. When the process is complete, the cheeses are *conciate* (dressed). First they are washed in the water used to cook a kind of homemade pasta called *pettole*. Next, they are coated in a mixture of oil, vinegar, wild thyme and ground chilli pepper. The coated cheeses are then placed in a terracotta amphora, although today glass containers may be used initially to discourage mould. They stay in the containers for a minimum of six months or up to two years. During this period, the containers have to be turned periodically to ensure they are evenly dressed. Some claim that Conciato Romano is Italy's most ancient cheese and that, despite its name, it dates from the pre-Roman Samnite culture. Certainly, the conservation and maturing techniques suggest a very ancient origin, perhaps dating back to the beginnings of livestock farming. Currently, production is limited. If there were sufficient supplies, Conciato Romano would be a valid alternative to formaggio di fossa (see entry), a product that it resembles in some respects.

Conciato Romano is a product that has been recovered from oblivion, like the cheese that emerges from the maturing pits in Romagna and Marche on 25 November, the feast of Saint Catherine. Both mature in anaerobic conditions, and both undergo refermentation. Yet Conciato Romano conserves its unique characteristics better. It has better balance flavour and more fragrance. Its distinguishing sensory features are strong reduction on the nose, aromatic notes of alcohol and ripe fruit, and exceptional personality on the palate, sometimes with a very pronounced pungency of flavour. The Slow Food Presidium was set up to support several producers who are reviving the production and amphora maturing of Conciato Romano cheese, to establish production regulations and to promote what is a unique product.

Rennet: paste, kid's
Outer rind: greasy from the oil solution, uneven, ochre yellow to dark brown in colour
Body: rock hard, pale to dark yellow in colour
Top and bottom: irregular
Height/weight: variable
Territory of origin: Monte Maggiore in the province of Caserta

The cheeses are packed into a terracotta amphora, where they remain for at least six months, or up to a maximum of two years.

Fior di Latte

A fresh, stretched curd cheese characteristic of south and central Italy, Fior di Latte can boast ancient roots in Campania. The cheesemaking procedure is similar to that used for cow's milk mozzarella, from which it differs in the shape and texture of its body. Whole cow's milk from one or more successive milkings over a period of 16 hours is inoculated with a whey-based starter culture and coagulated with calf's rennet. The curd is cut up and left to ripen, then stretched with the addition of near-boiling water. The cheese may be salted during or after stretching. The shape varies, depending on where the cheese is made, and can be a knot, a twist, rectangular or round, with or without a head. The smooth, shiny skin is milk-white in colour with straw-yellow tinges. The soft, slightly elastic body has a fibrous structure. Milk-white in colour, it exudes a milky white liquid if sliced or pressed lightly. Fior di Latte has a mild, delicately acidulous, flavour.

Rennet: paste or liquid, calf's
Body: elastic, soft, yielding, ivory white in colour
Top and bottom: smooth
Height/weight: variable / 50-500 g
Territory of origin: the provinces of Latina, Frosinone (Lazio), Campobasso (Molise), Avellino, Benevento, Caserta, Napoli, Salerno (Campania), Bari, Foggia, Taranto (Puglia), Potenza (Basilicata) and Cosenza (Calabria)

Fior di Latte di Agerola

Fior di latte produced in the Monti Lattari area has two special characteristics. The first is that cheesemakers use raw milk, some of it from prized Agerolese cows, the rest from Frisians. The second unique feature is that the curd is stretched at night. Souring, during which the curd acquires the bacteria that are indispensable for the product's flavour, occurs naturally, lasting for fully 12 hours. This is the feature that gives Fior di Latte di Agerola its unique character. The curd is then stretched late at night. The production cycle concludes with *mozzatura*, the skilled nipping (*mozzare*) of lumps of mozzarella between thumb and index finger to make cheeses of the desired size. The use of raw milk and natural souring give Fior di Latte di Agerola its distinctively fresh, milky aroma.

Rennet: paste or liquid, calf's
Body: elastic, soft, yielding, ivory white in colour
Top and bottom: smooth
Height/weight: variable / 50-500 g
Territory of origin: The Monti Lattari area, particularly the municipality of Agerola

Manteca

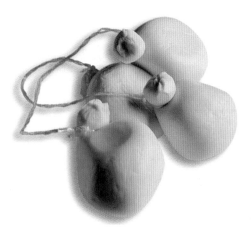

Manteca is a double-layered cheese whose centre is made of fat obtained from whey ricotta. This is encased in a soft, plastic-curd cheese. Both products are obtained from the cacio-cavallo podolico cheesemaking progress. Whey is placed in a pan and heated until the *manteca* (first ricotta) rises to the surface. It is collected in a cloth and allowed to stand overnight. The next day, the curd is transferred to a container known as a *giarra* and kneaded, first in hot water and then in cold, to separate the fat and allow it to solidify. The balls of fat are then wrapped in envelopes of plastic-curd cheese. In the past, this cheese provided a way of conserving milk fat. Manteca is white or straw-yellow in colour, has a mild flavour and is eaten as a table cheese. It is a typical dairy product of the provinces of Avellino and Salerno. Manteca from the Cilento area is particularly highly considered. Similar cheeses are also made in other regions of Italy, including Puglia and Basilicata.

Rennet: paste, lamb's
Body: fatty, plastic on the outside, creamy inside
Top and bottom: smooth, 6-8 cm in diameter
Height/weight: 10-12 cm / 400-500 g
Territory of origin: the provinces of Avellino and Salerno

Mozzarella di Bufala Campana DOP

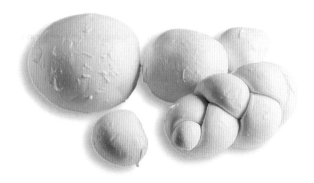

As early as the thirteenth century, the monks of San Lorenzo in Capua used to give bread and *mozza* to the members of the chapter who took part in their processions, but it was not until after the seventeenth century that mozzarella from buffalo's milk began to be produced on a large scale in the so-called *bufalare* or "buffalo pastures". Mozzarella di Bufala is a fresh, stretched curd cheese made up of very thin layers. It has an elastic texture in the first eight to ten hours after it is made, becoming softer and more fondant in texture as it matures. Whole buffalo's milk is inoculated with a starter culture of the previous day's whey, obtained by leaving the whey from cheesemaking to sour naturally at room temperature, and calf's rennet. The milk coagulates in 20-30 minutes. The resulting soft curd is milled into walnut-sized nuggets and left to ripen in warm whey for four to five hours, or until the curd becomes plastic, according to a rule-of-thumb "stretch test". The curd is put in boiling water and stretched by drawing it out continuously with a stick. After this, the cheese is shaped and cut into portions of varying weights, depending on production requirements. Mozzarella is pearl-white in colour, has a slightly sour taste and a mossy or feral nose. When cut, it exudes a few droplets of a whitish whey-like liquid. Mozzarella appears to have taken its name from the verb *mozzare*, meaning "to cut", a reference to the procedure of cutting the plastic curd into portions of the desired size. The cheese can be kept in its own liquid at room temperature for 24-48 hours in its own liquid. When sliced fresh, Mozzarella di Bufala Campana DOP exudes a sliver of whey with a delicate aroma of buffalo's milk enzymes.

Rennet: liquid, calf's
Body: plastic, soft, springy, with evident signs of leafing, porcelain-white in colour
Height/weight: 3-13 cm / 60-500 g
Territory of origin: the provinces of Caserta and Salerno, part of the provinces of Latina and Frosinone, and some municipalities in the provinces of Naples, Benevento and Rome
DOP status awarded on 12 June 1996, regulation no. 1107

When sliced, Mozzarella di Bufala DOP exudes a few drops of buttermilk and clearly shows the thin sheets of the inner structure.

Mozzarella nella Mortella

La muzzarella co' a mortedda, or indo a murtedda, is a charac-teristic cheese of the Lower Cilento, an area that is part of the Cilento National Park. The most important local cheese is cacio-cavallo, made mainly in summer on the high pastures using milk from Podolica or Podolica cross cows. Part of the milk drawn for caciocavallo is used to make a day-fresh cheese to be consumed at once, called *mozzarella stracciata*. Caciocavallo can be conserved on the high pastures for maturing, but mozzarella has to be taken down the mountain to population centres. In an age when there were no refrigerators or sterile packaging equipment, the cheese was wrapped in *mortella*, the myrtle that grows so profusely in this territory. The plant's smooth, non-porous leaves and branch-es not only provided an excellent natural covering, they also im-bued the cheese with their very special aromas and fragrances. Over time, this unique mozzarella became a dairy product in its own right in the galaxy of southern Italian stretched curd cheeses. The cheesemaking technique is the classic mozzarella method, but the curd is matured with all or most of the whey re-moved. The resulting cheese is drier and firmer, with a flat, irreg-ular, elongated shape, like mozzarella stracciata, and a white body. It is slightly more acidulous on the palate than standard mozzarella. There are distinct hints of fresh grass, and occasional-ly citron or lemon. But not all of these perceptions derive from the myrtle. The high-altitude pastures of the Lower Cilento include herbs from the floor of beech and chestnut woods while lower down the mountainside, the cows graze on Mediterranean scrubland. It is these herbs that give Mozzarella nella Mortella its principal aromatic components. The Slow Food Presidium was created to support the efforts of the few craft cheesemakers who continue to use exclusively raw local milk. Production regulations will protect the entire chain, from breeding to cheesemaking.

Rennet: paste or liquid, calf's
Body: plastic, fresh, firm, dry, ivory-white in colour
Top and bottom: irregular, wrapped in myrtle leaves
Height/weight: 15 cm / 100-150 g
Territory of origin: the municipalities of Novi Velia, Rofrano, Laurito, Futani, Montano Antilia, Celle Bulgheria and Camalonga in the province of Salerno

Wrapping mozzarella in myrtle dates back to an age when there were no refrigerators. The plant, which grows profusely in this territory, provides a natural covering and imbues the cheese with its very special aromas and fragrances.

Pecorino Bagnolese

The Bagnolese sheep is similar to the Barbaresca breed. Originally from North Africa, it is bred today mainly in Sicily. A native of Campania, the breed takes its name from the village of Bagnoli Irpino. This hardy sheep is very well-suited to harsh grazing conditions and has spread over the years from Irpinia to the rest of the region, as far as the provinces of Caserta and Salerno. Today, there are about 1,000 sheep on the Laceno plateau, so the breed is not endangered. However, it does deserve to be promoted in view of the remarkable quality of the dairy products it yields, including pecorino and fresh or especially salted ricotta. The lambs, fed exclusively on their mother's milk, are also much-prized by local cooks as their meat is outstandingly tender. In Irpinia, the most widely practised form of breeding is in the wild or semi-wild. The sheep are still taken to high-altitude summer pastures in the Monti Picentini, where they graze on grass, and are given supplements only in wintertime. Almost all of the breeders have only a few hundred sheep and for the most part produce Pecorino Bagnolese with a hard, firm-textured rind that is yellow tending to brownish in colour. The body is hard, fatty, straw-yellow in colour and is at its best after maturing for at least 60 days. The Slow Food Presidium aims to offer a focus for the breeders in Irpinia and encourage them to make pecorino using Bagnolese ewe's milk only. The milk is heated to about 40°C and coagulated in 20-35 minutes. The curd is vigorously broken up and removed with a strainer. It is then placed in the characteristic wicker baskets. After dry-salting, the cheese is taken to the maturing rooms. A simple, rustic cheese, Pecorino Bagnolese has a distinctive sensory profile. The fresh version is a staple on Irpinian tables, where it is served as a starter, or at the end of the meal, as is traditional in the south of Italy. It is also an ingredient in a number of recipes. When mature, it is markedly tangy and used principally as a grating cheese.

Rennet: liquid, calf's
Outer rind: hard, firm, yellow tending to brown or dark brown in colour
Body: fatty, uncooked, hard, straw-yellow in colour
Top and bottom: flat, 20-25 cm in diameter
Height/weight: 10-12 cm / 1.5-2.5 kg
Territory of origin: the municipalities of Bagnoli Irpino, Chiusano San Domenico, Montella, Nusco and Volturara Irpina in the province of Avellino

The Bagnolese sheep is similar to the Barbaresca breed. A hardy native animal, it is ideally to difficult grazing conditions. Today, there are about 1,000 sheep on the Laceno plateau.

Pecorino di Carmasciano

Ewe's milk is heated to a temperature of about 38°C and in-oculated with kid's or lamb's rennet. It coagulates in about 30 minutes. The soft curd is then milled into small pieces, left for a few minutes to settle, gathered up in cloths, put into moulds and pressed by hand. The rounds are cooked in warm whey and dry-salted by sprinkling the whole surface of the pressed curd with salt. After salting, they are left to mature on wooden boards in a cool place for a minimum of three months. Pecorino di Carmasciano has a pleasantly full, tangy flavour and a penetratingly intense nose. When the product has aged briefly, it may be eaten as a table cheese. Alternatively, it can be grated over pasta, rice or soup when more mature.

Rennet: liquid or paste, lamb's
Outer rind: hard, dark brown in colour
Body: uncooked, hard, firm, straw-yellow in colour
Top and bottom: flat, 20-25 cm in diameter
Height/weight: 8-12 cm / 1.2-2 kg
Territory of origin: the municipality of Calitri and the surrounding area, in the province of Avellino

Pecorino Laticauda

Pecorino Laticauda is named after the breed of sheep with whose milk it is made. The Laticauda sheep originally came from Africa and was probably introduced to the Campania region by the Bourbons. The milk is heated to 36-38°C and inoculated with rennet in paste. When the mixture has coagulated, the soft curd is milled into small pieces, wrapped in a cloth, placed in rush baskets and pressed by hand. After a few hours, it is cooked in warm whey and dry-salted. The next step is to place the rounds on wooden boards and leave them to mature in a cool, well-ventilated room. The body is ivory-white in colour. It has a mouth-filling, slightly tangy, flavour and an intense, pungent nose. When fresh, Pecorino Laticauda may be served as a table cheese but when fully mature, it is also grated over pasta, rice or soup, or used as an ingredient in the traditional regional cuisine.

Rennet: paste, lamb's
Outer rind: hard, firm, yellowy-orange in colour
Body: uncooked, soft, straw-yellow in colour
Top and bottom: flat, 20 cm in diameter
Height/weight: 12 cm / about 2 kg
Territory of origin: nearly all the municipalities in the Upper Sannio area of the province of Benevento

Pecorino Salaprese

The name *salaprese* (or *salabrese*) means "just salted". The cheese is not matured, and should be eaten shortly after production. Milk from native sheep is inoculated with rennet and coagulates in 20-30 minutes at a temperature of about 36°C. The curd is milled into sweetcorn-sized lumps, left to stand for a few minutes, then pressed into moulds to squeeze out the whey. After three or four hours, the cheeses are scalded in boiling whey and then dry-salted for about 24 hours. After drying briefly in a cool, well-ventilated room at a constant temperature, the cheeses are ready for the table. They have a characteristically soft, very pale hazelnut rind with an oily texture. The body is firm and doughy. It has no eyes and is white or very pale straw-yellow in colour. The flavour is milky, very delicate and free of any tanginess.

Rennet: paste, calf's or lamb's
Outer rind: soft, oily, very pale hazelnut in colour
Body: firm, soft, doughy, without eyes, white or very pale straw-yellow in colour
Top and bottom: flat, 14-22 cm in diameter
Height/weight: 4-8 cm / 0.8-2.5 kg
Territory of origin: the provinces of Avellino, Benevento, Caserta and Salerno

Provola Affumicata

Provola Affumicata is a brownish-coloured stretched curd cheese obtained from raw cow's milk. The cheesemaking process is very similar to that used for fior di latte (see entry). The main difference is the smoking. The cheese is placed in a closed room for a few minutes in contact with smoke from a damp straw fire. This procedure extends the product's shelf life and also imbues it with its distinctive sensory characteristics. The globular cheeses, weighing 400-500 grams, are conserved in buttermilk at room temperature for two or three days. The amount of whey in the cheese, which varies from one producer to another, determines the firmness of the body.

Rennet: paste or liquid, calf's
Body: plastic, soft, firm, brownish in colour
Top and bottom: rounded, smooth
Height/weight: 12-15 cm / 400-500 g
Territory of origin: the entire region, particularly the Volturno valley, the Sorrento peninsula, Vallo di Diano, Irpinia and the Sannio and Matese areas

Provola Affumicata di Bufala

This fresh, stretched curd cheese is produced mainly in autumn and winter. Raw milk from local buffaloes is inoculated with whey-based starter culture from the previous cheesemaking session. It is then heated to 35°C and coagulated with liquid calf's rennet. The curd is milled with a curd knife, part-drained and then left to ripen in the remaining whey. The rest of the whey is then removed and the curd is cut and heated in a vat of water to 83-85°C before being stretched. The cheeses are shaped and then smoked. The cheeses are tied with raffia and left in contact with straw smoke for about ten minutes. Provola Affumicata di Bufala is wrapped in parchment paper. After smoking, the skin acquires a colour that varies from ochre-yellow to tan, and is heavily streaked. The body is firm and does not exude whey when sliced. The cheese has a rich flavour and subtle aromas.

Rennet: liquid, calf's
Outer rind: thin-skinned, ochre-yellow tending to tan, heavily streaked
Body: plastic, soft, compact
Top and bottom: smooth, rounded, uneven
Height/weight: 12-16 cm / 400-500 g
Territory of origin: Cilento

Provolone del Monaco

This cheese takes its name, which means "monk's provolone", from the ancient dairy heritage of the province of Caserta, the home of Provolone del Monaco. In fact, the "monk" is a caciocavallo without the head. It is made in the Monti Lattari on the Sorrento peninsula . The traditional home of this cheese is the municipality of Vico Equense. Once, milk from Agerolese cows was used, and this nearly extinct breed is today slowly returning to local farms. The animals are almost exclusively stall-bred but farmers keep up the tradition of *andare per foglie* (collecting leaves). In other words, much of the fodder is procured by gathering the plants, brushwood and spontaneous vegetation that grows in these mountains. Raw milk from a single milking, at ambient temperature in summer or slightly heated in winter, is coagulated using kid's rennet made on the farm. The curd is milled into sweetcorn-sized lumps. At this stage, some cheesemakers let the curd settle to the bottom of the vat and remove the whey. Others either transfer it to a wooden vat, or knead it while it is still in the whey. In all cases, the curd is scalded with whey or very hot water. It is then extracted in a cloth and left to ripen before being sliced and washed with water at 90-95°C. Stretching is a demanding, time-consuming operation. In some cases, two cheesemakers are needed to stretch and twist the curd like a rope. When the curd is strong enough, it is modelled into the shape of a pear or tube. Finally, the cheeses are salted in a brine bath. When they have dried, they begin maturing. Four to six months later, the cheeses are ready for the table, but can easily continue to mature for 15-18 months. The Slow Food Presidium is striving to bring together in a consortium craft producers who will agree to source milk exclusively from local breeders. The aim is to promote the product and support the reintroduction of Agerolese cattle. Until only a few years ago, there were only 75 pure-bred Agerolese cattle. It has been possible, with great effort, to launch initiatives to improve and promote the breed.

Rennet: paste, kid's
Outer rind: smooth, hard, varying from pale straw-yellow to brown in colour
Body: plastic, stretchy when fresh, hard when aged, varying from pale to deep straw-yellow in colour
Height/weight: variable / 2-10 kg
Territory of origin: the Monti Lattari area in the province of Naples

Stretching is a demanding, time-consuming operation. In some cases, two cheesemakers are needed to stretch and twist the curd like a rope.

Riavulilli

Riavulillo is a characteristic dairy product of the municipality of Vico Equense in the province of Naples. It derives from the ancient tradition of making caciocavallo (see entry). The cheesemaking procedure is identical to that for small scamorza affumicata cheeses (see entry). When the cheese is being modelled into its distinctive shape, a filling of a black olive with chilli pepper is inserted into the stretched curd. After its traditional head has been shaped, the *riavulillo* (little devil) is tied with raffia. Excellent served as it is, this small cheese is even more tempting when lightly grilled. In August each year, the village of Arola holds a fair dedicated to this local delicacy.

Rennet: liquid, calf's
Outer rind: thin, ochre yellow in colour
Body: plastic, semi-cooked, tending to straw-yellow in colour
Top and bottom: smooth
Height/weight: 6-8 cm / 50-100 g
Territory of origin: the municipality of Vico Equense, in particular the villages of Arola and Ticciano, in the province of Naples

Scamorza

Scamorza is spherical in shape, with a prominent or vestigial head. It is produced all year round in much of southern Italy. In Campania, the Sorrento peninsula, the Upper Caserta area, the Sannio, Irpinia and Vallo di Diano are considered zones of excellence. The milk, which may have been pasteurised at 70-72°C for 20 seconds, is heated and inoculated with whey-based starter culture of naturally soured whey from the previous day's cheesemaking and liquid calf's rennet. The curd is milled and left to ripen on inclined surfaces, to allow the whey to drain off. The curd is then stretched, with the addition of near-boiling water, and shaped by hand. After cooling in water, the cheese is salted. It can be eaten immediately, or after brief maturing. Scamorza may also be smoke and/or stuffed (see entry for ri-avulillo). A similar technique is used in Sorrento to make *bebè*, so called because it resembles a newborn in swaddling clothes.

Rennet: liquid, calf's
Outer rind: thin, straw-yellow tending to brownish in colour
Body: elastic, uniform, straw-yellow in colour
Top and bottom: smooth
Height/weight: 8-12 cm / 150-250 g
Territory of origin: the entire region, in particular the Sorrento peninsula, the Upper Caserta and Sannio areas, Irpinia and Vallo di Diano

Scamorza di Bufala

Raw or heat-treated local buffalo's milk is heated to 38-39°C and inoculated with rennet and whey-based starter culture from the previous cheesemaking session. The curd is milled with wooden curd knives and the whey expelled. The curd is then cut into strips with steel knives. After ripening for 24 hours, the strips are stretched by hand using wooden spoons at a temperature of 94°C. The cheeses are shaped and then immersed in a brine bath for salting. After being tied with vegetable-fibre cords, they may be smoked using wheat straw only. The cheeses are then briefly matured. The finished product is globular or spherical in appearance, often with a head, and weighs 300-500 grams.

Rennet: liquid, calf's
Outer rind: smooth, varying from pale to dark brown in colour
Body: plastic, soft, compact
Top and bottom: smooth, rounded
Height/weight: 10-12 cm / 300-350 g
Territory of origin: the area defined by the regulations for mozzarella di bufala campana DOP

The producers

Agerolatte
Via Matteo Renato Florio, 15
Località Campora
Agerola (Naples)
Tel. +39 081 8791466
Fior di Latte di Agerola, Provola Affumicata, Provolone del Monaco

Giuseppantonio Arminio
Via Cavallerizza, 41
Bisaccia (Avellino)
Tel. +39 0827 89504
Scamorza

Pietro Bruno
Largo Croce, 11
Torraca (Salerno)
Tel. +39 0973 398107
Cacioricotta di Capra Cilentana

Antonio Campanile
Via Trugnano, 7
Tramonti (Salerno)
Tel. +39 089 876570
Fior di Latte, Ricotta

Campolongo dei Fratelli Gallo
Via Filaro
Frazione Arenabianca
Montesano (Salerno)
Tel. +39 0975 863212
Caciocavallo Silano Dop, Scamorza

Capodifiume di Angelo Mauro
Via Rettifilo, 272
Capaccio Scalo
Capaccio-Paestum (Salerno)
Tel. +39 0828 725682
Caciocavallo Silano Dop, Fior di Latte

Casearia Aversana
Via Nazionale Appia km 18,400
Giugliano (Naples)
Tel. +39 081 5069130
Caciocavallo di Bufala, Mozzarella di Bufala Campana Dop

Caseificio del Sole
Via Domitiana km 35.600
Castelvolturno (Caserta)
Tel. +39 081 5094048
Fior di latte, Mozzarella di Bufala Campana Dop

Cavaliere
Via Vena della Fossa, 1
Gragnano (Naples)
Tel. +39 081 8718211
Fior di Latte

Chirico
Via Nazionale
Località Ascea Marina
Ascea (Salerno)
Tel. +39 0974 971584
Mozzarella di Bufala Campana Dop, Mozzarella nella Mortella

Ciarlo "Le Follie del Latte"
Contrada Via Cuffiano
Morcone (Benevento)
Tel. +39 0824 951055
Pecorino Laticauda

Compolongo
Via Filaro
Località Arenabianca
Montesano sulla Marcellana (Salerno)
Tel. +39 0975 863212
Caciocavallo Silano Dop

Cooperativa Allevatori Bufalini Salernitani
Via Belvedere
Battipaglia (Salerno)
Tel. +39 0828 671033
Bocconcini di Bufala alla Panna, Burrino di Bufala, Mozzarella di Bufala Campana Dop, Scamorza di Bufala

Cordiale
Via Campi, 30
Frazione Sant'Agata dei due Golfi
Massalubrense (Naples)
Tel. +39 081 8080888
Fior di Latte

D'Anzilio
Strada Statale 18
Località Corno d'Oro
Eboli (Salerno)
Tel. +39 0828 347002
Mozzarella di Bufala Campana Dop

Delizie Alburnine
Via Provinciale
Castelcivita (Salerno)
Tel. +39 0828 975394
Mozzarella di Bufala Campana Dop

Ernesto Dell'Angelo
Via Bonelli, 91
Bagnoli Irpino (Avellino)
Tel. +39 0827 62209
Caciocavallo Podolico Picentino

Bruno Della Polla
Vico II Gramsci
Bagnoli Irpino (Avellino)
Tel. +39 0827 62466
Pecorino Bagnolese

Roberta Di Daniele
Via Cervito
Fisciano (Salerno)
Tel. +39 089 826224
Mozzarella di Bufala Campana Dop

Di Lascio
Via Cerro, 9
Località Ponte Barizzo
Capaccio-Paestum (Salerno)
Tel. +39 0828 871253
Fior di Latte, Mozzarella di Bufala
Campana Dop, Scamorza

Filippo Di Palma
Via Nazionale, 47
Padula (Salerno)
Tel. +39 0975 74047
Fior di Latte, Scamorza Affumicata

Erbanito
Via Palizzo
San Rufo (Salerno)
Tel. +39 0975 395348 - +39 333 9526790
Cacioricotta di Capra Cilentana, Fior di
Latte

Fattoria del Casaro
Via Licinella, 5
Località Uliveto Paestum
Capaccio-Paestum (Salerno)
Tel. +39 0828 722704
Mozzarella di Bufala Campana Dop

Fattoria dell'Alento
Località Isca dell'Abate
Perito (Salerno)
Tel. +39 0974 998425
Mozzarella di Bufala Campana Dop

Fior d'Agerola dei Fratelli Fusco
Via Locoli, 42
Località Santa Maria
Agerola (Naples)
Tel. +39 081 8791339
Fior di Latte di Agerola, Provolone del
Monaco

Gabriele
Corso Umberto I, 5-7
Vico Equense (Naples)
Tel. +39 081 8798744
Fior di Latte

Ezio Gambone
Strada provinciale San Francesco
Montella (Avellino)
Tel. +39 0827 69222
Fior di Latte, Provola Affumicata,
Scamorza

Giuseppe Giordano
Via Capitignano
Tramonti (Salerno)
Tel. +39 089 876280
Fior di Latte

Gustami
Via Bosco, 682
Località Arola
Vico Equense (Naples)
Tel. +39 081 8024047 - +39 081 8024499
Provolone del Monaco

L'Arenaro di Maria Carmela Di Feo
Via Fontana Medina, 28
Frazione Acquavella
Casal Velino (Salerno)
Tel. +39 0974 906116
Cacioricotta di Capra Cilentana

La Baronia
Strada Statale Appia
Località Molinella
Vitulazio (Caserta)
Tel. +39 0823 622595
Strada Statale Sannitica, 264
Località Truli
Castel di Sasso (Caserta)
Tel. +39 0823 659109
Mozzarella di Bufala Campana Dop

La Bella Contadina
Via Sant'Andrea
Frazione Brezza
Grazzanise (Caserta)
Tel. +39 0823 964200
Caciocavallo di Bufala, Mozzarella di
Bufala Campana Dop

La Bovalina
Via Ponte Fabbriche, 36
Sassano (Salerno)
Tel. +39 0975 72150
Fior di Latte

La Bufalat
Corso Europa
Località Matinella
Albanella (Salerno)
Tel. +39 0828 987285
Mozzarella di Bufala Campana Dop

La Cascina
Via Belvedere
Battipaglia (Salerno)
Tel. +39 0828 671394 - +39 0828 671713
Mozzarella di Bufala Campana Dop,
Scamorza

La Casertana
Viale Europa, 30
Casapesenna (Caserta)
Tel. +39 081 8164780
Fior di Latte, Mozzarella di Bufala
Campana Dop

La Contadina
Via Falagato, 2
Altavilla Silentina (Salerno)
Tel. +39 0828 987178
Mozzarella di Bufala Campana Dop

La Fenice
Via Vadopiano, 5
Presenzano (Caserta)
Tel. +39 0823 989318
Mozzarella di Bufala Campana Dop

La Mazzonara
Via della Francesca, 1
Cancello Arnone (Caserta)
Tel. +39 0823 856570
Mozzarella di Bufala Campana Dop

La Perla del Mediterraneo
Via Matinelle, 12
Località Ponte Barizzo
Capaccio-Paestum (Salerno)
Tel. +39 0828 871097
Mozzarella di Bufala Campana Dop

La Teggianina di Luigi Morbile
Via Pantano, 6
Teggiano (Salerno)
Tel. +39 0975 70044
Fior di Latte, Scamorza Affumicata

La Vallesina
Via Cammarota, 55
Vallo della Lucania (Salerno)
Tel. +39 0974 2158
Mozzarella nella Mortella

La Verde Fattoria del Monte Comune
Via Sala, 24
Località Moiano
Vico Equense (Naples)
Tel. +39 081 8023095 - +39 081 8023729
Fior di Latte, Provolone del Monaco

Latteria Santa Caterina
Piazza dei Dogi, 24
Amalfi (Salerno)
Tel. +39 089 871249
Fior di Latte

Le Camerelle
Contrada Camerelle
Strada Statale Benevento-Pietrelcina
km 5
Benevento
Tel. +39 0824 311426 - +39 0824 28471
Mozzarella di Bufala Campana Dop

Le Campestre di Livia Liliana Lombardi
Via Case Sparse, 4
Località Strangolagalli
Castel di Sasso (Caserta)
Tel. +39 0823 878277 - +39 349 7874994
Conciato Romano

Le Quercete
Via Nazionale per Gioia
San Potito Sannitico (Caserta)
Tel. +39 0823 911520
Pecorino Laticauda

Masseria Cardilli
Via Merchi, 3
Presenzano (Caserta)
Tel. +39 0823 989469
Mozzarella di Bufala

Masseria dei Trianelli di Luciano Di Meo
Via Forgioni, 3
Ruviano (Caserta)
Tel. +39 0823 860091 - +39 338 8127365
Casoperuto, Conciato Romano

Mini Caseificio Costanzo
Via Marconi, 47
Lusciano (Caserta)
Tel. +39 081 8142341
Mozzarella di Bufala Campana Dop

Antonio Naclerio
Via Case Naclerio, 3
Località Pianillo
Agerola (Naples)
Tel. +39 081 8791106
Fior di Latte di Agerola, Provolone del Monaco

Carmine Nigro
Località Rosole, 9
Bagnoli Irpino (Avellino)
Tel. +39 339 6148347
Pecorino Bagnolese

Salvatore Nigro
Via Tuoro
Bagnoli Irpino (Avellino)
Tel. +39 0827 62643 - +39 339 3191187
Pecorino Bagnolese

Olimpica Società Casearia
Via Carlo Levi
Lusciano (Caserta)
Tel. +39 081 8141877 - +39 081 8144747
Mozzarella di Bufala Campana Dop

Luigi Parlato
Via Aiello, 9
Località Arola
Vico Equense (Naples)
Tel. +39 081 8024063
Fior di Latte, Provolone del Monaco

Petrella
Via Santa Marta, 32
Aversa (Caserta)
Tel. +39 081 8111235
Mozzarella di Bufala Campana Dop

Ponte a Mare
Via Domitiana km 34,070
Castelvolturno (Caserta)
Tel. +39 0823 851525
Fior di Latte, Mozzarella di Bufala Campana Dop

Rivabianca
Strada Statale 18 km 93
Capaccio-Paestum (Salerno)
Tel. +39 0828 724030
Mozzarella di Bufala Campana Dop

Romagnuolo
Via Padula, 12
Serre (Salerno)
Tel. +39 0828 977005
Mozzarella di Bufala Campana Dop

Rosaria
Via Francesco Romano, 25
Eboli (Salerno)
Tel. +39 0828 366762
Mozzarella di Bufala Campana Dop

Ruocco
Via Lovieno, 43
Località Bomerano
Agerola (Naples)
Tel. +39 081 8791152
Fior di Latte di Agerola, Provola Affumicata, Provolone del Monaco

Russo
Via Alberi, 5
Vico Equense (Naples)
Tel. +39 081 8787055
Provolone del Monaco

Salati
Via Linora
Capaccio-Paestum (Salerno)
Tel. +39 0828 721094
Caciocavallo di Bufala, Mozzarella di Bufala Campana Dop, Scamorza di Bufala

Salicella
Strada Provinciale Mondragone
Località Sant'Andrea del Pizzone
Carinola (Caserta)
Tel. +39 0823 720620
Mozzarella di Bufala Campana Dop, Provola Affumicata di Bufala, Scamorza di Bufala

So.Ca.Me.
Via Marconi, 23
Sant'Arpino (Caserta)
Tel. +39 081 5013394
Mozzarella di Bufala Campana Dop

Fratelli Starace
Via Molinella, 20
Frazione Silla
Sassano (Salerno)
Tel. +39 0975 72536
Caciocavallo Silano Dop

Fratelli Taglianetti
Via Ponte Barbieri, 105
Via Ausella
Campagna (Salerno)
Tel. +39 0828 48053
Mozzarella di Bufala Campana Dop

Taverna Penta
Via Abate Conforti, 1
Località Sant'Antonio
Pontecagnano (Salerno)
Tel. +39 089 383268
Mozzarella di Bufala Campana Dop

Torrevecchia di Marafi
Via Marafi
Faicchio (Benevento)
Tel. +39 0824 819063
Pecorino Laticauda

Torricelle Piccola Società Cooperativa
Via Ponte Marmoreo
Capaccio-Paestum (Salerno)
Tel. +39 0828 811318
Caciocavallo di Bufala, Mozzarella di
Bufala Campana Dop, Scamorza di
Bufala

Antonio Valestra
Via Luigi Bozzotra
Località Monticchio
Massalubrense (Naples)
Tel. +39 081 8780119
Mozzarella di Bufala Campana Dop,
Scamorza

Vannulo
Via Galilei, 10
Località Rettifilo
Capaccio-Paestum (Salerno)
Tel. +39 0828 724765
Mozzarella di Bufala Campana Dop

Carmine Vivolo
Località Agnolivieri
Bagnoli Irpino (Avellino)
Tel. +39 333 5688383
Pecorino Bagnolese

Basilicata

Burrino

Caciocavallo Podolico
della Basilicata ●

Casieddu di Moliterno ●

Paddaccio

Pallone di Gravina

Pecorino di Filiano

Pecorino di Moliterno

Ricotta

Burrino

Burrino cheese has a double structure comprising an outside layer of soft, springy cheese and an inside layer of butter from the whey. The butter is worked by hand in very cold water, refrigerated so that it solidifies, and then inserted into an envelope of cheese, which is drawn together like a string purse and tied at the neck before being immersed in very hot water. Alternatively, the cheese may be part-cooked by heating the curd in whey or hot water. Burrino is white tending to yellow or ivory in colour on the inside and straw-coloured on the outside. It has a creamy consistency and a pungent aroma. Burrino made from the milk of Podolica cows is particularly highly prized. Burrino is also made using very similar techniques in Campania and Molise, where it is sometimes called Manteca, and in Calabria, where it is known as Butirro or Piticelle.

Rennet: liquid, calf's
Outer rind: smooth, fine, lustrous, white tending to straw-white in colour
Body: elastic, soft on the outside, creamy on the inside
Top and bottom: smooth, 6-10 cm in diameter
Height/weight: up to 15 cm / 250-500 g
Territory of origin: the entire region

COW'S MILK

Caciocavallo Podolico della Basilicata

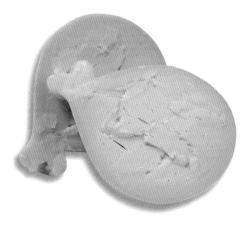

M ade using the characteristic stretched curd technique, caciocavallo is emblematic of the cheesemaking traditions of
southern Italy. The curd is obtained by heating and coagulating
milk. It is then cooked until it becomes plastic and can be han-
dled without breaking. Caciocavallo Podolico della Basilicata is
particularly prized, being made with the milk of the Podolica
cow, which can still be found in the southern part of the Apennines. Once it was the area's commonest breed, but today only
about 25,000 are left. There are two main reasons for this. The
first is the low quantity milk the breed yields, even though it is of
exceptionally high-quality, and the second is that its rustic nature
means it has to be bred in the wild or semi-wild. Yet the Podolica
is a breed that must be safeguarded, as it serves as a natural defence for the territory. In addition, the cheeses made from its
milk are excellent. The Slow Food Presidium for Caciocavallo
Podolico della Basilicata came into being at the initiative of AN-
FOSC, the association of cheesemakers who breed the animals,
with the aim of restarting the entire production chain. The association strives to encourage breeders in Basilicata to farm
Podolica cattle as a dual-purpose breed, for meat and milk. AN-
FOSC intends to put a cheese dairy at the breeders' disposal, and
above all to set up a cave for maturing caciocavallo cheeses. This
is a long-term project that depends on one fundamental condi-

tion: Podolica cows must acquire the milk quotas necessary to legalise the production and distribution of this outstanding cheese. Caciocavallo Podolico della Basilicata is a superb cheese for extended maturation. Larger cheeses weighing four to eight kilograms can be matured for four or even five years. The resulting product offers the palate an astonishing aromatic complexity. Some consumers prefer to temper the cheese's strong flavour with chestnut or strawberry tree honey, but this masks the full richness of the sensory perceptions offered by this wonderful cheese.

Rennet: paste, kid's or lamb's
Outer rind: straw-yellow tending to amber in colour as maturing progresses
Body: deep yellow, acquiring a crumblier texture after long maturing
Top and bottom: curved, 20 cm in diameter
Height/weight: 25-30 cm / 1.5-2.5 kg
Territory of origin: the municipalities of Abriola, Anzi, Calvello and Laurenzana in the province of Potenza, and the municipality of Accettura in the province of Matera

The Slow Food Presidium was set up to encourage the breeding of Podolica cattle in Basilicata, to put a cheese dairy at the breeders' disposal, and to set up a cave for maturing Caciocavallo Podolico cheeses.

Casieddu di Moliterno

The name Moliterno is thought to derive from the conflation of two Latin words, *mulctrum*, from *mulgere* meaning "to milk", and *ernum*, or "place". This shows how important sheep and goat farming has always been for the local economy in this part of Basilicata. The area is the home of the excellent Casieddu di Moliterno, as well as the better-known canestrato cheese. A traditional variant of cacioricotta (see entry), Casieddu di Moliterno is made only in the summer months by the shepherds of Val d'Agri in the province of Potenza. Goat's milk from two milkings is filtered using fern leaves, placed in a tin-plated copper vat called a *caccavo*, and heated to about 90°C. At this point, the cheesemaker adds a little basil thyme (*Calamintha nepeta savi*), a strongly aromatic herb belonging to the Labiatae family. The milk is cooled to 38°C and inoculated with kid's rennet in paste. When the curd has acquired the desired consistency, it is broken up into sweetcorn-sized lumps with a wooden stick known as a *scuopolo*. The curd is allowed to stand in the whey for a few minutes. It is then removed from the vat, pressed and shaped into balls 10-13 centimetres in diameter. Finally, the cheese is wrapped in fern leaves tied at the ends with stems of broom. Maturing may be extended to 60 days, in which case the cheese must first be dry-salted. Casieddu di Moliterno is normally served with its garnish of ferns. Depending on the maturing period, the small ball may vary in colour from chalk-white to straw-yellow. The smooth, firm body may present a few eyes. The nose combines aromas from the milk with the subtle notes of basil thyme. The same aromas come through on the palate, contrasting attractively with the sweet flavour of the goat's milk. The Slow Food Presidium for Casieddu di Moliterno involves a small group of local cheesemakers. It aims to ensure the future of this small-scale product by enshrining the cheesemaking procedure in a set of strict regulations and promoting the product in the Italian market.

Rennet: paste, kid's
Outer rind: hard, yellowish-grey in colour
Body: uncooked, hard or soft, depending on how long it has been aged, straw-white in colour
Top and bottom: smooth, 10-13 cm in diameter
Weight: 400-500 g
Territory of origin: the mid-mountain and hill slopes of Val d'Agri, especially the Moliterno area

EWE'S AND GOAT'S MILK

Paddaccio

Production of Paddaccio is extremely limited, with only a few hundred kilograms being made each year. The production period runs from June to September and the cheese is made in just a few villages, especially in the municipalities of Rotonda, Viggianello and Terranova di Pollino. The name of the cheese derives from its spherical shape (*padda* means "ball"). Once, Paddaccio was used as a medium of exchange, or as a gift in acknowledgement of favours received. The cheese is made from ewe's and goat's milk. The milk, mainly ewe's, comes from grazing animals. It is inoculated with farm-produced kid's or lamb's rennet in paste. Paddaccio should be eaten fresh. It has no rind. Its ivory-white colour shades into grey, presenting slight roughness on the surface. A little oily to the touch, Paddaccio is soft and creamy on the palate, with attractively tangy acidulous notes.

Rennet: paste, lamb's or kid's
Body: soft, ivory-white tending to grey in colour
Height/weight: 6-7 cm / 500-600 g
Territory of origin: the Pollino Park, in particular the municipalities of Rotonda, Terranova di Pollino and Viggianello in the province of Potenza

Pallone di Gravina

In ancient times, this cheese was made in the province of Bari, particularly around Gravina, hence its name. Today, it is produced in the province of Matera. The production process is similar to that used to make caciocavallo. The milk is coagulated, and then the soft curd is wrapped in a cloth and put on a board called a *tompagno* to allow the whey to drain off. When the curd has reached the required level of acidity, usually after two or three hours, it is cut into small slices and stretched in hot water. During this process, it is kneaded into its characteristic spherical shape. When the balls of firm curd have been salted in brine, they are left to dry in the rooms where they were made for about 15 days, and then transferred to a cellar to mature. Pallone di Gravina can be eaten fresh but is at its best when matured for at least a year.

Rennet: liquid, calf's, or paste, lamb's or kid's
Outer rind: hard, smooth, solid, straw-yellow tending to brown in colour, greyish-brown when mature
Body: plastic, uncooked, smooth, may have a few eyes, straw-yellow tending to gold in colour when mature
Top and bottom: smooth
Weight: 1.5-2.5 kg
Territory of origin: the entire province of Matera

Pecorino di Filiano

Pecorino di Filiano is an ancient cheese mentioned in documents from the days when Basilicata was part of the Kingdom of Naples. The milk is heated to a temperature of 35-40°C and coagulated with kid's and/or calf's rennet in a paste made on the premises. After 20-40 minutes, the soft curd is cut up finely with a wooden curd knife called a *scuopolo*, worked by hand and put in rush baskets in portions weighing two to six kilos. The curd is then cooked in hot whey, salted in brine, and placed in a cellar to age. The rind is golden yellow and the body of the cheese is firm and white or straw-yellow in colour. Pecorino di Filano is an excellent partner for local red wines, such as Aglianico del Vulture, Rosso Canosa and Rosso di Barletta.

Rennet: paste, lamb's or kid's
Outer rind: hard, lined, irregular, yellow tending to golden brown in colour
Body: firm, with small eyes, straw-white in colour
Top and bottom: flat, 10-30 cm in diameter
Height/weight: 8-20 cm / 2-6 kg
Territory of origin: the municipalities of Pescopagano, Castelgrande, Rapone, Atella, Ruoti, Ripacandida and the areas of Vulture and the Monticchio lakes

Pecorino di Moliterno

The soft curd, obtained by rennet coagulation of raw milk, is placed in the traditional rush baskets and pressed by hand to make it firm. The rounds are then cooked in hot whey for a few minutes and dry-salted for a period of 15-30 days. The cheeses are left to mature on wooden boards in a cool, dry room, where they are regularly turned over and brushed with oil and vinegar. The rind is hard, reddish-yellow and lined with furrows left by the rush baskets. The body of the cheese is soft and white or pale straw-white in colour, with a slightly tangy flavour. Pecorino di Moliterno made in the winter has a higher fat content and a creamier texture, which make it more highly prized.

Rennet: paste, kid's or lamb's
Rind: hard, lined, yellow in colour with streaks of red and brown
Body: uncooked, firm, soft, fat-rich, ivory-white or brown in colour
Top and bottom: flat, 20 cm in diameter
Height/weight: 10 cm / 2-3 kg
Territory of origin: the municipalities of the Mountain Community of Val d'Agri

Ricotta

The name Ricotta, from the Latin *recoctus*, refers to whey that has been re-cooked. Left-over whey from the day's cheesemaking is heated to a temperature of approximately 85°C, at which point the proteins separate from the whey and form little lumps that rise to the surface. This Ricotta is skimmed off using a strainer and transferred to rush baskets to drain, usually for three or four hours. At the end of this process, the product is ready for the table. To improve the yield of cheese obtained, a small amount of whole milk may be added to the whey when it reaches a temperature of approximately 60°C. Ricotta can also be dry-salted, matured for 15-30 days and used for grating, serving at table, or as an ingredient in first courses and desserts.

Body: moist, grainy
Top and bottom: irregular
Height/weight: 8-12 cm / approximately 500 g
Territory of origin: the entire region

The producers

Angiola Agrello
Contrada Tempa del Conte
Moliterno (Potenza)
Tel. +39 0975 67454
Casieddu di Moliterno

Agrituristica del Vulture
Contrada della Spina
Frazione Scalera
Filiano (Potenza)
Tel. +39 0971 808757
Pecorino di Filiano, Ricotta

Carmela Dandrea
Contrada Piani di Maglie
Moliterno (Potenza)
Tel. +39 0975 352174
Casieddu di Moliterno

Giacomo Dandrea
Contrada Piano di Vertola
Moliterno (Potenza)
Tel. +39 0975 67327
Casieddu di Moliterno

Domenico Fittipaldi
Contrada San Giovanni a Maglie, 5
Moliterno (Potenza)
Tel. +39 0975 67674
Casieddu di Moliterno

Istituto Sperimentale per la Zootecnia
Via Appia
Bella Scalo (Potenza)
Tel. +39 0976 72915
Pecorino di Filiano

Domenico Labanca
Contrada Tempa del Conte
Moliterno (Potenza)
Tel. +39 0975 67451
Casieddu di Moliterno

Rocco Panzardi
Contrada Paradiso
Moliterno (Potenza)
Tel. +39 0975 67216
Casieddu di Moliterno

Nicola Pessolani
Vico Napoleone, 1
Contrada Visciglieta
Abriola (Potenza)
Tel. +39 0971 923021
Caciocavallo Podolico della Basilicata

Maria Santoro
Via Aldo Moro, 1
Moliterno (Potenza)
Tel. +39 0975 67035
Casieddu di Moliterno

Aldo Senise
Contrada Castellana, 1
Rotonda (Potenza)
Tel. +39 0973 669120
Paddaccio

Calabria

Caciocavallo Silano DOP

Canestrato Cotronese

Caprino dell'Aspromonte

Caprino della Limina

Felciata di Morano

Giuncata

Pecorino del Monte Poro ●

Pecorino della Vallata
Stilaro Allaro

Rasco

Ricotta Affumicata

Ricotta Affumicata
di Mammola

Caciocavallo Silano DOP

Caciocavallo Silano is documented as far back as the Middle Ages. Today it is produced throughout the southern part of Italy and the following locations are all officially listed as territories of origin. In Calabria, the Upper Crotone area, Marchesato, Piccola Sila, Presilana, Monti Tiriolo, Serre, Alto Maesima in the province of Catanzaro, and Ferro, Sparviero, Pollino, Sila Greca Cosentina, Busento and Unione delle Valli in the province of Cosenza are all included. In Campania, some of the municipalities in the provinces of Avellino, Benevento, Caserta and Naples appear on the list. The provinces of Isernia and Campobasso in Molise are included, as are Foggia (including the Gargano and Sub Appennino Dauno subzones), Bari (north-east and south-east Murgia), Taranto (south-east Murgia) and Brindisi in Puglia, and Matera and Potenza in Basilicata. The milk is heated to a temperature of 35°C and kid's rennet is added. The resulting soft curd is cut, left to drain in the bottom of the cheese vat, then put on a board or in a bucket and allowed to ripen for several days until it reaches the required level of acidity. The curd is milled and stretched in hot water, then kneaded and cooled in cold water. The curd is salted in brine, a process that can last for several hours depending on the size of the individual rounds, which are then left to mature in a cellar at a constant temperature. The outer rind of the resulting cheese is hard and white, tending to ivory in colour while the body is golden yellow, tangy and crumbly in texture if it has been aged for a long time. Caciocavallo Silano DOP is eaten fresh, but is also an important ingredient in *pasta china*, a traditional dish in the Cosenza area.

Rennet: paste, usually kid's
Outer rind: smooth, shiny, straw-white tending to yellowy-brown in colour when mature
Body: uncooked, plastic, elastic, pale or dark straw-white in colour
Top and bottom: smooth, the larger of the two surfaces is 8-10 cm in diameter
Height/weight: 25-30 cm / 1.5-2.5 kg
Territory of origin: some provinces in Calabria, Campania, Molise, Puglia and Basilicata
DOP status awarded on 1 July 1996, regulation no. 1263

The designation Caciocavallo Silano covers the whole region of Calabria and includes industrial cheeses as well as products made by small-scale, premium-quality cheesemakers. When made with raw milk and very mature, the cheese is stretchy, crumbly and fondant in texture on cutting, with a richly aromatic nose.

Canestrato Crotonese

The first documented reference to Pecorino Crotonese dates from the second half of the eighteenth century. The milk from two milkings is coagulated with rennet in paste at a temperature of about 37°C for 30 minutes. The curd is broken into small pieces and part-cooked, then placed in the traditional cheese moulds made from woven rushes. The cheese is aged in refrigerated rooms at a temperature kept below 18°C, and at low relative humidity. The outer rind is hard and dark yellow in colour while the body of the cheese is white with very few eyes. It has a savoury, tangy taste. At Easter, Pecorino – or Canestrato – Crotonese is traditionally eaten fresh with raw broad beans and local red wines, such as Cirò, Val di Neto or Melissa.

Rennet: paste, kid's or lamb's
Outer rind: hard, lined by the rush moulds, brownish yellow to deep grey in colour
Body: part-cooked, hard, pale to dark straw-yellow in colour
Top and bottom: flat, 20-30 cm in diameter
Height/weight: 7-10 cm / 2-3 kg
Territory of origin: the province of Crotone and Rossano and Catanzaro Lido in the Sila area

Caprino dell'Aspromonte

Kid's rennet is inoculated into milk heated to a temperature of 36-37°C. Once coagulation has taken place, the soft curd is milled with a curd knife called a *ruotolo* into granules the size of a grain of rice. When the curd has sunk to the bottom, it is strained off and put in rush baskets, where it is pressed by hand. After a few hours, the firm curd is dry-salted, and the rounds are then left to mature on a rush rack (*cannizzo*) or a wooden rack in a cool room. The rind, which is white when the cheese is fresh and brownish yellow when mature, is clearly furrowed with marks left by the rush mat. The body of the cheese is white and supple, but tends to harden with maturing. The flavour is mild, with a slightly sourish taste and feral notes. Caprino d'Aspromonte is sold fresh as a table cheese or mature as a hard cheese for grating.

Rennet: paste, kid's
Outer rind: solid, lined by the rush baskets, yellow to grey-brown in colour
Body: uncooked, firm, ivory-white tending to brown in colour
Top and bottom: flat, 18-20 cm in diameter
Height/weight: 6-7 cm / 1-2 kg
Territory of origin: the municipalities in the Aspromonte area of the province of Reggio Calabria

GOAT'S MILK

Caprino della Limina

Caprino della Limina is an outstanding typical dairy product with a limited production area on the slopes of Monte Limina, where it is made exclusively from goat's milk. The cheese has a characteristic aroma and a strong, slightly tangy, flavour that varies depending on the period of production. The milk, just drawn if possible, is poured into a vat and inoculated with kid's rennet dissolved in a little water. It is left to stand for about one hour. When the curd has formed, it is stirred with a wooden spoon until completely broken up. Very slowly, the curd is collected by hand and separated from the whey. It is then placed in rush containers and pressed until well drained. The cheese is then removed from the mould and salted uniformly. It is then returned to the cheese mould for a day, removed and transferred to the cellar for maturing. The rind is brushed with olive oil throughout the maturing period, which lasts from eight months to one year.

Rennet: paste, kid's
Outer rind: pale straw-yellow in colour
Body: firm, milk-white in colour, softish until the third or fourth month of maturing.
Top and bottom: flat
Height/weight: 10-15 cm / 1-2.5 kg
Territory of origin: the municipalities in the Mountain Community of Limina

Felciata di Morano

A *filicèta*, as it is called in the local dialect, owes its name to the ferns (*felci*) that play such a significant part in its production and give the cheese its extraordinary aroma. The product's origins are ancient for it is associated with the long-established tradition of sheep and goat farming at Morano Calabro, where in 1810 the village's flocks had a total of 12,300 animals. Felciata di Morano is made in the summer months, when the animals are grazing on natural pastures. Goat's milk, mixed with a small proportion of ewe's milk, is filtered with ferns, and then heated in copper vats to 34°C. It is then inoculated with kid's or lamb's rennet and left to coagulate. When the process is nearly complete, ferns are placed on the curd. About half an hour later, the curd is removed with a traditional wooden implement known as a *cucchiera* and transferred to mulberry or walnut wood buckets, carefully alternating layers of curd and ferns. Today, glass or ceramic containers may also be used. Felciata di Morano should be eaten fresh, while it is still soft and warm.

Rennet: paste, kid's or lamb's
Body: smooth, soft, yielding, porcelain-white in colour
Height/weight: variable / 200-400 g
Territory of origin: the municipality of Morano Calabro in the province of Cosenza

Giuncata

Kid's rennet is added to raw milk and the mixture is allowed to coagulate for 45-60 minutes. Once a curd has been obtained, it is broken by hand into largish pieces. When the curd has settled on the bottom of the vat, it is strained off and placed in rush baskets. After two or three days, the firm curd is dry-salted by sprinkling salt over its surface. When the salting process is complete, the cheese is placed on wooden boards or a rush rack (*cannizzo*) for about ten days until it is ready to go on sale. If the product is to be matured, it may also be smoked to dry it out. Giuncata tends to go off fairly quickly and is therefore best eaten fresh as a table cheese. Mature Giuncata is also a popular hard cheese for grating over rice or pasta, or as an ingredient in various other recipes.

Rennet: paste, kid's
Outer rind: lined, fairly hard, brick-red in colour when smoked
Body: uncooked, moist, ivory or straw-white in colour
Top and bottom: flat, 8-15 cm in diameter
Height/weight: 3-6 cm / 200-400 g
Territory of origin: the entire region

Pecorino del Monte Poro

The Monte Poro area has an abundance of grazing land with a profusion of aromatic herbs. Sheep have always been bred in the wild here, and excellent traditional ewe's milk cheeses are made in particular in the municipalities of Drapia, Limbadi, Ricadi, Rombiolo, Spilinga and Zaccanopoli in the province of Vibo Valentia. The procedure used is the same as that employed for other Calabrian pecorino cheeses. The ewe's milk, sometimes mixed with goat's milk, is inoculated with kid's rennet produced on the farm. The curd is broken up into very small pieces and placed in the moulds uncooked. The cheeses are pressed vigorously by hand. The cheeses are always salted dry, the top and bottom being rubbed with sea salt. Before the cheese is left to mature, the rind is brushed with olive oil and chilli, which gives the surface its characteristic pinkish colour. The side is about 12 centimetres high and the top and bottom have a diameter of about 18 centimetres. Cheeses weigh 1.2-1.5 kilograms. Pecorino del Monte Poro is best consumed at five or six months as a medium-mature table cheese, to appreciate its aromatic intensity and fragrance on the palate. When sliced, it reveals sparsely distributed eyes, a grainy texture and a colour that ranges from milk-white to snow-white. The very fatty body has a distinctive aromatic profile, thanks to the olive oil and chilli with which the surface of the cheese is treated. Some cheeses offer notes of mint, wild flowers and forest floor whereas others are redolent of sun-dried hay. These aromas are often complemented by feral notes. On the palate, the cheese has a doughy texture. The flavour is slightly tangy with an attractive almondy note in the finish. The producers of Pecorino del Monte Poro are small farmers who sell the cheese locally. The Slow Food Presidium aims to provide them with regulation-compliant cheesemaking and maturing facilities so that this magnificent cheese can emerge from its current semi-clandestinity.

Rennet: paste, kid's
Outer rind: compact, yellow-gold with reddish streaks from treatment with chilli pepper diluted in olive oil
Body: elastic, with irregular eyes, ivory-white or straw-white in colour
Top and bottom: flat, 18 cm in diameter
Height/weight: 12 cm / 1.2-2.5 kg
Territory of origin: Monte Poro, in the municipalities of Drapia, Limbadi, Ricadi, Rombiolo, Spilinga and Zaccanopoli in the province of Vibo Valentia

Before the cheese is left to mature, the rind is brushed with olive oil and chilli. This gives the surface its characteristic pinkish colour.

Pecorino della Vallata Stilaro Allaro

This pecorino is made from October to July in the Upper Ionian area of Reggio Calabria. The whole, raw, filtered ewe's and goat's milk comes from Aspromonte, where the animals roam on extensive natural and artificial pastures. Coagulation takes place at about 30-35°C using kid's rennet in paste. After 60 minutes, the curd is milled into small granules. This is carried out without heating. The curd is left to stand and then removed from the whey by hand, exerting vigorous pressure. It is then transferred to baskets placed on an inclined board. The cheeses are dry-salted after 24 hours and then undergo continual pressing and turning over by hand for several days. After this, the cheeses are matured for four to ten months in a cool room. Pecorino della Vallat Stilaro Allaro is a hard cheese weighing one or two kilograms. Cylindrical in shape, it has a diameter of 15-20 centimetres. The side, which is straight or slightly convex, is 8-14 centimetres high. The flavour is subtle when the cheese is fresh, becoming savoury and tangy as maturing progresses.

Rennet: paste, kid's
Outer rind: hard, wrinkled, lined by the basket, white in colour when the cheese is fresh, ochre in mature versions
Body: compact, ice-white when fresh, straw-yellow in mature cheeses
Top and bottom: flat, 15-20 cm in diameter
Height/weight: 8-14 cm / 1-2 kg
Territory of origin: Upper Ionian area of Reggio Calabria

Rasco

Rasco used to be considered a delicacy. The herdsmen of the Sila area of Calabria made it from the top of the curd when their herds were in their summer pastures, at the express request of the local landowners. Inexplicably, this cheese has now disappeared. Luckily, small quantities are produced experimentally by the Institute of Animal Husbandry at Camigliatello sulla Sila. Freshly drawn milk is heated to 38°C and allowed to coagulate for 45-60 minutes. The resulting soft curd is then cut up into fairly large pieces, carefully wrapped in cloths, and placed in rush baskets, each containing about one kilogram. At this point, the rounds are turned over repeatedly and immersed in hot whey. Once dry, the cheeses are removed from the baskets, lightly salted and placed on rush racks called *cannizzi* in a room with an open fire to smoke for 10-13 days.

Outer rind: lined by the rush baskets used for draining, brown in colour
Body: firm, smooth, fatty, straw-white in colour
Top and bottom: flat, 5-8 cm in diameter
Height/weight: 5-8 cm / 300-800 g
Territory of origin: once, Rasco was produced all over the *vaccarizzi*, or summer pastures, of the Sila, but today it is almost impossible to find

Ricotta Affumicata

Whey is heated to 85-90°C so that the solids rise to the surface. About 10% ewe's or goat's milk is added to obtain a smoother, fuller-tasting product. The proteins are then strained off and placed in traditional rush baskets called *fuscelli*, where the mass is left to drain for at least 24 hours. It is then removed from the baskets, dry-salted, and put in a windowless chamber in which a fire is burning. After a minimum of three days' smoking, the cheese is moved to a well-ventilated room, where it is left to mature. It will be ready for the table in about one week.

Rind: wrinkled, hard, brown in colour from smoking
Body: smooth, firm, greyish-white in colour
Top and bottom: smooth, varying in diameter
Weight: 200-500g
Territory of origin: the entire region, but Ricotta Affumicata from the Crotone area is particularly highly esteemed

Ricotta Affumicata di Mammola

Continuing an ancient tradition, this smoked ricotta is prepared on a number of family-run farms. The main production period is from December to June. The cheese has a characteristic mushroom-like shape, comprising a 30-centimetre cylinder with an enlarged head. Whey left over from making goat's cheese is boiled and stirred for a few minutes with a fig branch. The resulting ricotta is taken off the heat and removed with a wooden spoon. It is placed in cylindrical rush moulds called *fasceji* and then wrapped in mountain ferns. It stands for a day, and is then removed from the moulds and salted. The cheese is transferred onto a one and a half metre-high structure over the hearth, where it is placed on a bed of mountain fern-covered chestnut mats. Fresh chestnut wood and heather are used for smoking, which usually lasts for 24 hours, and the ricottas are turned after 12 hours. The longer the cheese is smoked, the harder and firmer textured it becomes.

Outer rind: dark pink tending to gold
Body: soft, compact, white in colour
Height/weight: 6 cm / 0.7-1 kg
Territory of origin: the municipality of Mammola

The producers

A.B.Z.
Contrada Valle Dell'Arpa
Frazione Vena
Maida (Catanzaro)
Tel. +39 0968 77198
Ricotta Affumicata

Salvatore Arena
Contrada Torriglia
Frazione Caroniti
Joppolo (Vibo Valentia)
Tel. +39 0963 883152
Pecorino del Monte Poro

Callà
Località San Nicodemo
Mammola (Reggio Calabria)
Tel. +39 0964 414999
Caprino della Limina, Ricotta Affumicata di Mammola

Agostino Camarda
Contrada Marasa
Mammola (Reggio Calabria)
Tel. +39 0964 414404
Caprino della Limina, Ricotta Affumicata di Mammola

Raffaele Denami
Via Vittorio Veneto, 58
San Costantino Calabro (Vibo Valentia)
Tel. +39 0963 332116
Pecorino del Monte Poro

Dolci Pascoli di Giuseppe Barletta
Contrada Carbonara, 9
Morano Calabro (Cosenza)
Tel. +39 0981 30108
Felciata di Morano

Fratelli Ferraro
Località Limina
Mammola (Reggio Calabria)
Tel. +39 333 8998786
Caprino della Limina, Ricotta Affumicata di Mammola

Nicodemo Gorizia
Contrada Scali
Mammola (Reggio Calabria)
Ricotta Affumicata di Mammola

Ientile
Località Piani di Canolo
Mammola (Reggio Calabria)
Tel. +39 0964 414866
Caprino della Limina, Ricotta Affumicata di Mammola

Maiorano
Contrada Poggio Pudano
Crotone
Tel. +39 0962 946135
Canestrato Crotonese, Ricotta Affumicata

Francesco Mazzitelli
Contrada Carità
Zaccanopoli (Vibo Valentia)
Tel. +39 0963 600446 - +39 0963 603983
Pecorino del Monte Poro

Agostino Panzitta
Contrada Artesi
Joppolo (Vibo Valentia)
Tel. +39 0963 883480
Pecorino del Monte Poro

Vincenzo Roberti
Via Gramsci, 9
Celico (Cosenza)
Tel. +39 0984 435675
Caciocavallo Silano Dop

Romeo
Contrada Ciciari
Mammola (Reggio Calabria)
Tel. +39 0964 414144
Caprino della Limina, Ricotta Affumicata di Mammola

Francesco Ruffolo
Contrada Canalicchio
Bocchigliero (Cosenza)
Tel. +39 0983 92009 - +39 0983 92569
Caciocavallo Silano Dop

Alberto Schirru
Contrada Artesi
Joppolo (Vibo Valentia)
Tel. +39 0963 883589
Pecorino del Monte Poro

Simonetta
Contrada Cardeto
Mammola (Reggio Calabria)
Tel. +39 339 7382267 - +39 333 3097966
Caprino della Limina, Ricotta Affumicata di Mammola

Sità Camarda
Contrada Ghiro
Mammola (Reggio Calabria)
Tel. +39 333 4686678
Caprino della Limina, Ricotta Affumicata di Mammola

Antonio Vecchio
Contrada San Nicola Torriglia
Nicotera (Vibo Valentia)
Tel. +39 339 1999395
Pecorino del Monte Poro

Gennaro Vecchio
Contrada Freccia
Spilinga (Vibo Valentia)
Tel. +39 0963 883487
Pecorino del Monte Poro

Sicily

Caciocavallo
    Palermitano ●

Canestrato

Fiore Sicano

Maiorchino ●

Pecorino Siciliano DOP

Piacentino

Provola dei Nebrodi ●

Provola delle Madonie ●

Ragusano ●

Ragusano DOP

Ricotta Infornata

Tuma Ammucciata

Tuma Persa

Vastedda del Belìce ●

Caciocavallo Palermitano

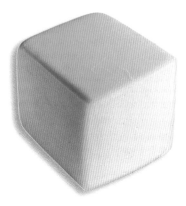

Caciocavallo Palermitano is produced in the prevalently wild, mountainous territory of northwest Sicily that extends from Godrano to the province of Trapani. This environment is the home of hardy beasts like Cinisara cattle, a breed that takes its name from Cinisi, one of the municipalities where Caciocavallo cheese is traditionally made. The medium-sized cows have a lustrous black coat, sturdy yet slender legs that hint at their agility, and a tireless capacity to graze. They yield a modest quantity of aromatic, fatty and remarkably protein-rich milk. Today, about 3,000 Cinisara cattle survive, rubbing shoulders on inland farms with a fair number of Modicana cows, or crosses of the two breeds. At each milking, the raw milk is soured in a wooden vat with lamb's, or less frequently kid's, rennet in paste. After 45 minutes, the curd is broken up into tiny lumps with a curd knife, removed and left to dry. It is cut into large slices and left to drain on a rush mat called a *cannara*. The curd is returned to the vat and covered with hot whey left over from ricotta making. About four hours later, it is removed again, laid on the *cannara* and pressed to produce a flat, elongated shape. The sheets obtained are then hung over a pole overnight, sliced and returned to the *piddiaturi*, the stretching vat, where they are moistened with hot ricotta whey. When the cheese has softened, it is stirred, with a stick called a *maciliaturi* and by hand, until it has acquired a perfectly closed pear shape (*'incuppata*). It is then reshaped on a flat surface by squeezing it between two moving boards and turning it continuously. In the end, the cheese will have acquired its characteristic rectangular shape. Smaller than ragusano DOP (see entry), Caciocavallo Palermitano weighs eight to ten kilograms and will be immersed in saturated brine for one day for each kilogram of its weight. At this stage, the cheese is ready to mature in a natural environment for a period of two to six months. The Slow Food Presidium was set up to promote this outstandingly characterful, native breed-based cheese and its complex traditional cheesemaking procedure. The Presidium will also strive to encourage the farming of Cinisara and Modicana cattle and indicate cheeses made exclusively from the milk of these breeds with a special mark.

Rennet: paste, lamb's or kid's
Outer rind: compact, lustrous, straw-yellow or yellow-brown in colour
Body: plastic, cooked, semi-hard, straw-yellow tending to gold in colour
Top and bottom: flat, rectangular, 30-45 cm in length
Height/weight: 12-18 cm / 8-10 kg
Territory of origin: the municipalities of Godrano, Cinisi and neighbouring areas in the province of Palermo, as far as the coastal hill country in the north-west of the province of Trapani

Cinisi is one of the municipalities with a long history of making Cacio-cavallo Palermitano. It has given its name to the Cinisara cow which, together with the Modicana, supplies much of the milk for this cheese.

Canestrato

The milk is heated to a temperature of 37°C, poured into a wooden barrel, and inoculated with a paste of lamb's rennet. The soft curd is strained off and put into moulds – in this case, rush baskets – that give the end product its characteristic shape. As it is put in the moulds, the curd is pressed by hand and black peppercorns or flakes of chilli pepper may be added. It is then cooked at a temperature of 80°C and left to dry on large wooden boards. The following day, the rounds are dry-salted with sea salt until they can absorb no more, and a layer of salt forms on the surface. Next, they are left to mature in very cool, well-ventilated rooms, such as cellars or natural caves, and remain there until they acquire the desired degree of maturity.

Rennet: paste, lamb's or kid's
Outer rind: wrinkled, lined by the rush baskets, ochre in colour
Body: solid, varying in consistency, may have very small eyes, straw-yellow in colour
Top and bottom: flat or slightly concave, 18-35 cm in diameter
Height/weight: 12-28 cm / 5-20 kg
Territory of origin: the entire region

Cow's milk

Fiore Sicano

Fiore Sicano, also known locally as *tumazzu ri vacca* (cow's cheese), is an uncooked cheese that acquires mould from native bacteria in the maturing rooms. According to one rather improbable story, the technique was "invented" by an absent-minded cheesemaker. Whole raw milk from two milkings is co-agulated with kid's rennet in paste. The curd is cut up and placed for about four hours in a wooden box, where it is turned over five or six times. The cheese is dry-salted over its entire surface. Fiore Sicano matures on holm-oak or oak shelves inside a basement room with very thick limestone walls. It is ready for the table after 60 days, but may mature for more than a year.

Rennet: paste, kid's
Outer rind: thin, elastic, grey in colour
Body: soft, compact, straw-yellow in colour
Top and bottom: flat, 18-20 cm in diameter
Height/weight: 4-6 cm / 1.5-1.8 kg
Territory of origin: the municipalities of Bivona, Cammarata, Castronovo di Sicilia, Palazzo Adriano, Prizzi and Santo Stefano Quisquina in the central part of the Monti Sicani

Maiorchino

Maiorchino was probably first made in the seventeenth century. It is one of Italy's great ewe's milk cheeses, both in
quality and for the sheer size of the round. Maiorchino is made,
using traditional methods, from February until about the third
week in June if the year goes well, but quantities are always limited. The animals graze on the rich spontaneous vegetation of
the Monti Peloritani, and the cheesemaking equipment is from
another age. The cheesemaker's tools are the *quarara*, a tin-lined
copper cauldron, a wooden stick called a *brocca*, a *garbua*, or
wooden hoop, a *mastrello*, a wooden board and a wood or iron
pin called a *minacino*. Raw ewe's milk, mixed with about 30%
goat's milk, is coagulated with kid's or lamb's rennet in paste.
The curd is milled into tiny granules and cooked in the cauldron before being transferred to hoops. The next stage is to
pierce the soft curd to encourage the whey to drain out. The
iron pin is used to prick the bubbles of air as they form in the
curd, which is then gently pressed on the surface by hand. This
is a slow operation that may take more than two hours. Piercing
is repeated after the cheese is cooked for a second time. The
cheese then spends 20-30 days being dry-salted and finally matures for up to 24 months on wooden shelves in cool, damp
basements. Maiorchino is cylindrical, with a flat or slightly concave top and bottom. The amber-yellow rind shades into brown

as maturing progresses and the firm, white body darkens to straw-yellow. The side is 12 centimetres high and the cheese is 35 centimetres in diameter, weighing 10-18 kilograms. When fresh, Maiorchino has faint, feral-dominated sensory perceptions mingling with notes of buttermilk. After maturing for a year, the aromas are more marked and persistent, revealing butter and herbs, as well as subtle sweet notes of apple fruit and vanilla. The complex production technique and long maturing period mean that Maiorchino is an expensive cheese to make, and risks disappearing altogether. The Slow Food Presidium aims to convince cheesemakers to resume production of a cheese with huge potential, but which for the time being is made exclusively to order.

Rennet: paste, kid's or lamb's
Outer rind: hard, firm, amber-yellow tending to brown in colour
Body: fatty, cooked, compact, white tending to straw-yellow in colour
Top and bottom: flat or slightly concave, 35 cm in diameter
Height/weight: 12 cm / 10-18 kg
Territory of origin: the municipalities of Basicò, Fondachelli Fantina, Mazzarrà Sant'Andrea, Montalbano Elicona, Novara di Sicilia, Santa Lucia del Mela and Tripi in the province of Messina

After the milk is cooked in the tin-lined copper quarara, *it is transferred to hoops. An iron needle called a* minacino *is used to prick the air bubbles that form in the mass.*

Pecorino Siciliano DOP

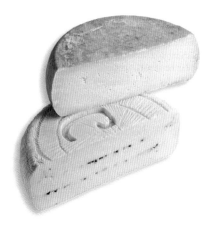

Pecorino Siciliano DOP can boast an ancient tradition, for it is documented as long ago as the days of the ancient Greeks. Pliny, the first writer to classify Italian and non-Italian cheeses, called it one of the best products of his age. Pecorino Siciliano is made from whole raw ewe's milk. Usually, the milk from the evening milking is stored in a cool place and mixed with milk from the following morning's milking. Some sheep farms, however, make cheese twice a day. The milk is heated to a temperature of 37°C and a paste of lamb's rennet made using traditional techniques is inoculated, in a proportion of 100 g of rennet per 100 kg of milk. After 25-30 minutes, the soft curd is cut into lentil-sized lumps with a curd knife called a *rotula* and put in a vat of hot (75°C) water. The curd is collected into rush baskets called *fascedde*, pressed by hand and cooked in whey at a temperature of 85°C for about three hours. The baskets are then placed on sloping boards for 24 hours to allow the remaining whey to drain off. The next stage is dry-salting, after which the cheeses, now known as Pecorino Primo Sale, is ready for the table. However, the cheese may also be matured, which involves a second salting ten days later, and sometimes also a third after two months. The cheeses are aged for a minimum of four months. Pecorino Siciliano DOP is used for cooking. It is a crucial ingredient in various traditional Sicilian first course dishes, such as *gnocchetti* (small potato dumplings), *maccheroni al sugo* (macaroni with meat sauce) and *bucatini alla contadina* (country-style pasta).

Rennet: paste, lamb's
Outer rind: wrinkled, lined by the rush baskets, ivory-white in colour
Body: uncooked, elastic at first, becoming more solid with maturing, ivory-white in colour, with reddish streaks, often studded with whole black peppercorns
Top and bottom: flat or slightly concave, 18-35 cm in diameter
Height/weight: 12-28 cm / 4-12 kg
Territory of origin: the entire region
DOP status awarded on 12 June 1996, regulation no. 1107

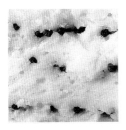 

Pecorino Siciliano DOP can be eaten fresh from the dairy, when it known as Tuma, as Primo Sale after two weeks' maturing, or semi-mature after ageing for 50 days. Only cheeses that have matured for at least four months, with or without peppercorns, can bear the DOP mark.

Piacentino

T he milk is heated in a container known as a *quadara* and coagulated with kid's or lamb's rennet, usually produced on the premises. The soft curd is broken up vigorously with a *ruotula* (curd knife) into rice-sized granules and then 10% hot water is added. The *lacciata* (curd) is allowed to settle on the bottom of the pan and stand for about a quarter of an hour. It is then strained off, put into rush containers, and cooked rapidly in hot whey. After two or three days, the cheese goes to be dry-salted for about one month, and is then matured. Piacentino can be eaten fresh as a table cheese, or may be used for grating.

Rennet: paste, kid's or lamb's
Outer rind: hard, wrinkled, brown-yellow in colour
Body: uncooked, soft, straw-yellow shading into gold or saffron in colour
Top and bottom: slightly concave, 18-30 cm in diameter
Height/weight: 22-35 cm / 6-14 kg
Territory of origin: the municipalities in the hinterland of the province of Enna

COW'S MILK

Provola dei Nebrodi

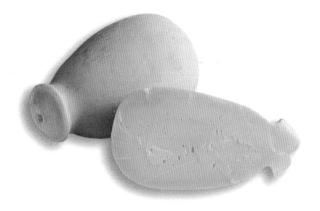

A classic Sicilian caciocavallo, Provola dei Nebrodi is produced by craft cheesemakers in the Monti Nebrodi area, who hand down the cheesemaking technique from generation to generation. Raw cow's milk is inoculated with lamb's or kid's rennet and coagulated. It is then stretched, hot water being thrown onto the soft curd during stretching. Before stretching, the curd is kneaded thoroughly. The technique is similar to that used for breadmaking and as a result, the cheese tends to flake in the mouth. Provola dei Nebrodi cheeses may vary in size, depending on the production area. In the northwest part of the Nebrodi mountains, at Mistretta, Castel di Lucio and Caronia, cheeses weigh about one kilogram. In the central area of Floresta, Ucrìa and Castell'Umberto, the weight rises to one and a half to two kilograms. At Basicò and Montalbano Elicona in the eastern Nebrodi, Provola cheeses can weigh up to five kilograms. Oval in shape, Provola dei Nebrodi has the classic caciocavallo "head", by which the cheese is tied and hung for storage. The rind is smooth, lustrous and amber-tinged straw-yellow in colour. Mild in flavour at first, Provola dei Nebrodi becomes tangier as maturing progresses. Provola dei Nebrodi is an excellent cheese for the table, and also features in a number of local recipes. When fresh, it is a fine partner for a white wine from Etna and after maturing it is delicious with a mid-bodied red.

SICILY

However, very mature Provola dei Nebrodi demands a sweet or dried-grape wine. In this case, it can be successfully matched with a well-aged Marsala. The aim of the Slow Food Presidium is to promote this ancient cheese and its wild, forest-clad territory. Pastures, mainly native cows and the traditional cheesemaking technique come together to create a natural cultural ecosystem that embraces all aspects of the territory: humans, animals, flora and soil. The Presidium is committed to identifying and improving where appropriate the many local variants, encouraging producers to mature cheeses for longer periods and raising awareness of Provola dei Nebrodi among consumers all over Italy, and especially among restaurateurs and buyers.

Rennet: paste, lamb's or kid's
Outer rind: smooth, lustrous, amber-tinged straw-yellow in colour
Body: plastic, raw, straw-yellow in colour
Top and bottom: smooth, curved
Height/weight: variable / 1-5 kg
Territory of origin: the entire Monti Nebrodi area

The curd is kneaded thoroughly. When it is ready, the cheesemakers shape the cheese swiftly and skilfully. It takes a few minutes to shape a standard cheese and 15-20 minutes to make one of the pony, basket or dove shapes traditionally given to children.

Provola delle Madonie

The Madonie area is one of the most biodiverse in Italy. From its heights, the eye can range as far as Etna, the Nebrodi chain and the Eolian islands. Provola delle Madonie is rounder and flatter than its neighbour, provola dei Nebrodi (see entry). A classic cow's milk stretched curd cheese, Provola delle Madonie has a pot-bellied flask shape and a smooth, thin rind with a straw-yellow colour. A large number of cheesemakers still use craft methods. Whole raw milk is heated to 37-38°C in a traditional wooden vat and coagulated with sheep's rennet in paste. When the curd has thickened sufficiently, it is cut up into hazelnut-sized lumps and left to stand. Hot water or whey is poured over it. The soft curd is then placed to drain on a wooden board. It is cut into thin slices, which are placed in the vat and water heated to 85°C is poured over. At this point, the curd is stretched manually with the aid of a stick. When it has become elastic, the cheese is shaped into small pears – the classic provola shape is roundish, with a very short neck – which are tied in pairs and hung over (*a cavallo*, in Italian) a pole to mature for at least 10-15 days in cool, well-ventilated rooms. There is also a slightly smoked version. Firm, soft, elastic and mild in flavour, Provola delle Madonie is a fine accompaniment for the local durum wheat bread made with natural yeasts (*lu criscenti*) and baked in a wood-fired oven. Fresh Provola delle Madonie has fragrant milky aromas, so a very light, dry wine is recommended. The mature version can be enjoyed with a classic Nero d'Avola red. The Slow Food Presidium brings together the best craft cheesemakers and aims to draft production regulations that will ensure the traceability and high quality of the cheese. Slow Food has also set up a Presidium for the local manna, the sweet sap of the manna ash, with the aim of promoting the extraordinary food and agricultural products of the Madonie Regional Park.

Rennet: paste, lamb's
Outer rind: smooth, thin, straw-yellow in colour
Body: firm, soft, elastic, ivory-white tending to straw-yellow in colour
Top and bottom: smooth, curved
Height/weight: 10-30 cm / 1-1.2 kg
Territory of origin: the Madonie massif in the province of Palermo

*Classic Provola delle Madonie cheeses are roundish, with a very short neck. They are tied in pairs and hung over (*a cavallo, *in Italian) a pole to mature for at least 10-15 days.*

Ragusano

Ragusano is made from November to May, during the fodder season, when the local pastures abound with more than one hundred different kinds of plants. The cheese is a rectangular block weighing 12-16 kilograms and bears the marks of the cords used to tie it and hang it from the ceiling to mature. Whole raw milk from two milkings is heated to 36°C and inoculated with lamb's or kid's rennet in paste. When a *ruotula* (stick) stands up in the mixture, the curd is broken up into sweetcorn-sized lumps. It is left to stand on a wooden board, then scalded in hot water or boiling whey. The firm curd matures for 20-24 hours and is then sliced, placed in a wooden or copper vat called a *staccio*, and scalded with water at 85°C. The curd is kneaded by hand with a stick. When it begins to stretch, it is shaped into a ball. The cheese is transformed into rectangles with the aid of a *mastredda*, a wooden board on which it is placed and knocked into shape with heavy blocks of wood. To obtain the desired corners, the cheesemaker must turn the cheese every 10, 30 and 60 minutes for 6-8 hours. Ragusano has a hard, thin, rind that is smooth, firm and golden-yellow in colour. The body, which is slightly flaky because of stretching, is straw-yellow in colour. It has an extraordinary richness of aromas, which range from fresh mushrooms to toastiness, orange, freshly cut grass, pot marigold, anthemis, mallow, geranium and jasmine. The complexity of the flavours and aromas intensifies with the passage of time. The finest Ragusano will have matured for 8-24 months. Sadly, Ragusano is part of a fragile ecosystem. Modicana cows have almost disappeared, the farms are losing the focal role they once played and the cheese is mainly consumed locally. Large-scale production using modern technology in industrial dairies never matches the quality and unique personality of the farmhouse cheese. The Slow Food Presidium was set up to protect this gastronomic, environmental, historic and cheesemaking heritage. Presidium's producers use only raw milk from cows of Modicana breed raised in their own farm.

Rennet: paste, lamb's or kid's
Outer rind: hard, thin, smooth, firm, golden-yellow in colour
Body: cooked, plastic, elastic or hard, straw-yellow in colour
Top and bottom: flat, rectangular
Height/weight: 10-15 cm / 12-16 kg
Territory of origin: all the municipalities in the province of Ragusa and some municipalities in the province of Siracusa

The curd is placed in the wooden or copper staccio *and cooked in very hot water. It is then kneaded by hand or with a stick. When it begins to stretch, it is shaped into a ball.*

COW'S MILK

Ragusano DOP

As long ago as the sixteenth century, cheeses from Ragusa were being exported and traded as far away as Zara (Zadar) in Dalmatia. Ragusano DOP is essentially a caciocavallo with a very unusual shape, called *scaluni* (step) in the Sicilian dialect. The shape must have been particularly practical in the years after the First World War, when the cheese was in great demand from Sicilian emigrants to the United States. Transatlantic customers persuaded producers to increase the size of the cheeses, which up until then had weighed seven to eight kilos each. Ragusano DOP is made with whole raw milk from cows, usually Modicana animals that have been raised practically wild in the aromatic herb-rich pastures of the Monti Iblei area. The milk is heated to a temperature of 34°C and coagulated with kid's or lamb's rennet in 60-90 minutes. Next, the soft curd is broken into small pieces in two stages, hot water being added to the curd in the pan in between. When it is ready, the curd is strained off, left to ripen, then stretched and shaped into its characteristic form. It is then salted in brine and left to mature for a varying period of time. After as little as one week, the fresh version is ready for the table, but it can be aged for up to four months. Mature Ragusano DOP has a mouth-filling, tangy flavour. Ragusano DOP may be served in slices or slivers with vegetables, and can also be used for grating. It can also be cut into thick slices, coated in breadcrumbs and fried. Ragusano DOP's territory of origin has been identified as the municipalities of Acate, Chiaramonte Gulfi, Comiso, Giarratana, Ispica, Modica, Monterosso Almo, Ragusa, Santa Croce Camerina, Scicli and Vittoria in the province of Ragusa, and the municipalities of Noto, Palazzolo Acreide and Rosolini in the province of Siracusa.

Rennet: paste, kid's or lamb's
Outer rind: firm, thin, blond to straw-yellow in colour
Body: cooked, plastic, elastic or hard, straw-yellow or golden yellow in colour
Top and bottom: flat, rectangular
Height/weight: 10-15 cm / 12-16 kg
Territory of origin: parts of the provinces of Ragusa and Siracusa
DOP status awarded on 11 July 1996, regulation no. 1263

The finest Ragusano DOP is made from the milk of Modicana cows, a native Sicilian breed that is highly adaptable and perfectly at home in Ragusa's poor quality but aromatic herb-rich pastures.

Ricotta Infornata

Sea salt or *agra* (acid whey) is added to whey from the milk of cows, ewes or goats, or to a mixture of the three, and the solution is heated to a temperature of 90°C. When the solids have risen to the surface, and the froth has been removed, they are poured into rush baskets, which are then placed on a sloping board. The mass is left to drain for one or two days and then transferred into a greased pottery container. It is now baked in a stone oven at 180-200°C for about 30 minutes. When a delicate reddish-brown skin has formed, the Ricotta Infornata is taken out of the oven and left to stand. It is customarily eaten fresh, but in the province of Messina it is usual to let it dry in the sun and then mature, so it can be used as a cheese for grating.

Outer rind: thin, reddish-brown in colour
Body: creamy, ivory-white in colour
Top and bottom: smooth, 10-12 cm in diameter
Height/weight: 3-5 cm / variable
Territory of origin: the entire region

Tuma Ammucciata

This cheese is made with milk from the Girgentana goat, using the traditional *tuma* technique and is left to mature until a light outer rind has formed. The bottom is removed from a container that was once used for cereals, and is called *tumminu*, *munniedrru* or *quartu* depending on its size. The container is cut on the side and a cord is tied round it. A small quantity of chalk mixed with water is poured in, the tuma is immersed in it, and more liquid is added. When the chalk is dry, the container is opened and the tuma is matured in the block. Chalk is hygroscopic and porous, ensuring ideal humidity for slow, uniform maturing. After three months' in the chalk, Tuma Ammucciata is ready for the table. The technique has its origins in the need to keep ewe's milk, goat's milk and mixed milk cheeses safe from the incursions of bandits and landowners, and makes use of a mineral that is readily available in the Agrigento and Caltanissetta areas. The cheeses were *ammucciate* (hidden) in the walls of the cheesemaker's home.

Rennet: paste, kid's
Outer rind: thin, compact, smooth with marks left by the basket, white in colour
Body: soft, compact, with sparsely distributed eyes, white in colour
Top and bottom: flat, varying in diameter
Height/weight: 8-10 cm / 1-3 kg
Territory of origin: the municipality of Campobello di Licata in the province of Agrigento

Tuma Persa

At present, this cheese is only made by one craft producer, who resumed production using the cheesemaking methods described in a text from the 1930s. A raw or semi-cooked, soft, pressed curd cheese from whole raw or heat-treated cow's, ewe's or mixed milk, Tuma Persa is at its best in the version obtained using cow's milk only. Maturing is crucial for this cheese. Once it has been transferred to its hoop, it is *persa* (forgotten) for eight to ten days. The mould that appears is brushed off roughly and the cheese is "forgotten" again for a further eight to ten days. The cheese is then very carefully washed and brushed before salting. The rind is ochre-yellow at first, but darkens after receiving a *curatina,* or coating of olive oil and ground pepper. Tuma Persa has a soft, compact body that tends to crumble. It has very few eyes and is never salted. Neither mild nor tangy on the palate, Tuma Persa has a lingering, aromatic finish that is vaguely reminiscent of blue cheese.

Rennet: paste, kid's
Outer rind: ochre-yellow shading into dark yellow
Body: soft, firm, crumbly, with few eyes, white tending to straw-yellow in colour
Top and bottom: flat
Height/weight: 10-14 cm / 7-9 kg
Territory of origin: the Monti Sicani area of inland Sicily

EWE'S MILK

Vastedda del Belìce

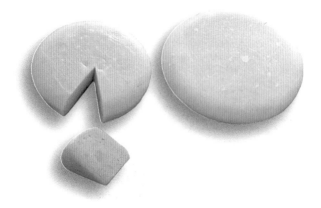

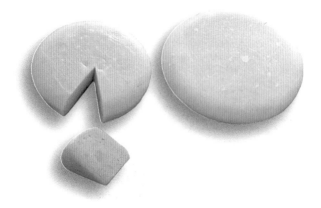

Italy's only stretched curd ewe's milk cheese, Vastedda del Belice has a name that probably derives from the dialect term *vasta*, meaning "spoiled". Cheesemakers in the Belice valley created Vastedda to recycle defective pecorino by stretching it at high temperatures. The milk comes from the local Belice sheep and the cheesemaking style varies from zone to zone, as well as from cheesemaker to cheesemaker. Usually raw milk from one or two milkings is coagulated at about 35-36°C using lamb's or kid's rennet made on the farm. The curd is broken up into lumps the size of a grain of rice with a wooden stick. It is allowed to stand for a short time, and then gathered up in a linen cloth and placed on a board. One hour later, it is cut into pieces and placed in a container, usually made of wood, and covered with whey heated to 55-60°C to encourage fermentation. Maturing can vary, depending on the time of year, external temperature and humidity. When the desired acidity has been achieved, the curd is sliced in a wooden container, to which very hot water (90°C) is added, and kneaded with the help of a wooden stick called a *vaciliatuma*. When the curd has reached the desired consistency, it is cut into portions that are shaped by hand into balls. The balls are placed in a deep pottery dish, where they acquire their characteristic flattened oval shape, called *vastedda* (like a flat loaf). One hour after shaping, the cheese is ready for the table. It should be enjoyed within three days of production. Vastedda has a very satisfying, subtly attractive fragrance and the palate reveals buttery notes against a backdrop of herbs from the Belice valley, including grasses and valerian. It is used as an ingredient in a number of local recipes, but chunky slices of cheese can also be savoured on their own, dressed with extra virgin olive oil, tomato and oregano. The Slow Food Presidium was set up with few producers. Subsequently, other cheesemakers joined to expand the group. The main aim of the Presidium is to rationalise the production, cheesemaking, maturing and transport processes for Vastedda.

Rennet: paste, lamb's or kid's
Outer rind: thin skin, white or straw-yellow in colour
Body: plastic, soft, lustrous, white or straw-white in colour
Height/weight: 2 cm / up to 3 kg
Territory of origin: the municipalities of Calatafimi, Campobello di Mazara, Castelvetrano, Gibellina, Partanna, Poggioreale, Salaparuta, Salemi, Santa Ninfa and Vita in the province of Trapani, Menfi, Montevago, Sambuca di Sicilia and Santa Margherita di Belice in the province of Agrigento and Contessa Entellina in the province of Palermo, all in the territory of Valle del Belice

The curd is shaped by hand into balls, which are placed in a deep pottery dish. They acquire a characteristic flattened oval vastedda *(flat loaf) shape.*

The producers

Filippo Abbate
Contrada Portella del Pero
Castelbuono (Palermo)
Tel. +39 0921 671576 - +39 320 1794238
Provola delle Madonie

Sebastiano Abbate
Via Calatafimi, 22
Contrada Bruca
Buseto Palizzolo (Trapani)
Tel. +39 0923 854060
Caciocavallo palermitano

Giuseppe Adragna
Via Giovanni Verga, 40
Alcamo (Trapani)
Tel. +39 0924 24130
Pecorino Siciliano Dop

Carmelo Agostino Ninone
Contrada Mulino di Mirto
Mirto (Messina)
Tel. +39 0941 919100
Canestrato, Provola dei Nebrodi, Ricotta Infornata, Ricotta Salata

Sebastiano Agostino Ninone
Via San Rocco, 40
Mirto (Messina)
Tel. +39 0941 919403 - +39 0941 919606
Canestrato, Provola dei Nebrodi, Ricotta Infornata, Ricotta Salata

Giacomo Agostino Tindaro
Contrada Oliveto
Località Fiumare
Mirto (Messina)
Tel. +39 335 6651139
Canestrato, Provola dei Nebrodi, Ricotta Infornata, Ricotta Salata

Paolo e Michele Aparo
Contrada Damma
Siracusa
Tel. +39 0931 717240 - +39 338 3302887
Canestrato, Pecorino Siciliano Dop, Ricotta

Mario Arcidiacono
Via Carlino, 96
Mascali (Catania)
Tel. +39 095 969526 - +39 347 0578358
Pecorino Siciliano Dop

Vincenzo Barreca
Contrada Abbate
Geraci Siculo (Palermo)
Tel. +39 0921 643721
Provola delle Madonie

Calogero Bavetta
Via Aquileia
Montevago (Agrigento)
Tel. +39 0925 38897
Vastedda del Belìce

BioNebrodi
Via Libertà, 237
Mistretta (Messina)
Tel. +39 0921 381881
Provola dei Nebrodi

Fratelli Borrello
Contrada Forte, 7
Sinagra (Messina)
Tel. +39 0941 594844 - +39 0941 594436
Canestrato, Provola dei Nebrodi, Ricotta Infornata, Ricotta Salata

Vito Calì
Via Conceria, 16
Cesarò (Messina)
Tel. +39 095 697323
Canestrato

Matteo Cangelosi
Contrada Pontesecco
Castelbuono (Palermo)
Tel. +39 0921 671166
Provola delle Madonie

Antonino Cangemi
Vicolo Battumari, 8
Partanna (Trapani)
Tel. +39 0924 921454
Vastedda del Belìce

Giuseppe Cappello
Via Vittorio Emanuele, 2
Basicò (Messina)
Tel. +39 0941 85013
Provola dei Nebrodi

Giuseppe Caldarella
Piazza Giuseppe Puglisi, 9
Godrano (Palermo)
Tel. +39 091 8208338 - +39 091 8208107
Caciocavallo Palermitano

Casalgismondo di Maria Rita D'Amico
Contrada Casalgismondo, 1
Aidone (Enna)
Tel. +39 0935 87900 - +39 0935 892118
Pecorino Siciliano, Piacentino

Salvatore Cascone
Via Michelangelo, 77
Contrada Serra Grande
Chiaramonte Gulfi (Ragusa)
Tel. +39 0932 927566
Ragusano

Salvatore Cirrito
Via Umberto I, 72
Collesano (Palermo)
Tel. +39 328 9380072
Canestrato, Provola delle Madonie

Angelo Cocuzza
Via Sico, 32
Contrada Valle del Previte
Gagliano Castelferrato (Enna)
Tel. +39 0935 693089
Pecorino Siciliano Dop, Piacentino

Consorzio Allevatori Costanzo
Via Roma, 2-4
Viale Regina Margherita
Randazzo (Catania)
Tel. +39 095 7991206 - +39 095 7991721
Pecorino Siciliano, Ricotta Infornata

Consorzio Terre dei Nebrodi
Contrada Drià, 70
Castell'Umberto (Messina)
Tel. +39 339 5260741
Canestrato, Maiorchino, Pecorino,
Provola dei Nebrodi, Ricotta Inforna-
ta, Ricotta Salata, Tuma

Giuseppe Criscione
Contrada Galermi
Ragusa
Tel. +39 0932 669284
Ragusano

Salvatore Di Pasquale
Contrada Cardita Friscionello
Ragusa
Tel. +39 0932 619269
Ragusano

Carmelo Duca
Contrada Bisanti
Geraci Siculo (Palermo)
Tel. +39 0921 645965
Provola delle Madonie

Vincenzo Evola
Via Pietro Sbacchi, 238
Carini (Palermo)
Tel. +39 091 8664971
Caciocavallo Palermitano

Rosario Floridia
Contrada Scorsone
Ispica (Ragusa)
Tel. +39 0932 951151
Ragusano

Salvatrice Floridia
Contrada Pernicia
Rosolini (Siracusa)
Tel. +39 0931 851032
Ragusano

Forte
Via Termini, 2
Castelvetrano (Trapani)
Tel. +39 0924 905506
Pecorino Siciliano Dop

Mario Fabrizio Galati
Contrada Costa Mandorla
Giardinello (Palermo)
Tel. +39 091 8984272
Caciocavallo Palermitano

Giacomo Gatì
Contrada Montalbo
Campobello di Licata (Agrigento)
Tel. +39 0922 877604
Tuma Ammucciata

Giorgio Guastella
Contrada Schifazzo
Ragusa
Tel. +39 0932 667381
Ragusano

Salvatore Gulino
Contrada Raffino
Ragusa
Tel. +39 338 7010547
Caciocavallo Ibleo, Ricotta

Il Cavalcatore
Contrada Cavalcatore
Enna
Tel. +39 0935 620606
Piacentino

Salvatore Interrante
Contrada Cinquanta
Menfi (Agrigento)
Tel. +39 0925 71416
Vastedda del Belìce

Grazia Invidiata
Contrada Santa Anastasia
Collesano (Palermo)
Tel. +39 0921 661536
Provola delle Madonie

Giuseppe Latino
Via Farinata, 38
San Marco d'Alunzio (Messina)
Tel. +39 0941 797315
Canestrato, Ricotta Infornata, Ricotta
Salata

Salvatore Lissandrello
Contrada Cornocchia Canalicci
Ragusa
Tel. +39 0932 64517
Ragusano

Antonino Lo Curto
Contrada Santagata
Collesano (Palermo)
Tel. +39 339 4064973
Provola delle Madonie

Giuseppe Longo
Via Ramusa, 37
Cesarò (Messina)
Tel. +39 095 696927
Canestrato

Giuseppe Maltese
Via Roma, 41
Cinisi (Palermo)
Tel. +39 091 8665564
Caciocavallo Palermitano

Melchiorre Mangiaracina
Corso Umberto, 212
Sambuca di Sicilia (Agrigento)
Tel. +39 0925 946059
Vastedda del Belice

Giuseppe Mantegna
Contrada Celsa
Geraci Siculo (Palermo)
Tel. +39 0921 689706
Provola delle Madonie

Gaetano Mazzurco
Contrada Malaterra
Bronte (Catania)
Tel. +39 338 5215825
Pecorino Siciliano Dop

Mario Mirabile
Contrada Fanuso
Santa Lucia del Mela (Messina)
Tel. +39 090 935886
Maiorchino, Pecorino, Ricotta Inforna-
ta, Ricotta Salata

Carmela Mommo
Strada Statale 120 km 181
Contrada Gurrida
Randazzo (Catania)
Tel. +39 347 1958943
Pecorino Siciliano Dop

Carmelo Mommo
Contrada Balzi Soprana
Bronte (Catania)
Tel. +39 095 690124
Pecorino Siciliano Dop

Nieli
Contrada Sparano
Noto (Siracusa)
Tel. +39 0931 872285
Canestrato, Pecorino Siciliano Dop,
Ricotta

Progresso e Natura
Contrada Valle Cuba
Castel di Lucio (Messina)
Tel. +39 0921 382222
Canestrato, Provola dei Nebrodi, Ricot-
ta Infornata, Ricotta Salata

Antonino Pappalardo
Contrada Difesa
Bronte (Catania)
Tel. +39 095 693626
Pecorino Siciliano Dop

Passalacqua
Contrada Baronaggio
Castronovo di Sicilia (Palermo)
Tel. +39 091 8218290
Fiore Sicano, Pecorino Siciliano Dop,
Tuma Persa

Vincenzo Piazza
Via Cavaliere, 4
Caltabellotta (Agrigento)
Tel. +39 347 4623635
Vastedda del Belice

Pro.Mad.
Contrada Conigliera
Castelbuono (Palermo)
Tel. +39 329 7792816 - +39 329 3820651
Provola delle Madonie

Luca Rosselli
Via Giuseppe Clemente, 64
Erice (Trapani)
Tel. +39 0923 532390
Caciocavallo Palermitano

Vito Calogero Savoca
Via Vittorio Emanuele, 137
San Teodoro (Messina)
Tel. +39 095 696722
Canestrato

Giovanni Schembari
Via Gioberti, 91
Contrada Camemi
Ragusa
Tel. +39 0932 619005
Ragusano

Antonio Scudieri
Via Nazario Sauro, 11
Castel di Lucio (Messina)
Tel. +39 0921 385007
Provola dei Nebrodi

Salvatore Luigi Sidoti
Contrada Radu
Alcara Li Fusi (Messina)
Tel. +39 0941 728191
Provola dei Nebrodi

Giovanni Spata
Via Colajanni, 139
Contrada Menta
Ragusa
Tel. +39 0932 655007
Ragusano

Antonio Tirrito
Via Palazzo Municipale, 50
Castronovo di Sicilia (Palermo)
Tel. +39 091 8217840
Pecorino Siciliano Dop

Giovanni Tuminello
Contrada Rabbuina
Ragusa Ibla (Ragusa)
Tel. +39 0932 654893
Pecorino Siciliano Dop, Ricotta

Giovanni Tumino
Contrada Cilone
Ragusa
Tel. +39 0932 251123
Caciocavallo Ibleo, Ricotta

Salvatore e Giovanni Tumino
Via degli Oleandri, 23
Contrada Cardita
Ragusa
Tel. +39 0932 619278 - +39 0932 619304
Ragusano

Valvo
Contrada Salerno, 1
Enna
Tel. +39 0935 20400
Piacentino

Sardinia

Bonassai

Callu de Cabreddu

Caprino a Latte Crudo

Casizolu ●

Casu Axedu

Casu Marzu

Fiore Sardo DOP ●

Fresa

Gioddu

Gransardo

Greviera

Ircano

Murùtzulu

Pecorino di Osilo ●

Pecorino Romano DOP

Pecorino Sardo DOP

Peretta

Ricotta Gentile

Ricotta Mustia

Semicotto Caprino

Triza

Bonassai

Bonassai was developed by the Bonassai Institute of Animal Husbandry and Cheesemaking, whose production methods are so well established they are now considered traditional. Pasteurised milk is inoculated with a starter culture and coagulation is complete in about 30 minutes. The soft curd is first broken up roughly with a *lira* curd knife, and then cut into to walnut-sized nuggets with a *spanarola* curd knife. After this, it is poured, still in its whey, into moulds. The cheeses are placed in a warm room, where the temperature encourages draining. They are turned over regularly. When they have dried out, the cheeses are salted in a brine bath and left to mature for 20-30 days in a very damp, cool place.

Rennet: liquid, calf's
Outer rind: thin, wrinkled, straw-white in colour
Body: soft, fatty, milk or ivory-white in colour
Top and bottom: flat, 18 cm along each side when square, 9 by 18 cm in the rectangular version
Height/weight: 5-6 cm / 2-2.5 kg
Territory of origin: a number of municipalities in the provinces of Nuoro, Sassari and Cagliari

Callu de Cabreddu

Callu de Cabreddu is still made according to the traditional methods once used by the prehistoric pastoral tribes
that originally inhabited the island. When a kid is butchered,
its vell, or fourth stomach, is emptied, cleaned thoroughly,
filled with raw milk and hung up to mature *su cannittu* (on
reed stands) in a cool place. The cheese is then aged, a process
that lasts until the skin of the stomachs stiffens to an almost
board-like hardness, usually after at least four months. During
ageing, Callu de Cabreddu is smoked so that the fumes from
the outside and the natural enzymes in the milk combine to
encourage coagulation, producing a creamy cheese with a
tangy taste and a pungent smell. Callu de Cabreddu is eaten
fresh as a spread and may also be used on canapés as a starter.

Rennet: natural, from the kid's fourth stomachs
Outer rind: the vell, or dried kid's stomach
Body: uncooked, soft, grey-white in colour
Top and bottom: flat, 12-18 cm in diameter
Height/weight: variable
Territory of origin: the central part of Sardinia in the provinces of Oristano,
Nuoro and Cagliari

Caprino a Latte Crudo

Raw milk is heated directly over a flame to a temperature of 36°C and coagulated by inoculation with kid's rennet that has been diluted with water and filtered. The soft curd is broken either by hand or with a wooden curd knife and the granules are left to settle on the bottom of the vat. The curd is then divided into lumps, put into moulds, salted in brine and then placed on a *canniciato* (rush rack) and smoked over a holm-oak wood fire. The outer rind is yellow or brown and the body of the cheese is firm and white or straw-yellow. It is tangy in flavour, depending on the length of time it has aged in the underground cellars used for this purpose. Caprino a Latte Crudo can be eaten as a table cheese or used as an ingredient in a wide range of recipes.

Rennet: kid's, diluted in water
Outer rind: firm, varying in hardness, yellow or brownish-yellow in colour
Body: uncooked, hard, ivory-white or pale straw-white in colour
Top and bottom: flat, 20-30 cm in diameter
Height/weight: 12-18 cm / 1.5-3.5 kg
Territory of origin: the entire region

Casizolu

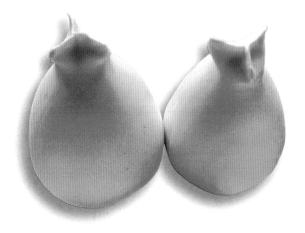

Sardinia is synonymous with sheep and ewe's milk cheeses, but there are rare exceptions. One can be found in the Montiferru area, where Casizolu, a fine stretched curd cow's milk cheese, has a long tradition. Traditionally, Casizolu is made by women. Those same women also bake bread, butcher pork and even today many have a loom in the home, on which they weave linen or cotton cloth, carpets and wool blankets. The womenfolk use freshly drawn milk for Casizolu. The curd is stretched in boiling water to make the characteristic fat-bellied pear shape. It is a long job, requiring effort and patience. It also ruins the hands, and means getting up very early indeed. After inoculating the milk with lamb's or kid's rennet, the maker has to wait for just the right point of fermentation, which could occur in the evening, at night or as the sun rises. When the curd has been stretched, the *s'abbagasu*, or white whey, is not discarded because it makes a tasty broth for fragrant cheese soups. Casizolu has to be shaped with care. The skin should be smooth, shiny and wrinkle-free. It is laid on a cloth, or in a basket of bran, so that it keeps its shape, staying there for two or three days. Then it is hung from the ceiling and finally stored in the cellar. Maturing may last anything from 30 days to 15 months. The body is straw-yellow with a few eyes, tending to flake with maturing. When the cheese is well matured, it reveals notes of grass and buttermilk mingling on the nose with woodland and leafy aromas. The palate has good length and a twist of almond in the finish. Casizolu has all it takes to become a great cheese. The raw material is fantastic, for the milk comes from Sardo Modicana or Bruno Sarda cows that spend the whole year grazing in the wild. The producers who are members of the Slow Food Presidium have formed an association and drafted production regulations that guarantee the entire cheesemaking chain.

Rennet: paste, lamb's or kid's
Outer rind: thin, smooth, intense straw-yellow in colour
Body: elastic, with a few eyes, tending to flake as maturing progresses, straw-yellow in colour
Height/weight: 20 cm / 2-3 kg
Territory of origin: the municipalities of Bonarcado, Cuglieri, Paulilatino, Santu Lussurgiu, Scano di Montiferro and Seneghe in the province of Oristano

This ancient, much-prized stretched curd cow's milk cheese is a typical product of Montiferru, where it is traditionally prepared by women.

Casu Axedu

The milk is heated to a temperature of 35-36°C, inoculated with whey from the previous day's cheesemaking, and co-agulated with kid's rennet. After about 30 minutes, the soft curd is broken into rectangles and left to drain overnight. The next day the curd is shaped and will be ready for the table only a few hours later. Casa Axedu has a slightly acidic taste. Sometimes, it is left to drain for 48 hours and then steeped in very salty brine, where it can be conserved for a long time. If it has undergone this treatment, the cheese is called *fiscidu* and is used as an ingredient in various local soups, or as a filling for the area's traditional potato ravioli.

Rennet: paste, kid's
Body: uncooked, soft, slightly acidic, white or straw-white in colour
Top and bottom: rectangular, flat
Height/weight: 4-7 cm / 150-300 g
Territory of origin: almost the entire region

Casu Marzu

Casa Marzu is produced seasonally throughout the region, particularly in the province of Nuoro. The basis for the product is pecorino cheese, generally fiore sardo (see entry), which has gone off because of infestation by the maggots of the cheese fly, *Piophila casei*, a process actively encouraged by the cheesemaker. As the maggots eat their way through the body of the cheese, they turn it into an extremely tangy, aromatic cream. Casu Marzu can be kept for a maximum of four months, after which it develops an unpleasant smell and taste. It is an un-cooked cheese, obtained by a combined proteolytic and lipolytic ageing process, and has a creamy body that varies in colour from yellow to brown. The flavour is distinctly tangy.

Body: uncooked, creamy, yellow to brown in colour
Territory of origin: the whole region, especially the province of Nuoro

Fiore Sardo DOP

Fiore Sardo can be manufactured industrially with a mixture of pasteurised, or occasionally raw, ewe's and cow's milk, but traditionally this cheese is made exclusively from freshly drawn, raw ewe's milk. Native Sardinian sheep are believed to be descended directly from the wild mountain sheep that today still inhabit the most inaccessible parts of the island, and the origins of this cheese go equally far back in time, possibly even to the Bronze Age Nuraghe period. Production is authorised throughout the whole region but traditionally Fiore Sardo is made by mountain shepherds in the huts, known as *pinnette*, whose central open fires give the authentic version its characteristically smoky overtones. A Slow Food Presidium will soon be launched to keep the shepherd's traditional cheesemaking technique alive. Today, Sardinian shepherds still make the cheese in the time-honoured fashion. Milk from one milking is poured untreated into a cheese vat – once, a wooden tub was used and the vat is the only concession to modern technology – and coagulated with a paste of kid's or lamb's rennet. The soft curd is broken with a curd knife called a *chiova*, left to drain, and then cut with a cheese "saw" called *sa sega casu*. The now firm curd is shaped in moulds, officially described as "two truncated cones joined at their wider base", whose diameter is inferior to the diameter of the cheese in the centre. The moulds are immersed in hot water so that the outer rind thickens, and then salted in a brine bath. After salting, Fiore Sardo is left to age, first on a rush trellis suspended over the fireplace in the *pinnetta* where it was made, then on a platform under the roof of the dairy, and finally in underground cellars where the cheeses are periodically turned over and greased with olive oil, which may be mixed with sheep fat. The ageing process lasts for two to eight months.

Rennet: paste, lamb's or kid's
Outer rind: dry, hard, intense yellow to deep brown shading into black in colour
Body: firm textured, with no eyes, varying in hardness according to maturing, straw-yellow or white in colour
Top and bottom: flat, 12-25 cm in diameter
Height/weight: 13-15 cm / 1-5 kg
DOP status awarded on 1 July 1996, regulation no. 1263

If aged for a long time, the body of Fiore Sardo tends to become rock hard and crumbly, making it ideal for grating.

Fresa

Fresa is very similar to stracchino (see entry). The milk is heated to a temperature of 36-37°C and coagulated in 30-40 minutes by adding calf's rennet. The soft curd is broken by hand into fairly large pieces, and allowed to drain before being gathered up and put into moulds. The rounds are then either dry-salted or salted in a brine bath. The outer rind is yellowish. The body has a deep straw-yellow colour and a slightly acidic taste. Fresa is one of Sardinia's very few soft cheeses and can be eaten either fresh or fried. There is also a version made with ewe's milk.

Rennet: liquid, calf's
Outer rind: thin, very pale straw-white in colour
Body: uncooked, moist, straw-yellow in colour
Top and bottom: flat
Height/weight: 5 cm / 1-1.5 kg
Territory of origin: the municipalities of Bonoria, Bortigali, Bosa, Macomer, and Silanus

Gioddu

L egend has it that a shepherd from central Sardinia once left a cork bucket full of freshly drawn ewe's milk in the corner of a pen and forgot all about it. The following day, he tasted the milk before throwing it away and decided that it was rather good. This was how Mizzurado (improved) or Gioddu cheese was created. Today, it is made by heating ewe's milk to a temperature of 80-95°C, then cooling it to 45°C. In former times, red-hot stones were put into the vat to heat it. When the milk has reached the required temperature, the cheesemaker adds a starter culture whose ingredients are a secret closely guarded by every family that makes Gioddu. However, the basic culture is the same as the one used to make yoghurt. After the desired degree of coagulation has been reached, the soft curd is broken up. At this point, Gioddu is ready for the table but it may also be left to ripen for a few days.

Rennet: milk-enzyme starter culture
Body: grainy, almost liquid in consistency, cream-white in colour
Territory of origin: the entire region

Gransardo

Strictly speaking, Gransardo is not a traditional product as it was created only recently. It is a very high-quality cheese made using the classic grana technique (see entry for grana padana DOP). To make Gransardo, ewe's milk from two milkings, one part-skimmed by allowing the cream to rise to the top, is sourced from dairy farms in the zone of origin. After filtering, it is heated to 60°C and inoculated with a thermophilic starter culture and coagulated at 34-36°C with lamb's rennet. The curd is milled into lumps the size of a grain of rice. The soft curd is then heated to 50°C and transferred to the portioner, where it is pressed. The cheeses are placed in moulds and turned over several times, ripening for several hours in heated rooms. Two days later, they go into brine baths for salting. Maturing lasts for at least 20 months and takes place at a temperature of 10-13°C and humidity of 80-90%. Gransardo is at its peak after maturing for 38-42 months.

Rennet: paste, lamb's
Outer rind: hard, smooth, not very thick, brownish in colour
Body: grainy, with small, sparsely distributed eyes, straw-yellow in colour
Top and bottom: smooth, 33-36 cm in diameter
Height/weight: 16-20 cm / 16-18 kg
Territory of origin: the province of Sassari

Greviera

In the latter half of the nineteenth century, the arrival of tech-nology and breeds of cattle from the mainland triggered pro-found changes in Sardinian livestock farming. One of the prod-ucts invented at that time was Greviera, which today is made by a small group of farmers in the Ozieri area. The milk comes from Bruno Alpina cows crossed with the more rugged local breeds. A starter culture of whey from the previous day's cheesemaking is added to whole raw milk from the evening and the following morning's milkings. The milk is heated to about 35°C and inocu-lated with liquid calf's rennet. The resulting curd is cut into sweetcorn-sized grains. The soft curd is cooked at 46°C and trans-ferred to moulds, taking great care to make sure they are correctly sealed. During the first 24 hours of draining, the cheeses may be pressed to expel the whey. The cheeses are salted in a brine bath and mature for at least three months in well-ventilated, moderately warm rooms, during which time they are frequently turned over.

Rennet: liquid, calf's
Outer rind: thin, hard, uneven, pale brown in colour
Body: firm, elastic, liberally scattered with eyes, cream-yellow in colour
Top and bottom: flat or slightly convex
Height/weight: 17 cm / 3 kg
Territory of origin: the municipality of Ozieri

Ircano

The cheesemaking technique for Ircano involves pasteurising milk by heating it to 72°C and keeping it at this temperature for 15-30 minutes. The milk is then cooled to 36-38°C and a starter culture of milk enzymes is added, to be followed immediately by rennet. When the soft curd has reached the required consistency, about 30 minutes after the rennet has been inoculated, it is cut into walnut-sized lumps. At this point, it is transferred into hexagonal or cylindrical moulds. These are then ripened for two or three hours in a room kept at a temperature of 37-45°C. Next, they are salted in a brine bath and left to mature. When ready for the table, Ircano has a slightly acidic taste.

Rennet: liquid, calf's
Outer rind: thin, white
Body: uncooked, soft, white
Top and bottom: flat
Height/weight: 7-8 cm / 1.5 kg
Territory of origin: the municipalities of Guspini, Tertenia and San Nicolò Gerrei

Murùtzulu

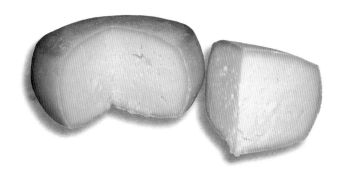

In the Lugudorese dialect of Sardinia, *murùtzulu* means a portion of soft curd in a mould. It is also known as *fresa*, not to be confused with the cheese of the same name (see entry), *pischeddu*, from the name of the mould used to make it, or *casu de 'acca* (cow's cheese). Murùtzulu cheese is made in winter using raw milk from grazing Bruno Sarda, Sardo Modicana cows and their crosses. Whole milk is coagulated at 36-37°C with calf's rennet. When the curd has formed, it is cut up vigorously into sweetcorn-sized lumps. The soft curd is allowed to settle on the bottom of the vat and then extracted and transferred to truncated cone-shaped moulds. It is then squeezed by hand to expel the whey and turned over several times. Salting is by immersion in saturated brine. The cheese is allowed to dry and then matures in the cellar on wooden boards. Murùtzulu is ready for the table after three or four weeks, but maturation may continue for up to a year. During maturation, the cheeses are periodically cleaned and brushed with olive oil.

Rennet: liquid, calf's
Outer rind: thin, irregular, bright yellow tending to brownish in colour
Body: with unevenly distributed eyes, bright yellow in colour
Top and bottom: flat
Height/weight: 9-10 cm / 1.5-3 kg
Territory of origin: Montiferru and neighbouring areas

Pecorino di Osilo

This pecorino is produced around Osilo, as well as in some of the neighbouring municipalities, Sassari, Ploaghe, Nulvi, Codrongianos and Tergu. Smaller than the classic Sardinian ewe's milk cheese – it is narrower in diameter and has a higher side – Pecorino di Osilo has a thin, straw-yellow rind and straw-yellow body. It is soft, fatty and oily in texture, intense on the nose, and has a very aromatic flavour. But shape is not the characteristic that sets Pecorino di Osilo apart from other Sardinian ewe's milk cheeses. The cheesemaking process involves protracted pressing of the soft curd, sometimes with a rudimentary mechanical press, after it has been milled into tiny granules. This gives the cheese a doughy texture that it conserves during maturation, which should ideally last for five to six months. The cheeses are periodically turned over and washed with water and brine during maturing. The surface is also brushed with a mixture of oil and vinegar. Pecorino di Osilo has the characteristic aromatic profile of a ewe's milk cheese. There are hints of wool, dry wood and in some cases aromatic herbs. The palate has very marked sensory perceptions. Pecorino di Osilo is buttery and fondant in texture, with attractive hints of roasted hazelnuts. Happily, this cheese is still widely made. More than a hundred farmers produce it, and the quality is high. On the negative side, production is fragmented and well below its potential level. Most of the farmers send their milk to large dairies as they do not have the facilities or equipment to make and sell their own produce. The Slow Food Presidium was set up to help cheesemakers to organise themselves into an association and equip themselves with legislation-compliant facilities and production regulations. It is only in this way that one of Sardinia's most interesting dairy products will be able to gain visibility and become a development opportunity, as well as a tourist attraction, for a splendid but little-promoted territory.

Rennet: liquid or powder, calf's
Outer rind: thin, straw-yellow in colour
Body: soft, fatty, oily, straw-yellow in colour
Top and bottom: smooth, 16-22 cm in diameter
Height/weight: 11-13 cm / 1.4-2 kg
Territory of origin: the municipalities of Codrongianos, Nulvi, Osilo, Ploaghe and Tergu in the province of Sassari

The cheesemaking process involves lengthy pressing of the soft curd. This gives the cheese a doughy texture that it conserves during maturation, which should ideally last for five to six months.

Pecorino Romano DOP

Pecorino Romano is made from October to July using a mixture of fresh ewe's milk from the morning and evening milkings. The freshly drawn milk is filtered, heat-treated, poured into a cheese vat and inoculated with a starter culture of left-over whey. It is then heated to a temperature of 39°C and coagulated by inoculation with lamb's rennet in paste. After 25-30 minutes, the soft curd is broken into rice-sized granules and re-cooked by heating it to a temperature of 45-48°C. Next, the curd is transferred to draining vats. When all the whey has run off, it is cut into lumps, put into moulds and pressed. The pressed curd is stamped with the DOP mark and then dry-salted several times in purpose-built rooms called *caciare*. The master salters who carry out this task are much respected professionals. After salting, the cheeses are ready for ageing. Pecorino Romano cheeses destined for the table are aged for five months and those for grating are aged for at least eight months. During the maturing process, the rounds are washed with a brine solution and may be wrapped in a protective film. Pecorino Romano for export is carefully selected and encased in a dark plastic material that recalls the old custom of massaging the cheeses with oil and grease or ashes as they aged.

Rennet: paste, lamb's
Outer rind: smooth, straw-yellow tinged with green in colour
Body: firm-textured, sometimes with a few eyes, fairly elastic in the early stages of maturing becoming firmer and drier, white or straw-white in colour
Top and bottom: flat, 25-30 cm in diameter
Height/weight: 20 cm / 20-35 kg
Territory of origin: the Agro Romano countryside, the province of Grosseto and the entire region of Sardinia
DOP status awarded on 1 July 1996, regulation no. 1107

Pecorino Romano acquires a rock-like appearance and consistency if sufficiently mature.

These Pecorino cheeses do not have the classic black wrapping that distinguishes rounds destined for the export trade. Today, the coating has a purely decorative function.

Pecorino Sardo DOP

Pecorino Sardo is eaten both fresh and mature as a table cheese, and the mature version can also be used for grating. The DOP regulations call for whole ewe's milk, which may be inoculated with a natural starter culture, and is coagulated with the addition of calf's rennet. When the curd has reached the required consistency, it is cut into walnut-sized nuggets, for the fresh version, or into sweetcorn-sized granules, if it is destined to become mature Pecorino Sardo. Next, the curd is poured into tube-shaped moulds to make cylindrical cheeses with a flat top and bottom. The rounds are salted, sometimes dry but more often in a brine bath. They are then allowed to age for a period of 20-60 days, for fresh Pecorino, and 2-12 months for the mature version, which may also be smoked. Fresh Pecorino Sardo has a smooth, thin outer rind that is white or pale straw-white in colour. Inside, it is soft, white and firm-textured, with sparsely distributed eyes. The flavour is mild, aromatic and slightly acidic. The minimum permissible fat in dry matter is 40%. Mature Pecorino Sardo has a thicker, straw-yellow rind that shades into brown as it matures. The body is firm, white or straw-white, and presents a few scattered eyes. Soft and elastic in texture when young, Pecorino Sardo becomes harder, and on occasion grainy, as it ages. The flavour is pleasantly tangy and the minimum fat in dry matter is 35%.

Rennet: liquid, calf's (large-scale, industrial dairies) or kid's or lamb's in paste (small-scale cheesemakers)
Outer rind: thin, straw-yellow, darker in more mature cheeses
Body: elastic, semi-cooked
Top and bottom: flat, 15-20 cm in diameter
Height/weight: 6-13 cm / 1.7-4 kg
Territory of origin: the entire region
DOP status awarded on 1 July 1996, regulation no. 1107

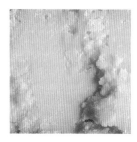 

More than seven million sheep graze on the pastures of Sardinia. Most of the milk they yield goes to make Pecorino Sardo cheese.

Peretta

After the milk has been first heated, then cooled to a temperature of 37°C, it is inoculated with a whey-based starter culture and rennet, although not all makers use the starter. When it has coagulated and set, the soft curd is cut into hazelnut-sized lumps. To obtain Peretta's characteristic elastic texture, the curd is allowed to ripen for about 24 hours, after which time it becomes plastic and pliable. Next, it is stretched and modelled into the shape of a pear with a small head. The now firm "little pear" curds are immersed in cold water for a short time to harden them. They are then salted in a brine bath. The next stage is to hang the cheeses to age for up to 15 days. Peretta is generally eaten fresh but may also be used as an ingredient in the preparation of stuffing for ravioli, or to make *sebada*, a traditional Sardinian fried sweet.

Rennet: liquid or powder, calf's
Outer rind: thin, smooth, straw-white in colour
Body: firm-textured, soft, straw-white in colour
Top and bottom: curved
Height/weight: variable / 0.5-1 kg
Territory of origin: the entire region

Ricotta Gentile

This version of ricotta is made by pouring whey into a double-bottomed cheese vat and heating it to a temperature of 80°C. As it is heated, the whey is stirred constantly until the protein starts to rise to the surface. When the proteins have solidified, they are carefully transferred with a strainer into truncated cone-shaped moulds. The resulting ricotta is left for a short time in a cool (5-10°C) room before being packed for sale. Ricotta Gentile is also known as Ricotta Romana because its basic ingredient is the left-over whey from the production of Pecorino Romano. White in colour when ready for consumption, it has a soft creamy texture and a mild flavour. Ricotta Gentile may be eaten fresh or used as an ingredient for ravioli stuffing, cakes or other sweets.

Body: buttery, creamy white in colour
Top and bottom: smooth, 10 cm in diameter (top), 20 cm in diameter (bottom)
Height/weight: 8-10 cm / 1.5-2 kg
Territory of origin: the provinces of Nuoro, Cagliari, Sassari, and Oristano

EWE'S MILK WHEY

Ricotta Mustia

Whey is heated to a temperature of 82-85°C and stirred constantly. When the proteins in the whey begin to rise to the surface, stirring stops and the mass is left to stand and solidify for five to ten minutes. After coagulating, the mass is transferred into cylindrical moulds. It is drained overnight under pressure from a wooden disc. Next, the cylinders are dry-salted and 24 hours later, they spend five or six hours to the smoking room, where a fire of aromatic herbs is burning. The table-ready product is cylindrical in shape. It has an amber colour, a soft, firm texture and a slightly piquant taste.

Outer rind: fine, medium-firm in texture, amber-yellow in colour
Body: soft, pressed, brownish-white in colour
Top and bottom: flat, 16-18 cm in diameter
Height/weight: 2 cm / 0.8-2 kg
Territory of origin: the entire region, particularly the province of Sassari

Semicotto Caprino

Goat's milk is heated to a temperature of 38°C and inoculated with a small amount of whey starter, followed by calf's rennet. When the mixture has coagulated to the required consistency, the soft curd is first broken up and then semi-cooked for a few minutes. Next, it is cut, put into moulds, and left to drain in a warm room for several hours. The following day, the rounds are salted by steeping them in a brine bath for about 48 hours. The product is now ready for maturing in a temperature and humidity-controlled cellar. The body of Semicotto Caprino is white and firm. If aged, the cheese has a strong flavour, but the palate is more delicate in the fresh version. Semicotto Caprino is produced throughout Sardinia, and is sometimes made with a proportion of ewe's milk.

Rennet: liquid, kid's
Outer rind: hard, smooth, dark brown in colour
Body: hard, semi-cooked, white in colour
Top and bottom: flat, 20-25 cm in diameter
Height/weight: 10-15 cm / 3-4 kg
Territory of origin: the provinces of Nuoro and Cagliari

Triza

In the Lugodorese dialect of Sardinina, *triza* corresponds to the Italian word *treccia*, meaning "plait". Triza cheese is made in the Montiferru area using raw milk from grazing Bruno Sarda, Sardo Modicana cows and their crosses. Once, it was obtained from soft curd left over from making casizolu (see entry), but today it is made in larger sizes, in particular for the Easter celebrations. The milk is coagulated at 36-37°C by inoculation with calf's or kid's rennet. The curd is cut into lumps the size of grains of rice and then removed in a cloth. It is left to ripen in terracotta containers. When the curd has reached the right degree of acidity for stretching, it is sliced and manipulated into plaits modelled on the traditional Easter palms with the aid of a little hot water and a wooden spatula. Salting is by brief immersion in saturated brine. Triza should be eaten within about one week of production.

Rennet: paste, calf's or kid's
Body: compact, white tending to straw-yellow in colour
Height/weight: variable / 0.3-1 kg
Territory of origin: Montiferru

The producers

Allevatori Sulcitani Società Cooperativa
Località Sirai, 14
Carbonia (Cagliari)
Tel. 0781 698294-0781 698356
Pecorino Romano Dop, Pecorino Sardo
Dop, Ricotta Gentile, Ricotta Mustia

Luigi Altea
Via Spano, 1
Osilo (Sassari)
Tel. 079 42541
Pecorino di Osilo

Aresu
Vicolo Vittorio Emanuele III, 1
Donori (Cagliari)
Tel. 070 981066
Pecorino sardo Dop

Giovanni Borrodde
Santu Lussurgiu (Oristano)
Viale Domenico Alberto Azuni, 121
Tel. 0783 551202
Casizolu, Triza

Cooperativa La Rinascita
Strada Provinciale, 25
Onifai (Nuoro)
Tel. 0784 97564
Pecorino Romano Dop, Ricotta Gen-
tile, Ricotta Mustia

Marcello Cuozzo
Via Cagliari, 23
Oristano
Tel. 0783 212441
Pecorino Sardo Dop

Fogu Casearia
Zona Artigianale S'Utturru
Oschiri (Sassari)
Tel. 079 734149
Fiore Sardo Dop

Pinuccio Mangatia
Via Università, 68
Sassari
Tel. 079 234710
Pecorino di Osilo

Andrea Niedda
Regione Binzas de Mela
Ozieri (Sassari)
Tel. 079 770481
Greviera

Antonio Onni
Via dei Dragoni, 17
Santu Lussurgiu (Oristano)
Tel. 0783 550528
Murùtzulu

Pischina Appiu di Salvatore Inzis
Corso Umberto, 2
Cuglieri (Oristano)
Tel. 0785 38025
Casizolu

Gianpaolo Piu
Viale Domenico Alberto Azuni, 199
Santu Lussurgiu (Oristano)
Tel. 0783 551115
Casizolu, Triza

Luigi Pulinas
Via Asilo Infantile, 33
Osilo (Sassari)
Tel. 079 42491
Pecorino di Osilo

Giuseppe Sanna
Via Merello, 17
Paulilatino (Oristano)
Tel. 0785 555587
Casizolu

Se. Pi.
Strada Statale 131 km 76,100
Marrubiu (Oristano)
Tel. 0783 858037
Fiore Sardo Dop

Mario e Pasqualino Testoni
Via Duca degli Abruzzi, 24
Osilo (Sassari)
Tel. 338 5946995
Pecorino di Osilo

Gavinuccio Turra
Via Campicello, 13
Osilo (Sassari)
Tel. 079 42695
Pecorino di Osilo

Bibliography

Atlante dei prodotti tipici dei parchi italiani, Ministry of the Envronment - Slow Food Editore, Savigliano 2002

Atlante dei prodotti tradizionali trentini, Autonomous Provincial Authority of Trento, Trento 2000

Cesari Sartoni, M., *Dizionario del ghiottone viaggiatore*, Fuori Thema/Tempi Stretti, Bologna 1994

Cibario del Friuli Venezia Giulia, Ersa, Udine 2002

Costardi, G. F., Rocca, G., *Il controllo igienico-sanitario del latte e derivati. Tecnica e legislazione*, Edagricole, Bologna 1987

Dispensa del Po. I sapori del grande fiume, Slow Food Editore, Bra 2002

Fiori, G., *Formaggi italiani*, Eos, Novara 1999

Gambera, A., Surra E., *Le forme del latte*, Slow Food Editore, Bra 2003

Guarnaschelli Gotti, M. (ed.) *Grande Enciclopedia Illustrata della Gastronomia*, Selezione del Reader's Digest, Milan 2000

Il Buon Paese, Slow Food Editore, Bra 2000

L'Arca. Quaderni dei Presìdi, Slow Food Editore, Bra 2000, n. 1-2

L'Arca. Quaderni dei Presìdi, Slow Food Editore, Bra 2001, n. 3-4-5

L'Italia dei Presìdi, Slow Food Editore, Bra 2004

Ottogalli, G., *Atlante dei formaggi*, Hoepli, Milan 2001

Pozzetto, G., *C'era una volta il formaggio di fossa, c'è ancora?*, Panozzo, Rimini 2000

Puglia, V. (ed.) *La dispensa del Molise*, Department of Agricolture, Forestry and Fisheries of the Molise Regional Authority - Slow Food Campania, San Martino Valle Caudina 2004

Zannoni, M., *Il parmigiano-reggiano nella storia*, Silva, Collecchio 1999

Links:

Atlas of tipycal products of Italian parks: www.atlanteparchi.com (in Italian)

Slow Food Foundation for Biodiversity:
www.fondazioneslowfood.it/welcome_en.lasso

Abruzzo:
www.ruralnet.it/Territorio/Prodotti%20tradizionali/Elenco%20Prodotti.html

Piedmont: www.saporidelpiemonte.it/prodotti/04.htm

Tuscany: germoplasma.arsia.toscana.it/Prodotti_tipici/BancaDati.htm

Index of Cheeses

The Seal that makes a difference.

Red Seal:

Parmigiano-Reggiano cheese which has been aged for more than 18 months. This cheese has a somewhat distinctive milk base, with vegetable notes such as grass, cooked vegetables and at times flowers and fruit. It is ideal served with aperitifs or dry white wines and as an accompaniment to fresh fruit such as pears and green apples.

Silver Seal:

Parmigiano-Reggiano cheese which has been aged for more than 22 months. The cheese has a balanced mild yet full-flavoured taste, with a crumbly, grainy texture that melts in your mouth. It is an ideal accompaniment to well structured red wines and excellent when served as shaved Parmesan cheese petals in fruit salad. It is superb if served with any dried fruit.